Young Children's Health and Well-being

Young Children's Health and Well-being

Angela Underdown

Mc Graw Hill

Open University Press
Maidenhead • New York

Open University Press
McGraw-Hill Education
McGraw-Hill House
Shoppenhangers Road
Maidenhead
Berkshire
England
SL6 2QL

email: enquiries@openup.co.uk
world wide web: www.openup.co.uk

and Two Penn Plaza, New York, NY 10121–2289, USA

First published 2007

A catalogue record of this book is available from the British Library

ISBN-10 0 335 21906 3 (pb)   0 335 21907 1 (hb)
ISBN-13 978 0 335 21906 3 (pb)   0 978 0 335 21907 0 (hb)

Library of Congress Cataloging-in-Publication Data
CIP data applied for

Typeset by YHT Ltd, London
Printed and bound in Slovenia
by DELO tiskama by arrangement with Korotan-Ljubljana

The *McGraw-Hill* Companies

For my parents, Vera and Jack Allwork

Contents

Foreword

Early childhood is a critical period of the life course in which the developing brain and body are undergoing rapid change, making them vulnerable to adverse influences. The physical, intellectual, social and emotional development of the child is set on a trajectory during this period that, though not irreversible, has a profound effect on subsequent health and well-being in childhood and throughout the life course. The factors affecting early childhood health and well-being are multifaceted and complex, and influenced by the interaction of the child with his or her carers and immediate environment, and through the broader community and culture in which they live. Much literature about early childhood development focuses exclusively on the quality of the relationship of the child and carer, usually the mother. This focus, however, is too narrow to understand the complexities of children's health and well-being. The main carers themselves are products of their own childhood environments, and have in turn been influenced by the social, economic and cultural conditions in which they live. A broad, holistic view of the macro- as well as micro-environment in which child rearing takes place is thereby central to a proper understanding of its complexity, and should be the basis of policy that is aimed at enhancing and not undermining early child health and well-being.

It is a special pleasure for me to write the Foreword for this book as Angela Underdown has succeeded in taking such a broad, holistic approach. From the first paragraph, the book is imbued with a commitment to the principles underpinning the UN Convention on the Rights of the Child (UNCRC) and informed by an ecological systems approach. The UNCRC is a vital document that establishes the indivisible rights of all children. It is concerned not simply with how parents and carers treat children but with the provisions made at state level for the welfare and protection of children and the promotion of their rights. Within this book the infant and young child are recognized as social actors and Chapter 3 refers to research about the crucial importance of the sensitive recognition of infant cues and signals, and the role that this plays in supporting the development of emotional regulation. Chapter 8 is a reminder that children with emotional and behavioural difficulties are expressing their distress. Although essentially an overview, the book provides enough detail and references for the interested reader to pursue the subject in more depth. The key individual and societal factors that influence child development and health, such as parenting and poverty, are described and the main aspects of them discussed. The book also uses case studies and qualitative data to enrich and bring to life some of the issues under discussion. Consistent with the UNCRC, Chapter 9 offers a fascinating account of how listening to young children's voices plays an important part in promoting their health and well-being.

Students, and child health and care professionals will gain insight from this book, particularly from its comprehensive and holistic approach to child health and well-being. This should be a stepping stone to greater understanding and to deeper study of the interplay of the influences of familial and societal factors. It should also provide policy makers with an insight into some new and innovative ways of promoting children's health and well-being.

Nick Spencer
Professor of Child Health
University of Warwick
July 2006

Acknowledgements

I would like to thank all those who helped me in the writing of this book. In particular I owe a debt of gratitude to Peter Elfer for invaluable critical comments, tirelessly reading drafts, and for his friendship and encouragement. I would also like to thank Ann Lexton for sharing her depth of knowledge and expertise about young children in distress, and the importance of listening and safeguarding. I greatly benefited from the expertise, support and encouragement offered by Jacky Bright, Jane Barlow, Lucy Thorpe, Pia Christensen and Nick Spencer. Finally, I would especially like to thank my family, Nigel, Lucy and Helen, whose support and encouragement made this project possible.

A note on the text

Every Child Matters, the *National Service Framework* (NSF) *for Children, Young People and Maternity Services*, and the *Choosing Health* white paper apply specifically to England. Scotland, Wales and Northern Ireland may have other specific policies and legislation to meet the needs of the population living in those countries.

1 Young children's health and well-being in context

The true wealth of a nation can be measured by the health of its youngest citizens, and in the twenty-first century children's health is still largely determined by social, environmental and economic factors (UNICEF 2001c; Hall and Elliman 2003). Economic factors, such as living in poverty, and social factors, such as the warmth of parenting, support from family, friends and neighbours, the type of housing and the safety of the environment, have the greatest impact on health and well-being. Children's health and well-being is important in its own right; every child is entitled to positive health, both in childhood and as a foundation for the future. Mentally and physically healthy children are more likely to grow into fulfilled, productive members of society and ensuring this means taking a wide view of the determinants of health. This introductory chapter reflects on the child's right to health, reviews some definitions of health and well-being, explores how health may be measured, and uses Bronfenbrenner's ecological systems **theory** as a framework for considering the many factors that interplay to influence children's health and well-being.

What rights does the child have to health?

Traditionally children have been considered as the 'property' of their parents (Gittens 1998) and have consequently had few entitlements in their own right. The concept of children having specific entitlements has developed over the last century, culminating in the 1989 production of the United Nations Convention on the Rights of the Child (UNCRC) (UN 1989). The 54 articles of the UNCRC incorporate universal standards for children and young people under the age of 18 years. The convention has been described as a catalyst for national action (UN 1995) with countries undertaking to bring their national laws and policies into line with the convention and to submit regular progress reports to the United Nations. The UNCRC has been ratified by virtually all nations worldwide, leaving Somalia and the United States of America as the only countries not to adopt the declaration. Although the standards are universal, interpretations may vary according to differing cultural situations, but the notion of children having rights, which are respected by adults, is beginning to be reflected in policies and legislation (Franklin 2002). For example, the *Every Child Matters* (DfES 2003) consultation paper has underpinned the Children Act 2004, and reflects some aspects of the UNCRC. Children's rights to health care and health services are, therefore, a matter of legal responsibility in those countries that have ratified the Convention. Many of the articles allude to children's health and well-being and to the value and dignity of family life. The following abbreviated examples (UNICEF 2004) are taken from a leaflet published for children and young people, and give some indication of the scope of the Convention in relation to children's health and well-being.

- **Article 6** All children have the right to life. Governments should ensure that children survive and develop healthily.
- **Article 7** All children have the right to a legally registered name, the right to a nationality, and the right to know and, as far as possible, to be cared for by their parents.
- **Article 8** Governments should respect children's right to a name, a nationality and family ties.
- **Article 9** Children should not be separated from their parents unless it is for their own good – for example, if a parent is mistreating or neglecting a child. Children whose parents have separated have the right to stay in contact with both parents unless this might hurt the child.
- **Article 12** Children have the right to say what they think should happen when adults are making decisions that affect them, and to have their opinions taken into account.
- **Article 19** Governments should ensure that children are properly cared for, and protect them from violence, abuse and neglect by their parents or anyone else who looks after them.
- **Article 23** Children who have any kind of disability should have special care and support so that they can lead full and independent lives.
- **Article 24** Article 24 of the UNCRC (1989) details the child's right to health care, beginning with the basic necessities of clean drinking water, adequate nutritious foods and a clean environment. Article 24 sensitively alludes to the differing global expectations for children's health, stating in Section 1 that the child has the right to the 'highest attainable standard of health'.

The need to ensure children's survival has, to date, focused attention on children's physical health, with much less attention being given to social and emotional health. Over time the health and welfare services in the United Kingdom have reflected this emphasis with the development of comprehensive immunization programmes, welfare foods and child health clinics. However, in stating that a child has a right to the highest attainable standard of health, the UNCRC has set aspirational goals for children's social and emotional well-being alongside their physical health. In moving from considering health rather than sickness and disease, there is an implicit obligation to identify ways of preventing ill health and promoting health, rather than relying on a curative model. The UNCRC states that countries should assist one another in promoting children's health and well-being, which should mean that children worldwide can benefit from health care knowledge and developments.

How are health and well-being defined?

Health and well-being have different meanings for children and families according to where they live and the available resources. A child living in a poor family in certain parts of sub-Saharan Africa where there is currently an **AIDS** epidemic or famine might be considered healthy by the local community because he or she is free from disease and reasonably nourished. In the minority world of the more prosperous countries most people would not be comfortable to consider a child's health in such narrow terms. Health and well-being are not easy to define and individuals may have differing ideas about what health means. In 1948, the World Health Organization (WHO) provided the following definition of health: 'Health is a state of complete physical, mental and social well-being and not merely the absence of disease.' This definition was well received because it concentrated on a person being healthy, rather than not being ill, and it took a holistic view by including mental and social well-being rather than focusing only on physical health. However, this definition has been criticized (Seedhouse 1986) because it suggests a perfect state of health that is probably unachievable. The WHO (1986) added to the definition to more realistically reflect what is achievable, describing health as:

> the extent to which an individual or group is able on the one hand to realise aspirations and satisfy needs; and, on the other hand, to change or cope with the environment. Health is, therefore, seen as a resource for everyday life, not the objective of living; it is a positive concept emphasising social and personal resources, as well as physical capacities.

This definition views health as a resource for intellectual, emotional, social and spiritual development and as a foundation for enabling children to achieve personal goals and feel a sense of satisfaction. It takes a holistic view

of health but still acknowledges that there may be health limitations requiring people to adapt the environment or themselves. The social, emotional and economic environments in which children live interact with their
personal physical and psychological resources to shape their health and well-
being. For example, a child with a physical disability will experience greater
health and well-being if he or she lives within a society that adapts facilities to
ensure access and participation. Children's well-being relies to an extent on
being able to participate, to express their views and have a response. This
approach is reflected in many examples within this book.

Children's health entitlements

Children who are healthy, emotionally and physically, have the energy and
motivation to play, explore, experiment, learn and form relationships with
others. The building blocks for health depicted in Figure 1.1 are the basic
requirements for health, and show how emotional, social, physical and intellectual health are all interrelated. All these factors are necessary not only in
preventing ill health but also in the promotion of positive health and well-
being.

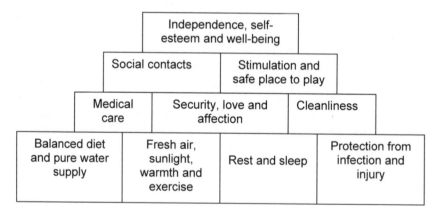

Figure 1.1 Building blocks for health

Defining well-being

Maslow (1970) described a hierarchy of motivational needs that must be met
before an individual can reach their full potential. Maslow's model (Figure
1.2) highlights the complexity of human needs and the fact that basic biological requirements such as having a balanced diet and a pure water supply
must be met before people can become concerned with higher-order needs

such as social contacts and self-esteem. Maslow's model is usually depicted as a triangle with basic physiological needs at the base and 'self-actualization' or self-fulfilment at the pinnacle. If children have all the building blocks of health as a resource they are more likely to feel at ease with themselves and be open to exploring new experiences.

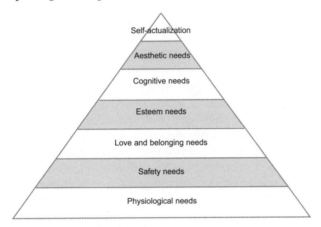

Figure 1.2 Maslow's hierarchy of needs

Well-being, therefore, involves experiencing healthy self-esteem, and feeling worthwhile and able to contribute positively. The biological relationships between physical health and emotional well-being are also becoming increasingly recognized. For example, research by Cohen *et al.* (1991) has shown that examination stress affects the immune system and makes it more likely that students will contract a viral infection like the common cold. Brunner (1997) cites other research that shows how children in post-war Germany fared differently depending on which orphanage they lived in:

> Under identical food rationing, those who lived in the Bienenhaus orphanage, initially under the control of the stern and forbidding Fraulein Schwarz, gained less weight and grew more slowly than children cared for at the Vogelnest orphanage by the affectionate Fraulein Grun. By chance Schwarz replaced Grun during the study and the growth rates reversed despite the provision of extra food at Vogelnest. (Brunner 1997: 1472)

Other, more recent, research has added support to this. Kim *et al.* (2003) reported that 23 Korean infants living in an orphanage who received massage, eye contact and talking for 15 minutes twice a day grew more quickly than 22 peers who received only the usual care. This growth increase was sustained when the infants were measured again at 6 months of age, indicating the important interplay between physical, physiological and psychological influencing factors.

Interestingly, in post-war UK and USA, where there is an abundance of food, overeating and weight gain are often linked with a lack of well-being. Toynbee argued in the *Guardian* newspaper (28 May 2004) that 'inequality is fattening and . . . people will only get thinner when they have things that are worth staying thin for – self esteem, social status and jobs'. Her article highlights just how complicated the relationships are between physical health and emotional well-being, and this links with research showing how eating high-fat food can be used as a comfort for distress (Cameron and Jones 1985). Stewart-Brown (1998) suggests that solutions to apparently intractable health difficulties, like inequalities in health and unhealthy lifestyles, may lie in researching emotional well-being and finding suitable interventions to promote well-being and positive mental health. Research (Bowlby 1969; Rutter and Smith 1995) has shown that unresolved distress in early childhood often leads to distress or mental health difficulties in adulthood, and Svanberg (1998: 543) argues that secure emotional attachment established early in life 'will provide the necessary resilience to cope with many adverse life events as an adult, without developing psychological or psychiatric symptomatology'. This approach views emotional well-being as part of mental health and one possible definition defines the concept of mental health as: 'a state of emotional and psychological well-being in which an individual is able to use his or her cognitive and emotional capabilities, function in society and meet the ordinary demands of everyday life' (Merriam-Webster 2006).

A study by Pavis *et al.* (1996) showed that the general public preferred the terms 'emotional and psychological well-being' to 'mental health' as they equated the latter term with mental illness. Perhaps this is hardly surprising, as the traditional medical model tends to look at what is wrong rather than what is right; as health has been viewed as a deficit model, with mental health professionals actually working with people who are mentally ill, perhaps the UK's National Health Service might more accurately be described as the National Sickness Service. The research into the importance of young children's well-being as a foundation for positive mental health is rapidly developing, however, and UK government policy (DfES 2004; DoH 2004a; DoH/DfES 2004) is beginning to reflect this. Finding appropriate, effective ways to promote children's well-being could be the key to major improvements in all-round health.

Signs of emotional well-being

Feeling unconditionally accepted, liked and loved is central to emotional health and, when a child feels emotionally healthy, he or she is more receptive to learning. Laevers (1997) believes that for learning and development to occur children need to be high on emotional well-being and high on involvement. According to Laevers, children's emotional well-being is characterized by:

- openness and receptivity
- flexibility
- self-confidence and self-esteem
- assertiveness
- vitality
- relaxation and inner peace
- enjoyment
- the child feeling connected and in touch with her/his self.

According to Laevers (1997), children who have these characteristics of emotional well-being are more likely to have a high level of engagement with life and learning. Children who are high on emotional well-being have 'space' in their minds to take on new ideas. Part of being healthy emotionally is 'feeling at one with yourself' so that children have the confidence to become interested and involved. Even very young babies are building up a sense of who they are and the self-esteem to enable them to explore and discover things for themselves. Laevers (1997) describes the signs of involvement as:

- concentration
- energy
- complexity and creativity
- facial expressions and composure
- persistence
- precision
- reaction time
- verbal expression
- satisfaction.

What indicators are there of children's health and well-being?

Children's health and well-being are actually measured very little. What tends to be measured most is children's ill health (morbidity) and the death rate (mortality). Infant mortality below the age of 1 year and again below the age of 5 years has been the major statistic for comparing child 'health' from one nation to another and for measuring a country's progress. Child mortality rates, particularly in the richer industrialized countries of the north, have

Table 1.1 Infant mortality and life expectancy in a selection of countries, 2005

Country	Infant mortality per 1000 live births	Life expectancy in years
Albania	21.5	77.2
Angola	191.2	36.6
Australia	4.7	80.4
Bangladesh	62.6	62.1
Canada	4.8	80.1
China	24.2	72.3
Finland	3.6	78.3
France	4.3	79.6
Germany	4.2	78.7
India	56.3	64.3
Japan	3.3	81.2
Kenya	61.5	48.0
Mozambique	130.8	40.3
New Zealand	5.8	78.7
Nigeria	98.8	46.7
Pakistan	72.4	63.0
Russia	17	66.4
South Africa	61.8	43.3
Sweden	2.8	80.4
United Kingdom	5.2	78.4
United States	6.5	77.7
Zimbabwe	67.7	36.7

Source: US Census Bureau (2006)

generally been falling over the last century due to improvements in the physical safety of maternity services, and in the treatment and prevention of infectious diseases such as **tuberculosis, polio, measles, whooping cough** and **diphtheria**. Many of these threats have been contained by improved living conditions and illness-prevention programmes like immunization, but the pattern of infant mortality is very uneven and the chances of survival and a healthy life are directly related to where a child lives. Consider the statistics in Table 1.1, which demonstrate the huge variation in the likelihood of surviving infancy and in life expectancy from one country to another.

The variation in the number of children dying before their first birthday is a dramatic indication of the health of a country. Compare infant mortality between Sweden and Angola. These shocking statistics are indicators of the hazards, such as measles, **malaria**, diarrhoeal disease, AIDS, war, famine and poverty, facing many of the world's children. In recognition of this the

United Nations marked the new millennium by setting Millennium Development Goals (MDGs) to be achieved by 2015. These goals include reducing the mortality rate for children under 5 by 66 per cent, and reducing maternal mortality by 75 per cent and reversing the spread of diseases such as HIV/AIDS and malaria.

Although the contrast between nations is stark there is also a hidden picture within individual nations (Spencer 2000), with infant mortality being higher in families in lower socio-economic groups. Babies born to families in the lowest socio-economic groups in the UK are more likely to be born early, have a lower birth weight or to die in the first year of life (Roberts 2000). In addition, life expectancy is 8.5 years less for a man in the lowest socio-economic group living in the north of England compared with that of a man in the highest grouping in southern England (DoH 2004a). Although statistics are published regularly to indicate child mortality rates, it is less easy to compare illness (morbidity) rates in differing countries, partly because of the variability of diseases and different countries' policies about which diseases have to be notified to the authorities. Measures of emotional health are even more disparate, although increasingly statistics relating to children and young people's mental illnesses and behavioural problems are being collated in the UK. The government has shown increasing awareness of the importance of positive mental and physical health in childhood and in 2004 published a policy paper, *Every Child Matters*, which emphasized five outcomes.

1. Being healthy: enjoying good physical and mental health, and living a healthy lifestyle.
2. Staying safe: being protected from harm and neglect.
3. Enjoying and achieving: getting the most out of life and developing the skills needed for adulthood.
4. Making a positive contribution: being involved with the community and society, and not engaging in antisocial or offending behaviour.
5. Economic well-being: not being prevented by economic disadvantage from achieving their full potential in life.

These outcomes are linked to new targets and health indicators for children, which include further reducing the infant mortality rate, reducing the number of teenage pregnancies by 50 per cent (TPU 2006), improvements in access to child and mental health services, and reducing the number of children under 11 years who are obese.

This paper laid the foundations for the Children Act 2004, which also makes provision for a new Children's Commissioner to act as an independent champion for children, particularly those suffering disadvantage.

Children in the UK had often been overlooked in health service provision, and services from one area to another were often fragmented. In 2004 a National Service Framework (NSF) was introduced to set national health standards for children, young people and maternity services. This NSF focuses on early child-centred interventions, and has a remit to tackle health inequalities and promote the health of children from conception to adult-hood. These ambitious policies are themselves in their infancy; it will be important to monitor how far the aims are achieved over the next few years.

What factors influence children's health and well-being?

Health and emotional well-being are not static and most children will ex-perience varying levels according to their individual interactions with others, and influences such as diet and the amount of sleep they have. While these fluctuations are usual, some children rarely experience well-being – for example, if they are living in a war-torn country where they fear for their own and their family's survival, or in a family where there is domestic violence. Alternatively a child who lives in a positive environment, with an established social network, may experience high levels of well-being, which act as a re-source for development. These themes are developed further in other chapters but first it is important to consider children's health and well-being within its contextual framework. The health and well-being of a child can never be viewed in isolation and systems theory offers a framework for understanding the sheer complexity of factors that interplay to influence health. For ex-ample, a fretful baby impacts upon the relationship between the parents, which influences the way stress is experienced at work and reflects on the infant's well-being again when they come home. The effects of this situation may also 'ripple outwards' to impact on others such as work colleagues, neighbours or the extended family. The influences upon health and well-being are 'bi-directional', and Bronfenbrenner (1979) has developed a model showing how these influences can broadly be represented by different layers or systems. Figure 1.3 shows the theory in diagrammatic form. It is followed by a short explanation of each of the systems.

Bronfenbrenner's theory of ecological development

American psychologist Urie Bronfenbrenner studied children's development within their environmental contexts. This 'ecological' approach focuses on how the child's unique characteristics interact with her or his surroundings. Bronfenbrenner's ecological systems theory views the child as developing within a complex set of relationships that are influenced by the various levels of the surrounding environment. Influences between individuals and each system are bi-directional and are mediated by many individual factors so no

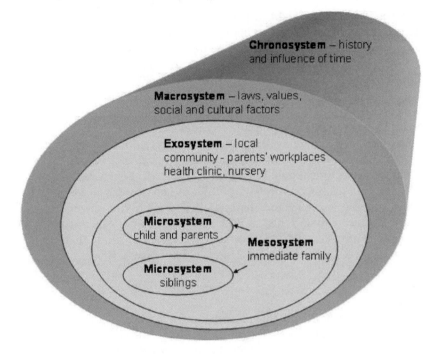

Figure 1.3 Bronfenbrenner's ecological systems theory

simple cause and effect models can be identified. (Some have recently re-named the model '*bio*ecological systems theory', to emphasize the importance of the child's own biological make-up.) Bronfenbrenner's theory focuses attention on a number of component systems, as described below.

The microsystem

The child is central in the innermost level of the environment, the micro-system, which reflects the immediate relationships and attachments experienced. All relationships are seen in this model as bi-directional and reciprocal, so adults affect children's responses but children's characteristics and beha-viour also influence adults' actions. Environmental factors impact upon the child right from the very beginning, with the pregnant woman developing a mental representation of her unborn child. This representation will initially be influenced by factors such as whether the child was planned and her re-lationship with her partner. The health of the expectant mother is closely linked to that of her unborn child, and research has shown detrimental links with factors such as stress, smoking and depression (Barker 1995). Infants are born ready to be social and to communicate (Murray and Andrews 2000) and, as active interpreters of their environments, the early relationships that the baby experiences are thought to play a role in the way that the brain cells (neurons) make connections and hard wire together (Schore 2001). Sensitive, warm interactions between young children and their main carers affect bonding and attachment, and may have long-term implications for health and well-being (Bowlby 1969, 1988; Stern 1998a; Schore 2001; Fonagy *et al.* 2004).

The mesosystem

No family can exist in isolation and the mesosystem refers to connections with settings such as the extended family, the nursery, childminder or school. Research (Runyan *et al.* 1998) has shown the crucial importance of strong support networks for children's health and well-being. For example, a child's well-being could easily be affected by either the positive involvement or the tension between a parent and the school. The mesosystem includes community involvements and this has been shown to be especially important for the whole family. Research (Johnson and Molloy 1995) shows that mothers are less likely to suffer from depression if they have a strong network of support.

The exosystem

The next layer of Bronfenbrenner's ecological systems model refers to influences that may impact upon the child's health less directly, but often forcefully. The parents' workplace is situated in the exosystem and if, for example, a parent was experiencing stress at work this may well impact upon the child, who might reflect the stress by developing difficult behaviour, resulting in more stress being placed upon the parents. (Of course this is not simple cause and effect as there would be many more influences involved.) Community health services are also part of the exosystem and a child living in poverty in a less industrialized country may have little access to health care, whereas in richer countries child health may be more closely related to whether parents choose to take up provisions such as immunization programmes or advice on nutrition.

The macrosystem

The macrosystem represents the culture, values and laws of the society in which the child lives. Culture could simplistically be defined as the 'rules and tools' of a society and, within that, the ways in which childhood is constructed and understood. What value is put upon children's health and well-being within any particular society? Teenage parents in the UK, for example, may feel discriminated against because the predominant culture suggests that parents should be older. The macrosystem reflects crucial policies such as how much financial support parents are given. For example, governments in the Nordic countries acknowledge the vital importance of the early parent–child relationship by offering extended maternity and paternity leave.

The global context
All these systems are embedded in the wider social context, which may have a major impact on the health of a nation. For example, when leaders practised oppressive policies within Iraq, much of the wider world responded by placing stringent sanctions on trade. A direct impact of this oppressive regime combined with the sanctions meant fewer health care provisions for young children and their families.

The chronosystem
The final system that Bronfenbrenner added to his ecological systems theory is the chronosystem, which refers to the influence of the passage of time. The child will change over time due to maturational processes, but these changes will also be influenced by the 'history' and culture of the family and wider community. Intergenerational influences will have an indirect impact on the child's health and well-being. For example, during the Second World War, many children in the UK were evacuated to safer areas in the countryside to ensure a better chance of survival. Although their physical safety was paramount, much less thought was given to the emotional impact of separation from their parents. The development of knowledge about children's emotional well-being would almost certainly influence against such practices happening today. The chronosystem reflects the impact of prior life events on later development, although these will be experienced and interpreted in unique ways by each individual.

A dynamic model

The environment is never static and the influences on health and well-being constantly interact with one another. Children who repeatedly experience positive exchanges may have a foundation of healthy self-esteem that enables them to cope more effectively when facing challenges. However, feelings of well-being vary to some extent according to day-to-day interactions. A dynamic systems model is an effective medium for considering how a multitude of factors impact on health and well-being. This book uses Bronfenbrenner's model as a framework for considering how a child's health and well-being is influenced by reciprocal processes of interaction both within and across systems. Young children's health and well-being are best considered within the social, political and cultural contexts in which the child is an active participant. Some social scientists (e.g. Prout 2005) have criticized the fact that the model may be viewed as static:

> despite encouragement to examine the interaction between levels, most social science continues to deal with children by focusing on one level only. For example, a lot of attention may be given to the

'micro' and the rest is dealt with as a more or less constant 'context'. Alternatively the wider context is studied but the linkages between this and local circumstances and practices are left unexamined or assumed. (Prout 2005: 65)

Bronfenbrenner's ecological systems model does provide a helpful theoretical framework for considering the interactional nature of influences on health and well-being but it should be employed critically and explored in the light of other developing theoretical approaches.

Risk and resilience

Bronfenbrenner's approach, therefore, views the child's health and well-being as developing within complex systems of relationships that are affected by multiple environmental levels, time and intergenerational patterns. A child's individual genetic predispositions, plus the fact that every child will make sense of each influence in his or her own way, by building on their previous experiences, means that it is very hard to predict the effect of any event on an individual child's well-being. All children have a right to be protected from circumstances that compromise their health and well-being, and situations such as living in poverty or relative poverty compound the risks of ill-health unacceptably. The first action in promoting children's health and well-being must always be to eliminate unacceptable risks and ensure every child has their entitlement to a standard of living that is good enough to meet their physical and mental needs. Article 27 of the UNCRC states that governments should help families that cannot afford to provide this. Not all risk can be eliminated and to begin to explore this further it is useful to consider some of the research into resilience and how this can underpin emotional well-being.

Resilience is often thought of as an 'inner strength' or the ability to cope in the face of adversity. Michael Rutter offers the following definition:

> Resilience seems to involve several related elements. First, a sense of self-esteem and self confidence; second a belief in one's own self-efficacy and ability to deal with change and adaptation; and third, a repertoire of social problem-solving approaches. (Rutter 1985, cited in Mental Health Foundation 1999: 10)

A number of research studies have examined the concept of resilience, and Newman (2004) overviews some key studies. Some of the factors (Rutter and Smith 1995) thought to promote resilience in young children include:

- easy temperament as an infant
- secure attachment

- affectionate relationships
- good communication skills
- problem-solving approach
- sense of humour
- religious faith/belonging
- positive attitude
- capacity to reflect
- wide support network
- supervision and firm, reasonable boundaries for behaviour
- higher intelligence
- lack of severe disharmony in family relationships
- support for education.

Werner (1996) studied a group of high-risk children through to adulthood and concluded that the single most important feature in developing resilience is having someone who really cares. The child who really 'matters' to another person, usually the parent, seems to have an invaluable resource for health and well-being. Building children's resilience, therefore, might involve eliminating unacceptable risk factors, such as poverty, and ensuring parents are offered appropriate support. Children who have been looked after by the state in the UK have had a poor health record largely due to the fact that many have had no consistent 'champion' to look out for them (see Chapter 6). The UK government recognized that children in the care of the state (because their families could not care for them) had greater health needs and were receiving some of the least effective care, so in 1998 the Quality Protects programme (DoH 1998) was launched, setting standards to improve the health and life chances of the most vulnerable and disadvantaged children. Few would dispute the fact that the family is central to supporting children's health and well-being, but in the UK the basic family unit is changing due to differing pressures and expectations (see Chapter 6). The Mental Health Foundation's report, *Bright Futures* (MHF 1999) suggests that families need more supportive services and networks if they are to nurture the next generation successfully:

> Not only has the family changed, but the social environment has changed in ways that make it harder for parents to provide the good care which will be the basis of their child's healthy physical and emotional development. There needs to be recognition that parenting is not an intrinsically private act, but that family life is constructed around a network of relationships within a larger setting of community, social and legal structures. Policies should not be based on blaming the child and parents when things go wrong, but on supporting parents in the parenting task. This justifies a range of

initiatives from more public provision for parent education through to national policies on employment, taxation, housing, health and social services which help parents. (MHF 1999: 21)

Change within the family has focused attention on the importance of supportive networks for health and well-being; this is sometimes referred to as 'social capital'.

Social capital

Social capital has only relatively recently been acknowledged as an important public health concept and refers to the beneficial effects of interpersonal relationships, social networks and support, trust, reciprocity, and community and civic engagement (Morrow 1999). The extent to which a family or an individual feels part of the community plays a major part in developing a sense of belonging and well-being, and affects the quality of family life. Bullen and Onyx (1999) define social capital as a developing process:

> Social capital is the raw material of civil society. It is created from the myriad of everyday interactions between people. It is not located within the individual person or within the social structure, but the space between people. It is not the property of the organisation, the market or the state, though all can engage in its production. Social capital is a 'bottom up' phenomenon. It originates with people forming social connections and networks based on principles of trust, minimal reciprocity and norms of action.

Social capital has been interpreted in different ways, and there is considerable debate as to whether it is an attribute of individuals or communities. Wilkinson (1996) argues that living in relative poverty affects health and well-being because it erodes social capital, and that social inequalities reduce social cohesion and undermine supportive networks. Living in a run-down community with few resources may well act as a barrier to building up supportive networks. Also, families struggling to survive financially are more likely to live in areas with high crime rates, leading to less trust within the community. Bronfenbrenner (2005) considers social networks to have a moderating effect and highlights the fact that they can change direction and exert negative or positive impacts. For example, he cites research that showed how supportive networks fostered the development of maternal responsiveness, but a subsequent investigation discovered that for 'mothers living under highly stressful environmental conditions, social networks not only ceased to exert a positive influence but become a source of stress' (Bronfenbrenner 2005: 79).

Bourdieu (1986) perceived social capital as a privilege that is based on the roots of economic well-being, whereas Putnam (2000) saw economic growth (or decline) as developing from social capital. This is an important distinction as there may be an implicit message that high levels of 'social capital' create cohesive communities rather than the more likely opposite action of economically secure communities being able to forge effective networks. Campbell (1999) suggests that social capital can act as a 'buffer' against disadvantage, but this could lead to a damaging approach where disadvantaged communities are blamed for not working together to help themselves. There is ample evidence that neighbourhood segregation, social discrimination (Collins and Williams 1999; House and Williams 2000) and poverty (Spencer 2000) are directly associated with poor health outcomes for children and families. However, Wallerstein (2002) claims there is no evidence that lack of social capital, independent of disadvantage or discrimination, causes poor health outcomes. Social capital can be undermined by poverty and social exclusion, which act as barriers to social cohesion (Horwath 2001). Focusing on social capital rather than social justice may compound the difficulties facing families living on low incomes in disadvantaged areas by concentrating on changing society rather than the economy. Policies that focus on social justice by ensuring that children and families have sufficient economic resources may result in families experiencing higher levels of self-efficacy and an increase in social capital (Morrow 1999).

Community capacity and community empowerment

Although social capital has gained prominence in the health literature, its interpretation is problematic. Wallerstein (2002) argues that two broader concepts – community capacity and community empowerment – are more useful in discussing health enhancing strategies. There are ten dimensions to community capacity: 'active participation, leadership, rich support networks, skills and resources, critical reflection, sense of community, understanding of history, articulation of values and access to power' (Wallerstein 2002: 73). This is a wider concept encapsulating social capital within 'rich social networks' and defining empowerment as: 'a social action process by which individuals, communities and organisations gain mastery over their lives in the context of changing their social and political environment to improve equity and quality of life' (Wallerstein 2002: 73). This broader concept is particularly valuable when considering pathways between powerlessness and poor health outcomes for children. For children, health-related behaviours need to be considered in the everyday contexts in which they take place – principally, for young children, within the home and nursery or school. Mayall (1994) reports how, within the home, children teach their parents to characterize them as individuals. This is often in contrast to the situation at school, where children are treated as part of a group within a predominately adult-directed social environment, leaving them powerless to negotiate. As children become more accepted as active participants, more exploration is needed into how capacity and empowerment can enhance health outcomes within the everyday contexts of their lives (see Chapter 9).

Conclusion

This chapter aims to give a broad introduction into the definitions and determinants of young children's health and well-being, set within a contextual framework so that some of the shaping influences can be highlighted. Historically, as far as health and well-being are concerned, children have been almost invisible as ensuring health has been considered the role of the adult or the 'professional'. Listening to young children and valuing their views as valid in their own right is supported by the UNCRC and by a growing body of research. The theme of listening to young children is developed throughout this book alongside the deep respect for the value of family life, which is set out in the UNCRC. Chapter 2 reviews research about the transition to parenthood and reflects on the possible impacts on family health and well-being when an infant is born. Different rituals that surround childbirth are discussed briefly, and post-natal depression and early support are reviewed. Chapter 3 explores theories and research about the foundations for emotional and social well-being, and reflects on how infants begin to learn to manage their emotional states. The effects of living in poverty or relative poverty are considered in Chapter 4. A global perspective is adopted as there is much to learn from the experiences of children's health and well-being in different locations. The terms 'developed' and 'developing' countries have been avoided where possible, as they may imply an inappropriate hierarchy. Most of the world's children live in the newly industrializing countries of 'the south' and the smaller proportion live in the richer countries, which include Australia, New Zealand, the UK, North America and most of Europe. The richer countries are sometimes referred to as the minority world: a reminder that most young children live in the less economically privileged majority world. Chapter 5 includes a range of issues about children's nutrition from breastfeeding to feeding difficulties and **obesity**. Families are changing rapidly in the twenty-first century and the possible impacts on children's health and well-being are discussed in Chapter 6. Child public health is concerned with improving the quality and length of life through health promotion and disease prevention within the population, and examples of these issues are reviewed in Chapter 7. Many children in the UK experience emotional or behavioural problems and in Chapter 8 a variety of perspectives about children experiencing stress are examined. Emotional and behavioural difficulties represent the way young children communicate distress and this chapter reflects on the various contexts that may impact upon this. For example, attention deficit hyperactivity disorder (ADHD) is much diagnosed in some cultures yet children's views are rarely reflected in research about the condition. Chapter 9 reviews research that considers outcomes when young children are involved in negotiating their own health and well-being. Finally, Chapter 10 concludes by pulling together some of the themes that have been developed throughout this book and considers how developments in the way childhood is conceptualized have implications for 'what works' in promoting young children's health and well-being. In recognizing each young child as a unique individual with their own likes and dislikes, the issue of young children's participation is highlighted as not only possible but key in developing health and well-being.

This book has taken specific examples from research that reflect some of the ways in which children's health and well-being is negotiated, but inevitably has left much out. There is infinite value in studying children's health and well-being cross-culturally and, while references are made to an international perspective, this book draws mostly on UK research. It is hoped that the issues raised will encourage further and deeper exploration.

2 The transition to parenthood

The safe arrival of a newborn infant is considered to be one of the happiest and most natural events in the human life cycle. Popular magazines carry many pictures depicting cute, smiling infants with relaxed parents, creating a mythical image of perfection and denying the more challenging aspects of becoming parents. Traditionally many cultures have surrounded childbirth with a number of customs and practices that are intended to control the unpredictability of nature and offer protection for the new mother and her child. The health and safety of the mother and infant are of paramount importance but, in the more industrialized world, this has often meant that birth becomes a medical event. Much energy is put into the physical preparations for the birth of the new baby but there is much less preparation for the inevitable emotional transitions facing partners who become parents. Increasing knowledge about the psychological processes that men and women face during the transition to parenthood, coupled with evidence about the effects of early interactions on infant development (see Chapter 3) mean that this is an important period in terms of the child's future mental health and well-being.

This chapter provides an overview of the transition to parenthood and highlights the support role of professionals, especially at a time when some traditional family and neighbourhood support networks have become less strong. It is argued that parents-to-be need accurate information about the emotional processes involved in the transition to parenthood, accessible practical support, and workplace and government policies that support parents. Using an ecological systems framework, the chapter starts by reviewing research evidence about the emotional changes parents-to-be may experience during pregnancy and when the new infant arrives. Special note is made of differing circumstances that may cause extra stress, such as when mothers are very young or infants born pre-term or with difficulties. Finally, attention is drawn to macro issues such as maternity and paternity leave policies and flexible working.

Changing relationships during pregnancy

In all cultures pregnancy and childbirth are embedded in rituals and customs that may be protective, but that can also exert powerful social and emotional pressures. American families, for example, may celebrate the impending birth by hosting a 'baby shower', when family and friends visit and literally shower the family with gifts for the new baby. This places the mother-to-be at the centre of attention but may also make her feel that she has to conform to expectations, grow the perfect baby and be the ideal mother. Other expectant mothers may experience the social pressures of not being 'good enough' because poverty, reflected in the lack of expensive equipment, is a powerful symbol of the inequality of life chances.

Feelings of closeness

During pregnancy, many women become preoccupied with the physical changes, and the excitement about creating a new life often causes the couple to feel very close emotionally. Many couples expect this closeness to last for ever, although Clulow (1991) refers to this period in the relationship as a fantasy state – perhaps before the storm of sleepless nights! In contrast, some men may resent their lack of control during pregnancy, and the attention being given to their partner. In these situations domestic violence sometimes becomes a feature of the relationship (Hedin *et al.* 1999).

Levels of stress in pregnancy

Stress during pregnancy is common. For example, one **longitudinal study** of low-risk parents-to-be in the UK showed that a substantial number of couples experienced 'psychological distress'. This study showed that couples had more concerns about emotional and relationship issues than aspects of the birth or childcare. It identified that support from external sources was low, forcing the couple to support one another, thereby increasing tensions between them. The study also showed that satisfaction with a couple's relationship declined after birth, and that lack of attention to the different needs of men and women in antenatal classes increased distress in both parent–parent and infant–parent relationships (Parr 1998). The parents' representations of their child – what they imagine the unborn infant will be like and how they imagine themselves as caregivers – have been found to be powerful predictors of how well couples will adapt to their new roles (Slade and Cohen 1996). Stress and depression during pregnancy have also been shown to be associated with poor outcomes for the infant. For example, a recent study showed that a high level of antenatal anxiety was a predictor of emotional and behavioural problems at 4 years of age in both boys and girls (Glover and O'Connor 2002).

Teenage pregnancy

In some parts of the world it is traditional that many women have their first child while still in their teens. However, in industrialized countries having a baby at a very young age is seen by many as a problem. In 1999 the UK government's Social Exclusion Unit published a ten-year strategy (SEU 1999) to reduce the number of teenage pregnancies. The rate of teenage pregnancies was the highest in western Europe (SEU 1999; UNICEF 2001b) and although every area of the UK was affected, the highest numbers of teenage births were found in the poorest areas and among the most vulnerable young people. The mortality rate for babies born to teenage mothers is 60 per cent higher than for babies of older mothers and infants are more likely to be born pre-term or have a low birth weight, or have a childhood accident and be admitted to hospital (SEU 1999). In the longer term, they are more likely to become teenage parents themselves (SEU 1999). In addition, teenage relationships in the UK have a higher chance of breakdown and single parents are more likely to live on a very low income. The SEU report describes one teenage mother's experience as follows:

> Although I loved my son I cried for many years after he was born because I lost my independence and my childhood, and I resented this. I lost many of my friends through no longer being able to socialise with them. I became very lonely and felt isolated. This life was not glamorous, instead it was lonely and for years I resented this because I wanted to go out clubbing and wear nice clothes. (SEU 1999: 62)

Some teenage pregnancies are planned, although one study found that the desire to have a baby was often strongly linked with young people seeking an opportunity to change their lives and gain a new role in life (Cater and Coleman 2006). Teenage parents' motivations for starting a family varied, but some felt that they could compensate for their own difficult experiences in childhood and that parenting was preferable to a low-paid, uninteresting job (Cater and Coleman 2006).

Although the transition to parenthood may seem much more difficult for teenagers, the adaptation that women and men make to their new roles usually depends more on other influencing factors rather than age. Every new parent has their own history of being parented (Slade and Cohen 1996) and this, combined with the available levels of emotional, social and financial support, is an important factor in how well the transition to parenthood is negotiated. In 2005 UK figures showed that the number of teenage pregnancies are not reducing in line with government targets, indicating that the

SEU's strategies may need reviewing. However, where young mothers have received effective support the experience can be more positive, with many new skills being mastered in childcare, budgeting and household organization, leading to an increase in confidence and opportunities for education and employment (Horgan 2001). The government has recognized the support needs of young parents in the National Service Framework for Children, Young People and Maternity Services (NSF) (2004), and Sure Start Plus projects have been set up to deliver coordinated support in some local areas. In particular the Sure Start Plus evaluation (2005) has shown effectiveness in:

- supporting young women in their decisions about pregnancy
- support for relationship and emotional issues including dealing with domestic violence
- improving family relationships
- improving housing situations
- increasing educational participation for those under 16 years.

In 2005 Sure Start Plus reported less success in involving young fathers and in specific health outcomes such as increasing the rates of breastfeeding or reducing smoking. These are areas that are high on the political agenda, requiring sensitive research that elicits parents' views.

The next section, discusses methods of preparation for parenthood.

Preparation for birth

Antenatal classes are one of the main 'official' sources of preparation for parenthood in the UK and a series of five or six two-hour classes are often offered by midwives. The aim of these classes is to prepare men and women for childbirth itself, by building the confidence and self-esteem that will enable parents to be in control of the labour and birth. The reality, however, may be somewhat different. Indeed, some have questioned the purpose of such classes, suggesting that they actually function to 'programme' the woman for a 'passive acceptance of medicalised childbirth' (Oakley 1980), while others have suggested that the teaching methods used in such classes 'often promote dependency amongst clients rather than nurturing the decision-making skills required by a consumer-driven maternity service' (Nolan 1997). It has been suggested that, in the UK,

> Less than half of pregnant women attend any sort of class, needs and service provision are mismatched, certain parents are missing out, men are excluded, the focus of the classes is too narrow, aims are unclear, the quality is poor and there is lack of specialised training,

management and support for those providing the services. (Parr 1998)

While women of different cultures may rely on various sources of support, a survey of white, Indian and mixed-origin women in South Africa showed that all groups, irrespective of ethnicity, felt that they had received poor preparation for most aspects of their experience of becoming a parent (Chalmers and Meyer 1994). In the UK, traditional antenatal classes have been found to address only the physical aspects of birth and often unintentionally exclude fathers-to-be (Combes and Schonveld 1992; Underdown 1998). In 2004, the Department of Health (DoH) published a ten-year strategy, the NSF (see the previous section), which provides standards for health services and points to the need for maternity services to provide 'good clinical and psychological outcomes for the woman and baby while putting equal emphasis on helping new parents prepare for parenthood' (DoH/DfES 2004). The Royal College of Paediatrics and Child Health (RCPCH) produced a report which stated that:

> Parenting starts with the unborn child and much more can and should be done to recognise potential problems and provide support to parents during the antenatal period. This requires antenatal services that provide time to talk with parents about their concerns and antenatal classes that address the emotional needs of parents and babies. (RCPCH 2002: 22)

Parents in Partnership Parent–Infant Network (PIPPIN) is a group-based parenting programme that is provided by some specially trained health visitors and midwives during the antenatal and immediate post-natal period. The aim of this programme is specifically to support and promote the emotional transition to parenthood. It is provided before and after the birth to groups of first-time parents for a period of two hours weekly, with one visit at home following birth – a total of 35 hours of support. The programme focuses on parent–infant communication and relationships (PIPPIN 2000), as opposed to the types of topic that are typically included in antenatal classes, such as the 'mechanics' of labour, delivery and infant care. It is based on a range of activities that are designed to raise the self-confidence and self-esteem of parents about their own parenting abilities and to promote the kind of nurturing parenting that research suggests is more likely to result in healthy attachment between parents and their infants. The results of a controlled study showed a significant increase in the psychological health of parents, increased confidence as a parent, increased satisfaction with the couple and parent–infant relationship, and more nurturing child-centred attitudes as regards infant care (Parr 1998).

Birth rituals and customs

Most cultural groups surround life transitions such as childbirth with a series of rituals that are intended to make order out of the 'chaos' caused by nature. Rituals are modified and changed over time, but it is useful to reflect and compare customs and the reasons why they were adopted. For example, traditionally in Jamaica the woman would have had a period of 40 days' seclusion following the birth, which was aimed at giving the new mother a rest and possibly preventing infection (Kitzinger 1982). Similarly, in 1967, Kelly reported how Nigerian mothers had special care from the babies' grandmothers and were secluded for two to three months after the birth. To mark the conclusion of this period of rest and attention, the mother and baby's reemergence into the community was celebrated with a feast in their honour; Kelly (1967) argued that these customs might have protected the mother against post-natal depression. This contrasts with recent practice in the UK in which women were frequently discharged from medical care after 24 hours and before they had rested or had a chance to establish feeding. A severe shortage of midwives in the UK meant that the physical safety of the mother and baby had to be prioritized, with medical practitioners concentrating on the physiological aspects of birth and treating the woman's body as a machine that has a task to perform. This machine was often perceived as 'faulty', as highlighted by the use of terminologies such as 'failure to progress' and 'incompetent cervix'. The *Changing Childbirth* report (Expert Maternity Group 1993) acknowledged that the woman should be the focus of care in order to maximize her control over the delivery. However, pregnant women may still feel disempowered during childbirth, with the expectant mother's 'condition' being treated in isolation from the rest of her life (Helman 2000) and with little account being taken of her new 'social' birth as a mother. The NSF (DoH 2004b) is intended to stimulate long-term improvements in the standards of services, and pledges that by 2009 all women will have a choice of where and how they have their baby and what pain relief they use. There is also a commitment that women will be supported by the same midwife throughout the whole pregnancy and that there will be an increased network of professional support (DoH 2004a).

Becoming parents

The past 60 years have seen wide-ranging changes in the roles of men and women, family life and support networks. Bronfenbrenner's ecological systems theory (1979) (see Figure 1.3) offers an effective framework for considering how men and women need to negotiate new relationships, not only with each other but with every system. Traditionally women have provided most of the caregiving, while men have had a greater role in the family's interactions with the outside world. Couples have to successfully renegotiate boundaries such as who works outside the home, who is responsible for organizing childcare, who does which domestic tasks, how much social life each partner has, in parallel with developing perceptions of their partner's identity as a parent as well as a lover. Parents who successfully adapt to these multiple demands may form a parenting alliance in which their new roles complement one another and they can work together. Not all couples are able to adapt easily to their 'social birth' as new parents, however, and evidence shows that the relationships of many couples are severely challenged and may break down after the birth of a baby (Cowan and Heatherington 1991; Belsky and Kelly 1994). Cowan and Cowan (1992: 212–13) researched the transition to parenthood and argued that the 'conspiracy of silence' that surrounds this period leaves the couple feeling that they are the only ones having a hard time, whereas the research showed that:

- new fathers as well as mothers are at risk of depression
- the level of stress and distress couples experience during pregnancy may predict difficulties with parenting
- conflict or distress in the family while the child is young are accompanied by poorer parent–child relationships and slower progress in the child's cognitive and social development up until and beyond starting school
- professional intervention with couples during the first year of parenthood, focusing on relationships, can have a significant impact on reducing the separation rate of couples, improving the quality of parenting and their child's adjustment and development.

Furthermore, there are many cultural contradictions surrounding pregnancy, childbirth and parenthood that may also make the transition to parenthood more difficult. For example, prevalent beliefs about pregnancy and motherhood being a totally 'natural' and happy time in a woman's life are frequently in sharp contrast to the woman's lived experience. In addition, while childbirth is viewed as 'natural', it has also been located within a pathological or illness model, which has implications for the way in which women and men experience and make sense of this event (Miller 2000). Consider the following case study in the light of research findings about the transition to parenthood.

Case study

Sonia and Raj had been living together for three years, both had good jobs and they were buying a flat together. They hoped, one day, to have two children and when Sonia became pregnant it was a little earlier than they would ideally have planned, but they were both delighted. Sonia continued work until 35 weeks and Raj spent the weekends doing up the spare bedroom as a nursery. They attended antenatal classes together at the clinic and had a tour round the local maternity ward. Raj was very attentive towards Sonia during her pregnancy and she enjoyed his protective comments and interest in their growing baby. Sonia had hoped for a normal delivery but in the end her cervix didn't open sufficiently to allow the baby to be delivered vaginally. Apparently 'failure to progress' is quite a common reason for a Caesarean section and it wasn't too bad as Raj was there to see their beautiful baby son, Sanjeev, enter the world. Sonia was a bit daunted to be home so soon – just three days after the operation – especially as she was still very tired and was trying to establish breastfeeding. It was difficult trying to get Sanjeev to latch on to the breast and Sonia became quite sore and very tearful before the midwife helped her to get the positioning right. Sonia had thought breastfeeding would be the most natural thing in the world – she had no idea that she would need to learn the technique. After two months Sonia found it hard to believe the changes in her life. She was totally absorbed with caring for the baby but Raj felt strongly that the baby should be in a routine and not breastfeeding all the time. Sonia thought Raj should help more with the chores and Raj argued that he was working flat out with his job and getting no attention from Sonia at all. In fact Sonia said making love was the last thing on her mind because she was so tired with the baby; Raj viewed this as another rejection. Six months on, the family have adjusted much more and are enjoying their new roles as parents. However, looking back Sonia and Raj feel quite shocked at how close they came to splitting up in those first weeks. On reflection, they realized that they had never discussed their views on childcare and neither of them had appreciated just how much a baby would impact on their lives.

New identities as parents

The 'fantasy of closeness' that draws couples together during pregnancy is often expected to continue after the baby is born. Following childbirth, however, there is frequently a polarization of goals and expectations as men and women negotiate their new roles (Belsky and Kelly 1994). Stern (1998b) explains how this experience of polarization is influenced by the 'motherhood constellation', which, he argues, is a temporary period in which the mother is preoccupied with several themes. One of these, the 'life growth theme', is biologically driven, making the mother's need to keep the baby alive her top priority (Stern 1986). This is what Sonia, in the case study, was experiencing in the first few months, when all her energies were focused on Sanjeev.

Couples are often unprepared for these fundamental changes in their senses of identity and, without the recognition that this may affect their relationship, there may be resentment and blame. As the case study demonstrates, for a few months after childbirth a mother may have little interest in leaving the baby to go out for an evening and she may be more interested in her partner's skills as a father than as a lover. Although the baby may be the focus, it is often the fundamental changes in the parents themselves that cause the disunity, and couples may need to mourn the loss of their earlier relationship before they can celebrate their new roles. In addition, there may be deep tensions between the cultural aspirations of a contemporary woman living in the industrialized world and the experience of biological drives associated with motherhood. These tensions may be exacerbated by the transition from being a 'competent woman', in control of her life to an 'incompetent', or inexperienced, mother. As support networks loosen and traditional rituals decline, the challenge to health professionals lies in ensuring the healthy emotional and social births of the mother and father.

Pre-term birth

Pregnancy reaches full term at 40 weeks and if an infant is born at 37 weeks' gestation or earlier this is classified as a **pre-term birth**. (This is a more precise word than premature, which has become a lay term to include babies who are born 'small for dates' as well as those who are born early). Most babies born up to eight weeks pre-term will have few difficulties, but as technology becomes increasingly advanced neonatal specialists have developed the skills to keep alive infants born after only 23 weeks of gestation and often weighing less then a kilogram. Parents of these tiny infants often face a confusing and frightening array of machinery and 'bleeping' equipment when they first enter the neonatal unit. Parents whose babies are born early have missed out on the natural preparation and this, combined with the stress of contemplating whether their baby will enjoy a healthy future, adds another dimension to the processes of the transition to parenthood. Parents of extremely small or pre-term infants, or those whose infant has a disability, will experience a sense of shock and numbness because the pregnancy has not turned out in the way expected. Mothers and fathers need time to adjust to this different experience and they may need to grieve for the full-term or the able-bodied infant they were expecting. If the baby is very fragile or ill parents may remain detached because they fear the pain of losing their infant. Many parents say that the worst part of having their baby cared for in a special hospital unit is feeling that there is so little they can do and having so little contact: 'It was painful not having my baby beside me. There was an ache because I was apart from my baby and I was not able to find the bond between her and me' (Redshaw *et al.* 1985).

As very pre-term babies grow and develop it is important to remember that they are younger than other children who may share the same birthday.

Case study

Amy was born at 26 weeks' gestation in mid-August, 14 weeks earlier than her estimated date of delivery in November. She weighed 880 grams and spent the first month of her life having her breathing supported by a ventilator and with extra oxygen. She came home from the hospital about the time she would have been born in November. Amy made excellent progress but her mother was constantly being asked 'When will she catch up? Is it at two years or five years that they catch up?' Amy's mother developed an answer to explain that Amy did not need to catch up – she was merely younger than her birth date suggested.

Lack of understanding puts additional pressure on parents and may place unfair demands on children. For some extremely pre-term infants there may be long-term impacts on their health and development, ranging from complex disabilities to more subtle developmental factors (Wocadlo and Rieger 2006). In the Netherlands, doctors do not routinely offer care to babies born before 25 weeks and some medical ethicists, such as Mary Warnock (Templeton 2005), believe that a similar approach in setting an age limit for actively promoting life-saving medical techniques should be adopted in the UK. This fiercely debated argument raises ethical, moral and religious issues as well as concerns about the rights of the child.

Post-natal depression

Many mothers experience what has commonly been known as the 'baby blues' around the third day after the birth. Mothers often report that they do not really know why they feel so tearful and frequently attribute the mood swings to hormonal changes, being in hospital or coping with the new role of being a mother. Most couples experience some temporary periods of sadness, concern and tiredness as they adjust to their new roles. The term post-natal depression (PND) has been used as a blanket term to cover an array of conditions, ranging from anything more enduring than the third-day 'baby blues' to the rare and serious **puerperal psychosis**. The recorded incidence of post-natal depression varies between cultures. In the UK rates are thought to be about 10 per cent (Cooper 2001), although detecting PND can be difficult so this may be an underestimate. Day (2001) highlights increased risk factors alongside the difficulties of detecting the condition in South Asian communities living in the UK. Research studies in Sweden (Wickberg and Hwang 1997) show that approximately 15 per cent of women experience post-natal depression, with some surveys showing that 9.5 per cent of men (Ballard *et al.* 1994) will also experience depression. There are various schools of thought about the causes of post-natal depression. The medical model views PND as an 'illness' triggered by hormonal changes in a woman, whereas the social model highlights the cumulative effect of environmental stresses such as lack of social support, the changing roles in the transition to parenthood, the responsibility of coping with the infant and running a home, lack of adult company or an unsatisfactory couple relationship. The social model views it as a difficulty in adjusting to all the new roles and stresses associated with parenthood. Maternal depression may result in the mother feeling despondent, unable to cope and losing her usual interest in life. This level of depression is strongly associated with a reduced capacity to function, including mother–infant relationship difficulties and, in some cases, rejection of the infant (Loh and Vostanis 2004). It is very important that parents with post-natal depression are supported as it is a debilitating illness that can affect all the relationships within the family.

Mothers with post-natal depression are likely to experience difficulty with relationships – both within the family and in forging friendships with others – and this may leave them socially isolated. Post-natal depression is strongly associated with poorer outcomes in both emotional and cognitive functioning in children (Caplan 1989). Depressed mothers were found to be less sensitive, less attentive and more critical of their infants. According to Murray (1992; Murray and Cooper 1997), the effects of untreated post-natal depression on children may include:

- impaired cognitive development from 1 year on
- less warmth and positive interaction between the child and the parent (in both directions)
- more insecure attachments
- behavioural difficulties from 18 months.

Post-natally depressed mothers' interactions with their infants have been found to be less sensitive, with mothers either being indifferent and passive or intrusive and always 'doing things to' the baby (Glover 2001). Murray (2001), however, stresses that not all depressed mothers are less sensitive in their interactions and that exploring mother–baby communication has revealed interesting information. In particular, developmental outcomes were improved if the mother's speech focused on the baby's experience, and showed understanding of the infant as someone with a personality and intentions of his or her own.

Mothers' feelings of depression may be made worse if they consider that their illness is affecting their child, so it is important to remember that infants are active interpreters of their worlds and they may be able to forge warm interactions with other family members that may buffer the impact of their main carer's depression. A healthy couple relationship has also been shown to impact on the bonding and attachment processes that are fundamental to a child's short- and long-term health and well-being (Heinecke 1992). In the UK it is common practice for new mothers to complete the Edinburgh Post-Natal Depression Scale (EPDS) (see Figure 2.1) to identify the possibility of post-natal depression (Cox 1994). The EPDS is a screening tool (see the criteria for screening tests in Chapter 7) in which mothers self-rate how they have been feeling in the past seven days in relation to the statements listed in Figure 2.1. However, there are some limitations to this screening scale (Seeley 2001).

- Staff need training to use it sensitively and interpret it correctly.
- Some mothers may have literacy difficulties and the scale was never intended to be read aloud.
- The questions could be misinterpreted.
- Some mothers may choose to rate the 'right' answers to indicate that there are no problems and thus conceal their needs.
- It may be less culturally appropriate for some groups. For example, in Punjabi there is no word for depression, it is less acceptable to talk about emotions and women may describe physical symptoms such as 'my sinking heart', 'my heart feels heavy' or 'I feel weak' (Day 2001).

It is important to identify post-natal depression so that mothers can receive early support to help them feel better and enjoy being with their infants. The earliest years of life are a critical period when young children are making emotional attachments and forming the crucial first relationships that lay the foundations for future mental health. These issues are discussed in detail in Chapter 3.

In the UK many couples find that the traditional support networks of the extended family are no longer present and older family members are working or living too far away to give any practical help. This means that health professionals, including health visitors, midwives, community doctors and practitioners such as nursery nurses, need to begin to focus on supporting couples during the transition to parenthood, and on promoting the parent–

Figure 2.1   Edinburgh Post-Natal Depression Scale

The questions are about how you are feeling and about your mood. Please tick the statement that comes closest to *how you have felt in the past 7 days*, not just how you feel today.

1. **I have been able to laugh and see the funny side of things:**
   - A. As much as I always could ....
   - B. Not quite so much now...
   - C. Definitely not so much now ....
   - D. Not at all...
2. **I have looked forward with enjoyment to things:**
   - A. As much as I ever did...
   - B. Rather less than I did ....
   - C. Definitely less than I used to..
   - D. Hardly at all ....
3. **I have blamed myself unnecessarily when things went wrong:**
   - A. Yes, most of the time...
   - B. Yes, some of the time..
   - C. Not very often ....
   - D. No, never...
4. **I have felt worried and anxious for no good reason:**
   - A. No, not at all..
   - B. Hardly ever ....
   - C. Yes, sometimes ....
   - D. Yes, very often ....
5. **I have felt scared and panicky for no good reason:**
   - A. Yes, quite a bit...
   - B. Yes, sometimes ....
   - C. No, not much...
   - D. No, not at all..
6. **Things have been getting on top of me:**
   - A. Yes, most of the time I haven't been able to cope at all...................
   - B. Yes, sometimes I haven't been coping as well as usual.....................
   - C. No, most of the time I have coped quite well.................................
   - D. No, I have been coping as well as usual.......................................
7. **I have been so unhappy that I have had difficulty sleeping:**
   - A. Yes, most of the time...
   - B. Yes, sometimes ....
   - C. Not very often ....
   - D. No, not at all..
8. **I have felt sad or miserable:**
   - A. Yes, most of the time...
   - B. Yes, quite often..
   - C. Not very often ....
   - D. No, not at all..
9. **I have been so unhappy that I have been crying:**
   - A. Yes, most of the time...
   - B. Yes, quite often..
   - C. Only occasionally..
   - D. No, never...
10. **The thought of harming myself has occurred to me:**
   - A. Yes, quite often..
   - B. Sometimes...
   - C. Hardly ever ....
   - D. Never..

infant relationship. Where families have few social capital resources, health and well-being may be actively promoted by enabling social networks to be built through a variety of initiatives at children's centres (see the section on universal services in Chapter 3). Research into initiatives to support parents in the transition to parenthood is still in its relatively early stages and the next section describes the European Early Promotion Project, which aims to identify families that may need extra support.

The European Early Promotion Project

The European Early Promotion Project (EEPP) has developed new methods for supporting parents by trained primary health care workers (most of whom are health visitors in the UK) conducting 'promotional interviews' immediately before and after all new births. The aim of these interviews is to identify those who are experiencing problems antenatally and/or post-natally with a view to promoting positive interaction between parent and child. For example, the health visitor might ask as part of the antenatal interview, 'How did you feel when you learned that you were pregnant?' This provides the opportunity for the health visitor to endorse any positive feelings or to explore and talk further about any negative feelings. The health visitor then works intensively using counselling techniques with those families identified during interview as being in need of further support. This method of intervening during the perinatal period is currently being evaluated in a number of European countries including the UK (Puura *et al.* 2002). Early evidence shows that primary health care workers found the training useful in increasing their understanding and skills, in addition to improving their sensitivity to families' psychosocial needs and their accuracy in identifying psychosocial problems. Families were also significantly more satisfied with services (Puura *et al.* 2002).

Maternity and paternity leave

Parental leave policies in the UK are being strengthened and fathers as well as mothers are becoming entitled to time off when they have a new child. The effects of supporting new parents with maternity and paternity leave and flexible working options are easier to measure in physical health terms than in terms of emotional well-being. Tanaka (2005) examined the aggregate effects of parental leave policies by analysing data collected between 1969 and 2000 from 18 OECD (Organization for Economic Co-operation and Development) countries on child health outcomes. The study concluded that the extension of paid parental leave had a significant effect on reducing infant mortality rates. The study reports that a ten-week period of paid leave reduced mortality rates by 4.1 per cent, whereas unpaid leave was found to have no effect. Tanaka (2005) suggests that periods of unpaid leave may have been cut short because the parent needs to return to work for financial reasons. The financial security offered by paid leave is likely to impact on family stress levels. More studies to estimate whether additional parental leave strengthens family relationships would be valuable.

Conclusion

The protective rituals and customs that have traditionally surrounded the transition to parenthood are, in many places, being swept away, raising questions about how families can best be supported in the transition to parenthood. The findings of two recent **systematic reviews** about the effectiveness of programmes during pregnancy and early childhood suggest that they should concentrate on supporting individual and family strengths, and not just focus on risk factors (Bakermans-Kranenburg *et al.* 2003; Barnes and Lagevardi-Freude 2003). They recommend the use of an ecological approach that involves macro-level changes such as enhanced maternity and paternity leave to enable couples to adjust to their new roles and to bond with and get to know their infant. Access to accurate information about the emotional processes involved in the transition to parenthood and classes that offer preparation to support understanding of each other's new role as parent would be valued by many parents (Combes and Schonveld 1992; Barnes and Lagevardi-Freude 2003). This type of support may help avoid the early breakdown of relationships that many couples face, leaving children with only one parent as main carer and with the resulting stress that ensues. Perhaps most importantly, there is a need to recognize the importance of the emotional transition that men and women must make when they become parents and the part this plays in promoting early infant mental health.

3 Foundations for emotional and social well-being

From the very beginning, infants are seeking interaction with others and are continually influencing and responding to their changing environments. It is now acknowledged that the earliest years of life are a crucial period when children are making emotional attachments and forming the first relationships that lay many of the foundations for future mental health (Bowlby 1969, 1988; Sroufe 1995; Steele *et al.* 1996; Stern 1998a; Fonagy *et al.* 2004). Infants need opportunities to attune to others, to learn to regulate or manage their emotions, and to attach to main carers who in turn can reflect and respond to them as individuals. This chapter explores theory and research about how infants and their main carers build healthy relationships, and reviews theories about attunement, attachment and reflective function. It is important to remember that all these theoretical models are continuing to be developed and challenged by new research and by other theoretical models. Questions are often asked about how critical the earliest years are for future emotional well-being and mental health. This is a highly controversial debate and, although there is much research continuing in the area, there are probably no clear answers. Recent research about brain development is considered in relation to constructivist and determinist theories of attachment. Finally, universal services and policies aiming to support families with young infants are explored.

Attunement

> A father is cradling his young son in his arms and, as they gaze intently at one another, the infant begins to smile and the father responds by gently stroking the baby's cheek and softly saying 'Hello you' as he smiles back.

Special moments like these are the threads of emotional development that are woven through everyday interactions within relationships. As the British paediatrician and psychoanalyst Donald Winnicott (1966) argued, 'there is no such thing as a baby, there is a baby and someone'. Infants and young children cannot be studied in isolation as if their development happens spontaneously. This father's loving and gentle response may well reflect his own history and experience of interactions with others. Daniel Stern (1998a), an American psychiatrist and psychoanalyst, describes attunement as an empathic responsiveness between two individuals, which subtly conveys a shared emotion.

Learning to manage feelings: emotional regulation

One of the key tasks that a baby begins to deal with during the first year of life involves learning to manage or regulate his or her own emotions. When a baby is newborn the urge to have her or his needs met is intense and parents often describe the 'hunger cry', which must be met instantly. Infants notice that certain patterns are repeated. For example, the main carer may make soothing noises as she prepares to feed, using some sensitive infant-directed speech such as 'Okay baby, your milk is just coming.' This may seem routine and, thankfully, it is for many infants, but it is also a crucial interaction when the main carer 'contains' the infant's difficult feelings. Bion (1962) described 'containment' as the way in which one person could take on board the powerful feelings of another and, by communicating with touch, gesture and speech, makes them more manageable. Winnicott (1960) described how parents 'hold in mind' the needs of the baby so the infant actually experiences a sense of security with someone who understands his or her needs, responds to distress signals and contains her or his difficult feelings. As this pattern is consistently repeated the infant learns what to expect and to trust their main caregivers to help manage his or her emotions. Babies who learn to co-regulate their emotions with their carer also gradually learn how to self-regulate their own emotions, which is a very important social skill.

To recognize the infant's cues the parents need to be in touch with their own feelings and to have time for playful interactions. It is the sensitivity of the parent–infant relationship, in particular, that will create the conditions for establishing healthy patterns of functioning (Stein *et al.* 1991; Murray *et al.* 1996). Murray has demonstrated that the more the parent is sensitive in identifying the infant's signals and cues at 2 months the better the outcomes for cognitive and emotional development (Murray 1992). As the child grows, attunement continues to be important. If the caregiver can recognize the child's emotional state and symbolize it in words this gives the child the vocabulary and the understanding to process and cope with her or his own feelings. By the second half of the first year infants are communicating more widely with others. In situations where there is uncertainty they will check the expression of their main carer and adjust their behaviour accordingly. This 'social referencing' (Klinnert *et al.* 1983) aids developing understanding of the intentions and feelings of others.

Attuned social play: an example

Learning to manage or regulate one's own emotional state is a key task in the early years and early interactive play routines (Murray and Andrews 2000) such as the 'I'll gobble you up' game (Figure 3.1) help infants to learn to regulate their own emotional behaviour in conjunction with others. In the sequence of photos in Figure 3.1, Cody, aged 4 months, signals to his mother that he is ready to play, and then the pictures show how he manages his anticipation, excitement and pleasure. The mother and Cody make eye contact; there is an air of suspense as the young infant knows something is about to happen; suddenly mum reaches forward and 'gobbles' Cody, who squeals with laughter; then the sequence is repeated, but with different timing so that the baby has the added suspense of not knowing when the 'gobbling' action will happen. Timing (Trevarthan and Aitkin 2001) is crucially important and the mother knows that, by varying this, she can add to the suspense and fun. Play like this helps an infant to observe other people and sensitively pick up on their cues. This everyday game is about co-regulating emotions, managing anticipation and suspense, waiting and trusting, and sharing laughter. Cody might be said to be in a high state of arousal, although Sroufe (1995), who studied the emotional development of 180 infants, prefers the word 'tension' to 'arousal' as it captures the active role of the infant in creating, as well as responding to, stimulation. Sensitivity includes subtly increasing or lessening contact according to the infant's cues about what he or she is feeling. It is very common to be really enjoying a game when the pair 'mistune', or perhaps the adult doesn't pick up quickly enough on the cue that the infant has had enough and the laughter is suddenly replaced with overwhelmed cries. The crying is often followed by 'containing' behaviour as the care-giver cuddles and soothes the infant. Sensitivity includes the timing of the response and the match with the infant's expressed emotional state (Crockenburg and Leerkes 2000) and although mismatches are common, most infants and caregivers 'repair' these and this can positively contribute to the development of adaptive processes. Hopkins (1996) highlights the dangers of 'too good' mothering and argues that being completely tuned in is not an ideal state: 'it is the experience of frustration and conflict in concert with their successful repair and resolution which are optimal for development'.

Interaction in different cultures

Although games like the one Cody is playing are traditional in the UK, these patterns will be culturally specific. Caregivers' interactions have been examined in a range of cultures around the world. For example, Keller *et al.* (1988) observed video-taped interactions between caregivers and infants aged

Cody is now able to take part in body games. He and his mother, Beki, have developed a number of routines around the home of 'I'll gobble you up'.

1 Beki checks to see that Cody is ready for play.

2 As she opens her mouth and lowers her head in the direction of Cody's foot, he laughs in recognition.

3 Cody's feeling of suspense builds up, as he waits ...

4 ... for the climax ...

5 ... and then relaxes in laughter with his mother.

Figure 3.1   An example of 'attuned' social play: the 'I'll gobble you up' game

Source: Murray and Andrews (2000: 72–73)

6 Cody braces himself for another approach.

7 He takes part in the build-up, opening his mouth wide in concert with Becki.

8 Cody tilts his head back in anticipation ... and ...

9 ... waits with bated breath ...

10 ... for the 'gobble, gobble' ...

11 ... and wriggles with pleasure at the end.

between 2 and 6 months in Germany, Greece, Venezuela (Yonomami Indians) and New Guinea (Trobrian Islanders). The findings showed that emotionally expressive interactions have a common dialogue structure in all of these cultures. While Marquesan mothers in the South Pacific found it less comfortable to engage in intense face-to-face interaction with their infant, Martini and Kirkpatrick (1981) described how mothers actively encouraged infants to interact with others, especially older siblings:

> Mothers consistently provided the infant with an interactively stimulating world, first by interacting, next by encouraging and making effective his attempts to make contact, and finally by directing others to interact with the infant. Caregivers ... shaped the infants' attention towards others and objects, and shaped their movements towards effective contact and locomotion. By the end of the first year, infants were becoming interactants able to accompany and learn from older children in an environment supervised by adults. (Martini and Kirkpatrick 1981: 209)

LeVine *et al.* (1994) contrasted the interactional patterns of mothers and infants from America with those of Gusii mothers from north-eastern Africa. American mothers praised and encouraged active participation, whereas the Gusii mothers valued calmness and avoided highly excited or negative arousal states. Infants of Gusii mothers characteristically have close physical contact throughout the early years and much less face-to-face talking or eye contact compared with American infants (LeVine 1994). While both types of interaction are likely to make infants feel safe and secure, Bronfenbrenner (cited in LeVine 1994) indicates that these varied cultural practices will influence differing patterns of development.

Effects of post-natal depression

As described in the previous chapter, some mothers may experience post-natal depression and Murray (2001) has found that this affects the sensitivity of mother–infant interactions. It is more likely that mothers with post-natal depression will either be remote and distant with the infant or be intrusive. Interaction is two-way, and babies who become used to having unresponsive, joyless interchanges may begin to behave in that way themselves, thus making it less easy for them to elicit any playful exchange. A study by Sharpe *et al.* (1995) found that there were significant delays in development particularly for boys of depressed mothers. It is important to stress, however, that post-natal depression is not always linked with poor-quality interaction and other factors in the child's environment need to be taken into account. Other relationships the baby has with, for example, the father (Hossain *et al.* 1994) or grandparents can act as a buffer and for infants raised in cultures where there are extended social networks there is even more opportunity to find quality interaction.

When attunements become attachments

Through day-to-day caregiving, the bond of love between parents and their infants usually becomes very strong. Ideally, infants learn that they can rely on the main adults in their social network to help alleviate their stress and to share their joy and sense of fun. Crockenburg (cited in Zeanah 2000) argues that the strategies infants use to regulate their emotional states underpin the development of attachment relationships and contribute to children's developing independence and 'mastery' in the second and third years of life. On the other hand, lack of warmth and sensitive care may prevent the development of emotional regulation strategies and be a factor in behaviour problems. Survival is the primary goal for the dependent infant and, in order to gain the protection and nurturing required, the infant needs to stay in close proximity to the main carer, who acts as a 'secure base' (Bowlby 1988).

Children who feel confident that their caregiver will be there to protect them gain the confidence to explore knowing that they can 'refer back' when they are unsure about new experiences. In the next section, attachment theory is discussed alongside research linking this to well-being and mental health.

What is attachment theory?

Bonding and attachment are different. Bonding is the binding love that a parent may feel for their infant, sometimes strongly even before he or she is born. 'Attachment' refers to the enduring 'tie' of affection directed towards a small number of close individuals, leading to pleasure in interactions and comfort by being close at times of stress. Babies become attached to familiar carers who respond to their physical and emotional needs and, by about 7 months, the baby will show her or his attachment behaviour by being very wary of strangers and clinging on to their main carers. In the 1950s John Bowlby, a British psychiatrist and psychoanalyst, first identified the crucial role that the loving attachment between an infant and his or her mother played in the foundation of mental health. Bowlby (1969, 1973, 1980) conducted a famous study where he found that 14 out of 17 juvenile thieves who had suffered maternal deprivation were particularly uncaring about the victims of their crimes and did not experience any guilt feelings. This led Bowlby to believe that the first relationship with the mother was the crucial foundation for people's mental health and that the main ingredient for secure attachment is parenting that is characterized by warmth, sensitivity, responsiveness and dependability. The baby gains a sense of belonging, or reassurance that the world is safe, when the behaviour of the adult is in tune with the inner state of the baby. By about 6 months emotionally healthy infants become more confident that their distress signals will be responded to appropriately and they begin to develop what Bowlby describes as an 'internal working model', which is a sort of blueprint of what to expect from relationships both in the present and in the future. Children who feel valued by having their distress signals answered will develop a sense of self-worth and the confidence to separate and explore knowing that their carer can be returned to for safety. These children are said to be securely attached to their main carers and usually they will be able to make friendships more easily with their peers. In contrast, children who receive insensitive, inconsistent or unresponsive care are more likely to form an internal working model in which other people cannot be relied upon, and children who are constantly let down will find it difficult to trust within relationships.

Bowlby's research was not well received initially in post-war Britain. Men had just returned from fighting in the Second World War (1939–45) and far from returning to the promised land 'fit for heroes' they found austere conditions and few jobs. Women had successfully taken on many traditionally male roles and Bowlby's work was much opposed by the feminist lobby, some thinking it politically timely to encourage women out of the workplace and back to the home to care for children. Eventually, the establishment became convinced about the importance of early attachment through the dramatic emotional impact of films made by Joyce and James Robertson (1989) of children separated from their parents. The Robertsons filmed the behaviour of children separated from their parents due to their admission into residential care or hospital. The medical world was shocked by the heart-rending despair and initially rejected the powerful visual evidence, but gradually accepted the sense of loss shown by the children. One child, John, who had come into a residential nursery for nine days became increasingly distressed, before sinking into complete despair and apathy and, when his mother did return, he rejected her. These films and Bowlby's research (1980) on attachment and loss have had a lasting impact on service design in the UK. Children were no longer expected to stay in hospital alone, camp beds were made available for parents and, more recently, full accommodation has often been provided for families when children are hospitalized. Similarly, in education, children starting nursery have 'settling-in' procedures when parents are encouraged to stay during the time it takes for their child to feel confident in the transition to nursery, and many nurseries have a member of staff who becomes the 'key person' for the child (Elfer *et al.* 2003). The damaging effect of multiple placements for children looked after by the state was realized and the health of children in the care of the state is explored in Chapter 6.

Developing attachment research

Bowlby's work was further extended by Schaffer and Emerson (1964), who found that the crucial first attachment did not necessarily have to be with the mother (although most are) and suggested that the crucial issue is that loving, warm relationships develop with somebody who is reliable and consistent. Later research confirmed the importance of early infant relationships, and researchers (Sroufe 1995; Steele *et al.* 1996; Stern 1998a) found that children also make attachments with other sensitive main carers and siblings (Dunn 1983). The majority of children will have a secure attachment, but there are also three types of insecure attachment: avoidant, resistant and disorganized (Ainsworth *et al.* 1978). Children who are securely attached develop the concept of their main carer as a 'secure base' who is available when needed. The theory suggests that this helps the infant to develop the confidence to begin to explore their environment. Psychologists studying attachment sometimes observe behaviour when parents and infants are reunited after a brief separation – a 'strange situation' for the infant. (The strange situation was devised by Mary Ainsworth (Ainsworth *et al.* 1978) to measure attachment security at around 1 year of age.) Ethically there are questions about whether infants should be put under stress (see Chapter 10) by contriving a brief separation and, in addition, it may be less valid for psychologists to interpret nowadays as contemporary infants have a variety of experiences such as day care (Clarke-Stewart 1989). In broad terms, a securely attached child will be distressed when a parent leaves and comforted by the parent on return, whereas an infant with an avoidant attachment will not be distressed by parental separation and will avoid the parent on return. These children have learnt that they need to be self-sufficient and to manage on their own. Children with an anxious-resistant attachment will stay close to their parent before departure and are angry and resistant on their return. These children are anxious about their parent and may lack the confidence to use them as a secure base for exploration. Finally, a more recently added category includes children with a disorganized or disorientated attachment, who respond in a confused, contradictory fashion on reunion. This attachment pattern seems to indicate the greatest insecurity, and Main and Hesse (1990) argue that in such cases the child cannot use the parent as a secure base because he or she is the source of fear. This means that when children with 'insecure disorganized' attachments are stressed they find it more difficult to make an effective strategy to contain and manage their fears. This last type of attachment is more common in children in abusive care situations or those who have received neglectful institutionalized care (Carlson *et al.* 1989).

Attachment determinists and constructivists

Perhaps one of the most controversial areas in early development is the debate about how important the first two or three years of life are for future healthy emotional and social development. There are two schools of thought: the 'attachment determinists', who believe the earliest years are a critical period of development with permanent consequences for future social development; and the 'attachment constructivists', who consider the period as important for setting patterns for later interactions (Barrett 2006). Constructivists consider that the earliest years are not the only key times and that, throughout childhood, there are opportunities to be creative in constructing social relationships (Barrett 2006). Bowlby (1973) acknowledged that, although it became more difficult to make attachments in later childhood, it was still possible. Recent biological research into the development of the brain has frequently been cited by determinists, who consider this as biological 'proof'; however, the research is in its early stages and must be viewed with caution.

The biological research

When infants are born their brains are still rapidly developing and as the nerve cells, or neurons, mature they begin to develop processes (axons and dendrites) that make connections with one another across fluid-filled spaces called synapses (Nelson and Bosquet 2000). These connections are reliant on social interaction and neurons hard wire electrical connections in the brain as a response to stimulation; those that are not 'used' are pruned away (Schore 1994). Most of the work into early brain development to date has been conducted on animals but a limited number of studies have examined the functional brain activity of infants who have suffered severe sensory deprivation. Chugani *et al.* (2001) studied the brain development of a small sample of Romanian orphans and found decreased levels of electrical activity in a number of brain regions including the frontal cortex. Although the children were found to be functioning within the low to average range of normal limits they were also found to have persistent cognitive and behaviour problems. In addition, infants cannot regulate stress hormones such as cortisol in the first few months of life and if prolonged stressful situations are experienced this may deleteriously affect the development of the brain (Gunnar 1998).

There is some evidence that the brain can reorganize itself (neural plasticity) if the deprivation is followed by enriching experiences. However, most of the evidence is from sensory and motor rather than emotional and social areas of development (Nelson, cited in Zeanah 2000). It is to be hoped that no children in the future will experience the severe deprivation that these orphans did, but the research has led to important questions about the crucial nature of sensitive interactions between infants and their carers. Nelson and Bosquet (2000) highlight the need for more research into the links between positive interactions and brain development, and Barrett (2006: 264) concludes that there is probably not enough evidence to be certain about the long-term effects of early experiences: 'although early experiences will play an important role in opening up opportunities for development, fortunately the human psyche, like human bones, is strongly inclined towards self healing'.

It is crucial that infants experience the best possible environment for early development and this is therefore an important area for continuing research.

Reflective function

Recent research has also highlighted the importance of parental reflective function. This suggests that the capacity of the parents to experience the baby as an 'intentional' being, rather than simply viewing him or her in terms of physical characteristics or behaviour, is what helps the child to develop an understanding of mental states in other people and to regulate his or her own internal experiences (Meins *et al.* 2001; Fonagy *et al.* 2004). Research by the author has used the Working Model of the Child Interview (WMCI) (Zeanah and Benoit 1995), which was designed to explore how parents perceive, interpret and experience their infant's distinctive characteristics. While this lengthy interview should always be considered as a whole, two differing responses to one question are reproduced here as they demonstrate examples of contrasting perceptions. Both mothers when interviewed had a 3-month-old infant and one question asked what was unique or different about their child. Two very different answers were recorded:

> Everything is unique about her – she has developed her own personality. She is her own person. She knows what she wants. When my mum comes round she won't go to sleep because she is so pleased to see her. She knows my mum will play with her and make her laugh. (Mother)

> There is nothing that is different about him. He is just a baby – I don't know if there is anything different about him, perhaps he cries more than other babies. He doesn't really have a personality. (Mother)
>
> (Underdown 2006, unpublished research)

The second mother had more difficulty in engaging with her infant as she was less able to be attentive to his individual preferences and characteristics. On another occasion the researcher arrived to interview a mother just as her baby was due to have a sleep; the infant was put into his cot but continued to cry so the researcher offered to come back later. The mother gave this response:

> No, no. I think it will be fine. You see this is what we call his sort of 'wind-down cry'; it's like his little protest at going in his cot. My partner talks about his cry like it's a motor bike. He says, is he revving up or revving down? He [the infant] saw you come in and he thought, she looks a nice lady, I wonder if she is going to talk to me, but he knows he is tired as well. Just listen, you will hear it's a winding-down cry. We couldn't get him to sleep at all at first and we used to rock him in our arms and then take him into bed with us. But that made us feel guilty because you're not supposed to do that you know because it's sort of dangerous, and my neighbour said 'They have got to learn to go to sleep on their own.' So we started putting him in his cot and just staying with him, saying 'shush', and sometimes I put my hand gently on his tummy so he knew I was there. We were just getting a routine when one night he got really revved up, there was no missing that something was wrong, he was shrieking, well I took him down the doctor's first thing in the morning and he'd got an ear infection. Poor little thing, well he really needed his cuddles then, poor little thing. When he was over it we thought we were right back to square one with the sleeping so we had to do it all over again. It was really hard having to do all that again. Now I just know what he wants. See he has gone off [to sleep] now. (Mother, 31, WMCI)
>
> (Underdown 2006, unpublished research)

This mother was describing how she was able to reflect from her infant's point of view and how she had tuned in to his communications, imagined what he must be feeling and had enabled him to move from co-regulating his falling asleep to managing to do it on his own. This was no easy process, requiring an ongoing, balanced interpretation of her infant's signals, supported by discussion with her partner and neighbour. The mother now appeared confident in knowing what her baby needed. Anders *et al.* (2000: 326) describe how biological and social regulation of sleep patterns occurs through consistent and predictable recurring interactions. It would seem that there is an association between infant sleep problems and family depression and stress (Anders *et al.* 2000). Undoubtedly there are many factors involved but it may be that stress makes the parent less able to pick up on infant cues and so the infant is less able to regulate sleep patterns, which causes more stress. Psychotherapy sheds more light on sleep issues, sometimes making links with security and attachment. For example, if a parent has suffered the loss of a loved one, they may have an unconscious fear of 'separating' from their infant by placing him or her in the cot to sleep alone. Cultural expectations of when infants are expected to sleep alone vary.

Every individual parent brings their own 'parenting history' to the relationship with their new infant. Some parent–infant dyads will tune in to one another quickly, while others may struggle much more to read each other's signals. For some infants and caregivers, the tasks of sensitive attunement and the co-regulation of emotions may be more difficult. Many infants will experience some sleep or feeding difficulties during the early days, and reading cues and signals will enable parents to help the infant to regulate these and adopt a secure pattern that suits the family. Factors like infant immaturity due to being born pre-term, some disabilities and parental depression may make communication more difficult. Babies who are born pre-term may be too immature to seek or be able to sustain attuned interactions (Klaus and Kennel 1982) and a few of these infants may experience longer-term difficulties in forming effective social relationships (Wocadlo and Rieger 2006). A small number of children may have autistic tendencies and do not make eye contact or seek social interaction in the same way as others. Infants with **autism** need even more practice with social interaction and this may be very challenging for parents who are trying to engage with their baby. Other infants may find that their overtures are not met with sensitivity by a caregiver who is able to read and respond to their signals. In some instances this may reflect that the parents themselves have never experienced any warmth or sensitivity when they were children and they may find it especially difficult to know how to engage with their infant. If an infant is never sensitively attuned to by their main carers this may contribute to problems with the regulation of sleep or feeding patterns, or to behavioural difficulties (Anders *et al.* 2000; Benoit 2000). Other research shows a clear relationship between poor maternal–infant relationships and outcomes such as emotional and cognitive difficulties (Caplan *et al.* 1989) and a range of mental health problems (Fonagy *et al.* 1997). Sensitively attuned interactions are, therefore, an important basis for emotional well-being. Although the reasons why some children regularly experience a greater sense of well-being than others are complicated because they include individual factors like temperament and resilience, most agree that well-being is intrinsically linked with the quality of the relationships that the child experiences. When infants enjoy fun and positive interactions, they may in fact be developing the orbito-frontal cortex of the brain, establishing patterns of emotional regulation and laying the foundations for subtle patterns of communication (van den Boom 1995). The first year of life is therefore a crucial period in which the attachments develop and the infant learns to co-regulate and self-regulate behaviour within the context of relationships with caregivers. Part of the development of attachment includes the infant's emerging desire to go exploring and begin to 'separate'. Once infants are mobile and enjoying the excitement of discovery, they usually keep their main carer in sight to return to in case of danger.

Emotional and social development in toddlers

Once secure and trusting attachments are formed, the young child can use this 'secure base' (Bowlby 1988) as a safe foundation for exploration of the world. By 15–24 months, the toddler is beginning to develop independence and often fluctuates between asserting his or her own wishes and needing comfort and 'babying'. There are many tasks for children to achieve, such as moving from being fed to feeding themselves, and at around 2 years, when muscle control and understanding are becoming suitably mature, toilet training takes place. Young children have to negotiate the shifts between dependence, interdependence and independence. These frequent shifts can be emotionally exhausting for the toddler (and the parents!) and frequently children may demonstrate some challenging behaviours as they try to assert their independence. Toddlers are often overwhelmed by frustration and will externalize their feelings by throwing a tantrum. This is developmentally appropriate for a 2-year-old but needs careful handling by the main carer so that the child can feel safe and his or her feelings are 'contained'. This usually entails the carer staying close until the 'explosion' of feelings begins to sub-side and then putting into words what has happened. For example, Pete managed to keep firm boundaries after 2-year-old Rosie had a tantrum by cuddling her while saying gently: 'I know you want some chocolate but we are just going to have dinner so it's not a good idea right now, but you can have some after dinner.'

While unconditional acceptance of the child, and keeping firm bound-aries, are important for healthy development they are also extremely chal-lenging for the adult. Some parents lack the confidence and skills to manage challenging behaviour effectively and so the externalizing behaviour does not diminish as the child's understanding and language development increases. This means that, for some children, difficult behaviour becomes entrenched and increasingly hard to manage as the child grows older (Gross *et al.* 1995). As the child moves through the toddler period the development of friend-ships with peers becomes increasingly important; attachment research in-dicates that children internalize their experiences from early relationships and these 'internal working models' continue to have a profound effect on many aspects of children's later mental health, including their behaviour (van-Ijzendoorn 1997). In summary, research indicates that children who enjoy attuned communications and secure attachments in their earliest years have increased well-being, which enables them to enjoy friendships and ex-plore the environment. Lewis *et al.* (1984) found that secure attachment at 18 months correlated with:

- the quality and the sensitivity of mother–child interaction at 6–15 weeks
- curiosity and problem-solving aged 2
- social confidence at nursery aged 3
- lack of behaviour problems (boys) aged 6.

Children with secure attachment relationships are more able to be independent, relate to their peers and engage in more complex and creative play; they are more resourceful and have healthier self-esteem.

Although these positive outcomes are linked with secure attachment, it is important to remember that 'behaviour is always a complex product of past experience and current circumstances' (Sroufe 1995: 190). In the next section consideration is given to practical methods for supporting early relationships.

How can early relationships be supported?

Parents are the most crucial resource in promoting children's health and well-being, and they should be valued, respected and supported in carrying out this most important work. Most parents are dedicated to doing their best for their children but many face challenges particularly as neighbourhood support networks and kinship groups have, in some areas, weakened and the pressure to compete in the workplace increases. Knowledge about children's mental health is advancing rapidly and parents have a right to be kept informed about this. However, while most people would agree that parenting positively is a challenging task, it is extremely difficult to evaluate what support parents want and whether it actually works. The Sure Start programme was set up in 1999 in England to work in partnership with parents to improve the health and emotional development of young children (Glass 1999). Although Sure Start promised a range of services to families it also acknowledged that families have distinctly different needs, both between individual families, in different locations and across time in the same family. Sure Start maintains that services should be offered right from the first antenatal visit; these should reflect what parents want and should be accessible at suitable times. The core aim of all support services is better outcomes for children, but the real challenge lies in finding effective and acceptable ways to deliver this.

Universal services

Services can either be universal or targeted. Universal services are suitable for everyone and aim to support early carer–infant relationships. Targeted services aim to support families who are experiencing difficulties. Some Sure

Start Children's Centres in the UK have set up programmes to support infant mental health and Figure 3.2 represents a four-tier model that is being used at Chelmsley Wood Centre, Solihull, UK. Tier 1 represents universal services that are open to all parents and infants. The idea of tier 1 services is to offer appropriate services to prevent difficulties from occurring. The transition to parenthood and the first months are often characterized by difficult adjustments (see Chapter 2), and universal services aim to support families when they are getting to know their new infant and renegotiating their relationships. The challenge lies in discovering whether early preventive services work and whether they are cost-effective. The early national Sure Start evaluation found that while the majority of families benefited to some extent, the most socially deprived families did not (Belsky *et al.* 2006).

Tiers 2, 3 and 4 represent targeted services for parents and children who are experiencing more difficulties than most and require some extra support; and these are explored in more detail in Chapter 8. If tier 1 services are effective they should reduce the number of children and families who require the more costly support at tiers 2, 3 and 4. Funding for universal services is often difficult as families may not have any 'diagnosable' problems so funders may consider the services to be a luxury. Health service commissioners usually require research-based evidence of effectiveness before spending public money, and proving that ill health has actually been prevented is a very difficult task. In the next section there is an overview of some tier 1 universal services aimed at supporting early adult–infant relationships, and research evaluation of effectiveness if available.

The Brazelton Neonatal Behavioural Assessment Scale

The Brazelton Neonatal Behavioural Assessment Scale (NBAS) (Brazelton 1995) can be used in hospital or at home, and involves a trained worker, such as a nursery nurse, midwife or health visitor, supporting the parents to discover the infant's individual behavioural characteristics and highlighting the baby's capabilities. This technique is used to increase the parents' interest in and knowledge about their baby, and may raise the parents' awareness of things such as their baby's characteristic body tone, how they are soothed, areas in which the baby interacts positively and areas in which they are less strong (Rauh *et al.* 1988; Brazelton and Cramer 1991). The use of this technique in hospital and at home with parents of low birth weight babies has been shown to improve parental perceptions of their infant's individual characteristics (Rauh *et al.* 1988).

Infant massage

Infant massage is traditional in many parts of the world. Teaching parents how to massage their infants may also be helpful, particularly if mothers are experiencing post-natal depression. One study, for example, showed that the

Possible provision

Specialist provision-community or residential based

- Residential parent/child assessment
- **Inpatient parental psychiatric treatment**
- Intensive community support

Specialist provision-community based

- Parent-/infant psychotherapy
- Family therapy
- Individual parent support
- Specialist parenting group – e.g. Mellow Parenting, Growing Together

Targeted provision

- Home visits
- Family support
- Being Together (with your baby)
- Play Link
- Watch Wait and Wonder group

Universal provision

- Ante- and post-natal screening for mental health difficulties
- Post-natal support for relationship difficulties
- Parent support, education and advice, e.g. parenting group, nursery matters, welcome to nursery, childhood matters, baby café, breastfeeding support
- Crèche facilities
- Play + Stay
- Baby massage

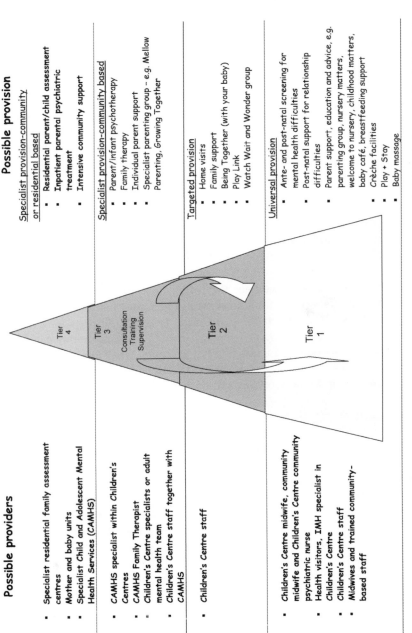

Possible providers

- Specialist residential family assessment centres
- Mother and baby units
- Specialist Child and Adolescent Mental Health Services (CAMHS)

- CAMHS specialist within Children's Centres
- CAMHS Family Therapist
- Children's Centre specialists or adult mental health team
- Children's Centre staff together with CAMHS

- Children's Centre staff

- Children's Centre midwife, community midwife and Children's Centre community psychiatric nurse
- Health visitors, IMH specialist in Children's Centre
- Children's Centre staff
- Midwives and trained community-based staff

Tier 4

Tier 3

Consultation
Training
Supervision

Tier 2

Tier 1

Figure 3.2   A model for infant mental health provision (IMH) within Chelmsley Wood Children's Centre, Solihull, England

use of infant massage resulted in less distress behaviour and less disturbed sleep patterns in infants, improvements in mothers' moods and behaviours and improved mother–infant interactions (Onozawa *et al.* 2001). Some mothers report that learning infant massage gives them a chance to observe and relate to their infant:

> I think it makes you more aware, it's made me more aware of like when I can't remember when my son started talking, and when I say talking – responding back to you, but through the massage I think that is when I noticed that she is actually responding to me. Like we were having mini-conversations kind of thing, she's gurgling and chatting away and I actually think, I don't know, I am sure that she has done it earlier than he did, now whether that's the benefit of the massage, I don't know, but I think it made me more aware of it, in that she definitely is talking to me, whilst it's going on. (Mother, 29)
> (Underdown 2006, unpublished research)

Infant massage teachers encourage the parent to consider the infant's cues and signals throughout the teaching session. The sessions often start with all the parents 'asking their infants' permission' to begin the massage and to watch for cues like eye contact and smiling, which show baby's enjoyment, or moving a limb or crying if a massage is not welcome. Many mothers, like the one quoted above, suggest that spending the time concentrating on their baby helped them to 'tune in' to their infant's likes and dislikes.

Songs and music

Infants love fun and laughter, and one way of encouraging early positive relationships is through songs, music and dance and, in many cultures, intergenerational family groups traditionally shared rhymes and songs. It seems perhaps that technology and the pace of lifestyles in the twenty-first century mean that some of these traditional customs are being lost. The Peers Early Education Programme (PEEP) helps parents to learn about songs, music and books, and is based on the growing body of evidence that links the early development of language, literacy, and personal and social development with outcomes relating to higher educational attainment and prosocial behaviour. Parents are invited to weekly group sessions where they are offered mutual support and group-based interactive activities with their baby, including sharing a book every day, songs and rhymes, listening games, playing with shapes, and using the library. A longitudinal study comparing a cohort of 300 babies from a PEEP area with a sample from a matched non-PEEP area showed improved verbal comprehension, vocabulary and self-esteem (Evangelou and Sylva 2002). Baby dance groups involve both parent and infant engaging in a structured series of interactions, which the baby is able eventually to anticipate. This provides parents and infants with the opportunity for joyful exchanges (Maattanen 2001).

The Solihull Approach

In the early weeks many parents experience sleepless nights and perhaps difficulties with establishing feeding. The Solihull Approach (Douglas and Ginty 2001) is becoming increasingly popular throughout the UK and provides health visitors with a new means of addressing these problems, based on the concepts of containment (Bion 1962), reciprocity (Brazelton *et al.* 1974) and behaviour management. Containing parental worries involves the worker acknowledging feelings in a non-judgemental way that enables the parent to reflect more on the difficulties rather than feeling overwhelmed. Reciprocity refers to the process whereby the parent and infant develop their communication and interactions to be in tune with one another. By focusing on the relationship between the parent and infant, they are supported to tune in to each other more effectively (Douglas and Ginty 2001). Emerging findings suggest that the approach is empowering to parents and enables them to change their own perceptions of difficulties and to find the best solutions (Whitehead and Douglas 2005). Dysregulation of sleeping and feeding is extremely common in early infancy as babies learn to co-manage and then manage these functions themselves. For some, feeding and sleeping problems may become serious if they continue over a long period, and the Solihull Approach is useful in preventing difficulties developing. (Feeding difficulties are discussed in more detail in Chapter 5.)

Parenting programmes

Antenatal classes (as discussed in Chapter 2) were the first programmes to be routinely offered, but recently there has been huge growth in the number of support groups in the UK. The popularity of these groups has gained momentum as more parents feel able to acknowledge that raising healthy young children is difficult. Programmes are usually group based, consisting of weekly sessions that are provided over the course of a few weeks. While the theoretical basis is varied, most aim to help parents to improve emotional and behavioural outcomes for their children either by supporting parents to explore new techniques that promote prosocial behaviour (behavioural programmes) or by helping parents to recognize the reasons that children behave in particular ways (relationship programmes). Research by Maccoby and Martin (1983) showed that those parents who set clear boundaries for their children's behaviour, but also show warmth and are able to listen and respond to their child's needs, have children who are more self-confident and have higher self-esteem. Hughes (2003: 256) argues that parenting classes can be about learning to conform and 'generally [mean] educators teaching parents who are working class and from culturally diverse backgrounds to conform to white, middle class norms of child rearing'. It could equally well be argued that it is easy to take a sceptical view of parenting support and that parenting classes may never attract parents who are isolated or excluded.

High-quality evaluation is needed. Research by Barlow and Stewart-Brown (2001) has shown that parents placed the greatest value in being able to share difficulties and gain ideas from other parents. Parenting programmes should not be about 'telling parents what to do', as there is no 'one right way' to parent, but about sharing approaches so that families can find answers to their own challenges. A study into the effectiveness of parenting programmes in poor, ethnically diverse areas (Scott *et al.* 2006) found that parents from all ethnic backgrounds were prepared to enrol provided that the course was well planned and attractive. Researchers found that behaviourally based programmes did not merely impact on individual parenting acts, there were also effects on the whole pattern of relating, so interactions became 'warmer', more sensitive and reciprocal, which enhances attachment security and emotional well-being (Scott *et al.* 2006). Despite the diversity in parenting programmes, they appear to offer an effective means of supporting parents to promote their children's social and emotional development. Another review reported that parenting programmes improved a number of aspects of maternal psychosocial health, including depression, anxiety/stress, self-esteem and the relationship with the partner (Barlow *et al.* 2002).

Conclusion

Ensuring that every person has the best possible environment for positive mental health is a shared responsibility. At the most intimate level in the microsystem, infants need the time and sensitive attention of a small number of adults. Although this chapter has concentrated on the microsystem, it is important to bear in mind the wider context. In the broadest context, macrosystem policies should reflect the growing understanding of infant development and ensure that there is a healthy, supportive environment so that families can thrive. The increase in the number of children with emotional and behavioural difficulties and with mental health problems (see Chapter 8) is testament to the importance of finding the most effective ways of preventing ill health and distress, and of developing appropriate early support services. Developing effective services depends on the high-quality training of people who have the personal characteristics to be available and empathetic with families, particularly those who are facing extra challenges. The universal services reviewed in this chapter aim to ensure that all parents are supported to lay the best possible foundations for their child's emotional and social well-being. Parents play a crucial role in nurturing children's emotional and social development, but being a parent is challenging and, if children's emotional well-being is to be nurtured, parents must also be nurtured and valued. This means having social policies that enable mothers and fathers to have sufficient parental leave (see Chapter 2) and a degree of flexibility in their work–life balance. Every child is entitled to high-quality childcare if parents are working, and this includes the opportunity for the child to make attachments with a small number of consistent workers. Early childhood workers and parents should have knowledge of how infant emotional and social development unfolds within relationships. Without this knowledge, care will be based on merely keeping infants safe rather than enabling them to engage in sustained relationships with key adults and peers. A triangle of trust between the child, nursery staff and parents will help optimize healthy emotional and social development. At a macro level, policies are needed that ensure adequate housing, sufficient income and neighbourhoods where there are opportunities to build supportive networks. The insidious impact of poverty on children's health and well-being has been shown to have lifelong effects (see Chapter 1). Supporting the positive mental health of future generations involves support for families at every systemic level.

4 Health inequalities in early childhood

Childhood is one of the most vulnerable periods of the human lifespan and a time when social and material disadvantages may have the greatest impact on health and development. There are approximately 1.5 billion children worldwide: 15 per cent live in the richer countries, leaving the majority of the world's children living in the less industrialized countries of the south. Poverty is the greatest threat to children's health worldwide and, even in more prosperous countries, children under 5 years of age are the group most likely to experience health problems due to living in a family with a low income. Living in poverty powerfully influences the quality of children's lives in a myriad of ways, with its impact on social, emotional, physical and spiritual health and well-being extending into adulthood (Attree 2004; Graham and Power 2004). In the first part of this chapter reference is made to the 'gradients' of adverse health outcomes across social groups; 'absolute' poverty is defined, followed by an overview of some of the health issues facing young children living at subsistence level. In the second part of the chapter 'relative' poverty is defined, some of the health challenges facing poor children living in a rich economy are identified and, using England as an example, policy and practice initiatives that aim to tackle health inequalities are reviewed. There is a strong association between poverty and well-being and even very young children may struggle with feeling different because of the realization that their family is more impoverished than others (Robinson *et al.* 2005). Wilkinson (1999: 58) argues that 'processes of social comparison and fears of inferiority and inadequacy in relation to others' are central to understanding the effects that poverty has on health and well-being.

Although there are differing health challenges in the industrially developed countries in the north and the industrially developing countries in the south, there are also strong reasons for adopting a global approach when examining children's health. Children's health evolves and as one threat diminishes another comes to the fore. Children were malnourished in Europe a century ago, through having too few nutrients, but now many are malnourished by having too many calories, often in the form of 'junk food'. Knowledge and progress can be shared to speed appropriate health improvement, and richer nations, in turn, can reflect on the many positive aspects of child health in the south, such as how strong community networks support families' emotional and social health. Knowledge of the global context of children's health also aids understanding of families involved in migration and asylum seeking, as well as the particular concerns of those transnational families whose child health issues span continents. This vast subject can only be covered in summary in this chapter but hopefully the complex links, the lessons from history and from differing cultural practices, and the interdependence of children's health and economic well-being will stimulate further reading and discovery.

Social gradients in child health

In both richer and poorer countries a fine grading of risk for child health outcomes can be identified across all social groups (Spencer 2000a). There is, for example, a social gradient in infant mortality in the UK with almost twice as many infants of teenage mothers in lower socio-economic groups dying compared with infants born to older mothers (aged 30–34 years) who are likely to be predominantly in higher-income groups (ONS 2005). Spencer (2000) argues that fine grading of risk is apparent across the whole socio-economic spectrum and is likely to be the result of the cumulative effects of risk and protective factors that are patterned through the life course and across generations.

> Poor children are at increased risk of mortality and morbidity in developed and developing countries. The relationship holds good for the 'new' mortality and morbidity (for example, sudden infant death, accidents and behaviour problems) as it does for the 'old' causes of death and ill-health (for example, infection and malnutrition). (Spencer 2000: 191)

This finely graded pattern of risk, which weights adverse health outcomes towards the most disadvantaged children, means that identifying and modifying single risk factors is likely to have only a modest impact on improving health outcomes. Wider social and economic policies that tackle the complexity of factors and reflect the mechanisms by which risk factors combine are more likely to be effective in addressing health inequalities.

Being poor in a poor country

Throughout the world young children's health is disproportionately affected by poverty. Although there are gradients of poverty in every country, a large minority of children may experience absolute poverty with a complete lack of resources and resulting in devastating consequences for children's health and well-being (Spencer 2000). Absolute poverty threatens children's very existence and, according to Haines and Smith (1997), of the 4.4 billion people living in countries in the south:

- 33 per cent lack access to clean water
- 66 per cent lack access to sanitation
- 20 per cent have no health care
- 20 per cent have insufficient nutrition.

Lack of these most basic resources impacts directly on mortality and morbidity. Children who are more at risk from disease (e.g. through contaminated water) and lack of immunizations are also more susceptible to infections due to poor nutritional status. (Lack of adequate nutrition means that children are generally in a weakened state and therefore less able to resist disease.) Comparable statistics for life expectancy and infant mortality can be found in Table 1.1. Child mortality rates tend to be highest in sub-Saharan Africa and South Asia (Black *et al.* 2003) and worldwide over 10 million children under 5 years of age die every year from preventable factors. Six causes (Bryce *et al.* 2005: 1147) account for 73 per cent of these deaths:

1. pneumonia, 19 per cent
2. diarrhoea, 18 per cent
3. malaria, 8 per cent
4. neonatal pneumonia or sepsis, 10 per cent
5. pre-term delivery, 10 per cent
6. asphyxia at birth, 8 per cent.

All of the above named causes are preventable but the answer does not lie simply in having more money for the basics such as food, water and shelter. Health staff must be trained and political stability is needed to establish systems to continuously deliver health care on a large scale rather than attempting to address individual issues (Ruxin *et al.* 2005). In 1985 Bob Geldof, a British rock singer, was horrified by the starvation affecting people in Ethiopia and drew fellow musicians together to raise money for aid by recording the song 'Do They Know it's Christmas? (Feed the World)'. Although the response for aid was immense and awareness was raised, more than 30 years later the health difficulties facing many children and families in Ethiopia and much of Africa remain. In 2005 children and families in Niger experienced a catastrophic famine because of a combination of drought and a locust plague destroying crops. Aid organizations have learnt that sustainable change does not come about by pouring money into disaster situations and that long-term improvements will happen only through strategic changes at every level. In 2005, Geldof organized more rock concerts across the world (Live 8), not to raise funds but to put pressure on the leaders of the eight richest nations when they met at the G8 summit in Edinburgh. This time the international agenda was to find appropriate strategies to 'make poverty history'. How rich countries help poorer countries to eliminate poverty is a highly complex issue. The giving of money from a richer nation to a poorer one can create a stigma, emphasizing the power differentials between them and, in some cases, creating impossible debts. The richer countries may argue that aid cannot be given if it is likely to be siphoned away from the people into corrupt regimes, instead of building the infrastructure for health care and education. Consider the four examples of children's health issues cited below and reflect on how any resolutions must impact at both local and global levels if sustainable change is to occur.

Infant feeding

Bottle-fed infants in the south have seven times the risk of dying from in-fection as those who are exclusively breastfed (Black *et al.* 2003). The sale of formula milk for infant feeding has placed millions of babies in the south at risk from diarrhoea, either due to the lack of facilities or the knowledge to make bottle feeds correctly. Water supplies may be contaminated and it may not be possible to effectively sterilize feeding equipment. Baby milk manu-facturers have advertised their products by displaying pictures of healthy-looking bottle-fed babies while supplying maternity hospitals with infant milk formula and attempting to influence health staff with samples and sponsorship. While much needs to be done at a local level to ensure families have accurate health information and adequate resources, change is also re-quired at the global level. Many of the major pharmaceutical companies market baby milks and foods in poorer nations and Health Action Interna-tional (HAI) campaigns against unethical marketing and the conflicts of in-terest created by manufacturers' sponsorships. In the UK, Baby Milk Action is a registered charity that aims to prevent infant mortality and morbidity by ensuring that there are effective controls on the marketing of infant formula, and a recent government public health white paper, *Choosing Health, Making Healthier Choices Easier* (DoH 2004a), plans to further restrict advertising. The International Baby Food Action Network (IBFAN) is a worldwide group working to improve the health and well-being of infants and their families through the protection, promotion and support of breastfeeding and optimal infant feeding practices.

Immunization

The development of immunization to protect against many childhood dis-eases has been one of the major public health success stories of the last century. However, fewer than 50 per cent of children in sub-Saharan Africa receive the measles vaccine (Blair *et al.* 2003) even though the cost is low and the death rate high (two to three children in every 1000 die in northern countries from measles compared to 300 in every 1000 in some African countries). Problems of supply, storage and staff to safely administer the vaccine all contribute to this failure to protect children. In addition, once local health staff are highly trained they may be attracted by the increased opportunities, salaries and living standards of working in richer countries. (Immunization is discussed further in Chapter 7.)

Injury

Children in the south face a high risk of being injured through accidents. Factors influencing this include the poor maintenance and safety record of transport, such as few seat belts fitted to cars, poor enforcement of traffic regulations, little access to health services and the large number of children working in unsafe situations. About 250 million children work long hours and in hazardous conditions, but merely banning richer nations from exploiting child labour would not resolve the issue. Many families rely on the child's income for survival and some children may develop healthy self-esteem from contributing, so all the systems involved need to be addressed before a solution can be found. (Child injury and safety is discussed in Chapter 7.)

HIV and AIDS

In many countries children's health has been further compromised by lack of health education about HIV and AIDS, resulting in the premature death of thousands of parents who were unable to access the antiretroviral drugs that would have ensured a longer lifespan. The AIDS epidemic has left many children orphaned and families may be headed by children not yet in their teens. Again, there are many more factors involved in tackling the AIDS epidemic than just ensuring that those in need get the drugs necessary to prolong their lives. Examples of effective methods to combat HIV/AIDS include safe sex campaigns in all communities, freely available condoms and following protocols to reduce transmission of the disease from mother to child (Ruxin *et al.* 2005).

How can these issues be resolved?

Although the disease patterns may differ, many of the public health problems facing children and families in subsistence economies are similar to those experienced by children and families in industrialized countries a century ago. Basic public health measures such as improvements in water supplies, availability of health services and immunizations, adequate nutrition and better housing will have a dramatic impact on health. International action is needed to ensure that these basic public health measures happen, and Blair *et al.* (2003: 75) highlight some of the international measures necessary to improve global child health:

- cancellation of debt owed by the poorest countries
- increased aid flows targeted at the poor, children, and health and education sectors
- support for the UNCRC
- arms control and support for a treaty banning landmines
- peaceful resolution of conflict
- malaria and AIDS vaccines
- cheaper antiretroviral drugs (to treat those who are HIV positive and those with AIDS)
- strengthening of primary health care
- reduction of marketing of infant milk formula and 'junk foods'.

The World Bank and the International Monetary Fund (IMF) have provided loans and many countries in the south, particularly in Africa, are left continually struggling to repay huge foreign debts. The size of the repayments and the interest on the debts has meant that spending on essentials such as child health and education has been cut back. There is now wide recognition that this cycle of debt has to be addressed before real progress can be made in alleviating the effects of poverty on the population. At the turn of the millennium the United Nations set measurable goals to reduce global poverty (see Chapter 1). These Millennium Development Goals (MDGs) aim to reduce poverty, promote maternal health, reduce child mortality and morbidity, and tackle major diseases such as HIV/AIDS and malaria, as well as ensure sustainability of environmental change. In addition, goals are set to promote gender equality and achieve universal primary education, both of which would have dramatic effects on child health. If the aim is to meet all the targets by 2015, richer countries not only have a part to play in debt relief and fair trade: there are also important roles in research and development for sustainable change so that countries can govern more effectively and invest in health care and education. The aforementioned G8 summit, held in Scotland in July 2005, brought together the leaders of the eight richest nations with a commitment to tackle world poverty appearing to be at the top of the agenda. Following the summit, the leaders pledged to fulfil one-quarter of the promise of $100bn debt cancellation that it had made six years previously. There was also a promise to increase total aid by $50bn (with half of this sum, around $25bn, to be directed towards Africa) in five years' time (http://www. jubilee2000uk.org/, accessed 29 July 2005). The world leaders of the richer nations have a responsibility to ensure that Article 24 of the UNCRC is met. This states that children have the right to good-quality health care, and to pure water, nutritious food and a clean environment so that they will stay healthy, and that rich countries should help poorer countries achieve this. While some progress was made towards this at the G8 summit many are frustrated by the slow progress in meeting basic health commitments to children and families.

Being poor in a rich country

'Relative poverty' means that some people experience a much smaller degree of wealth than others living in the same economy. Definitions of relative poverty are not fixed. It is often expressed as a proportion of the median national income, although some contest this very notion, arguing that it merely identifies the less well-off in rich societies (Spencer 2000).

The countries with the lowest levels of child poverty are Denmark and Sweden, with a rate of less than 3 per cent, and America and Mexico top the league with rates of more than 20 per cent of children living below the national poverty lines (UNICEF 2005). Just below this level, the UK, Portugal, Ireland, New Zealand and Italy all show exceptionally high rates of child poverty of between 15 and 17 per cent (UNICEF 2005). UNICEF (2005) makes special mention of the fact that the UK government has pledged to eradicate childhood poverty 'within a generation' and claims that the first target of a 25 per cent reduction by 2005 is likely to have been met. However, recent figures from the Joseph Rowntree Foundation (2006) indicate that, in 2005, 3.4 million children in the UK were living in poverty, and although 700,000 children were 'lifted' out of poverty between 1998 and 2005, this is a reduction of only 17 per cent.

The next section of this chapter takes an in-depth look at what it means to be living in relative poverty in the UK and offers an overview of how the government is aiming to tackle these inequalities. In England the Sure Start initiative, aiming to support families with young children under 4 in disadvantaged areas, was launched as the 'cornerstone' of the government's pledge to end child poverty. The progress of this initiative will be reviewed.

Childhood poverty in the UK

In 1979, one in ten children in the UK lived in a household with below half the average income, but by 1999 this had risen to one in three children (DSS 1999a). This dramatic increase in children living in families with insufficient income has had a devastating effect on children's health, with the gap between health experienced between those in highest and lowest income groups becoming ever wider. Spencer (2000) claims that there has been a feminization of poverty, with lone mothers experiencing a very high rate, and Bradshaw (2003) highlights the fact that child poverty is concentrated in certain types of family. An increased risk is indicated if the child lives in a family:

- headed by a lone parent
- where there is a child under the age of 5 years
- with more than four children in the family
- with a very young mother
- where there is either an adult or a child with a disability
- from a minority ethnic group (although 80 per cent of poor children in the UK are white (Bradshaw 2003), the risk for child poverty is higher in minority ethnic groups, especially those of Pakistani or Bangladeshi origin).

Issues such as disability often put added financial pressures on a family, and Parker (cited in BMA 1999) concluded in his study that 55 per cent of families with a child with a disability were living in, or on the margins of, poverty. The BMA report (1999: 103) also highlights the severe disadvantages of ethnic minority families whose children are disabled:

> The barrier of inadequate information and lack of interpreters, the reluctance to offer some services, such as respite care, because of misunderstandings about the role of the extended family and the poor housing and poverty exacerbate any problems of care.

Some families may face a temporary period in poverty, perhaps after parental separation or divorce, and financial circumstances may improve when a lone parent is able to take up employment or re-partner. While for some this period will be temporary, other families may face long-term unemployment, perhaps caused through illness or disability.

Changing family circumstances (see Chapter 6) often create challenging transitions and children may experience the effects of parental depression and loss of self-esteem either long term or in transitional periods. Thus the effects of poverty on the child must be viewed within the wider systems framework (as discussed in Chapter 1).

Changing patterns of health

A century ago, children's health in the UK was threatened by many of the same infectious diseases that still affect children in the south, such as tuberculosis, polio, measles, whooping cough and diphtheria, but today these threats have largely been contained by improved living conditions, hygiene and immunization (see Chapter 7). New threats to children's health emerge, reflecting the changing environmental and economic circumstances. No children in the UK should be at risk of starvation, yet the rate of childhood obesity, with its possible long-term emotional and physical ill effects, is soaring (BMA 1999). Accidents pose a major threat to young children's health, particularly affecting boys in families from lower socio-economic groups. Children in poorer neighbourhoods have fewer safe places to play and exercise, and face increased danger from traffic. The apparent rise in the number of children experiencing emotional and behavioural difficulties is of major concern, resulting in countless children feeling distressed, causing problems with forming relationships, and leading them to underachieve at school. Emotional and behavioural problems are now the foremost cause of functional disability in children (Bone and Meltzer 1989) and there is a much higher incidence in families with a low socio-economic status (DoH 1998). Domestic violence is prevalent in all **socio-economic groups**, but research (Hester *et al.* 2000) has indicated that it is more likely to occur in homes where there is stress, depression or alcohol abuse, and these factors are more often present in families experiencing relative poverty. Between 75 and 90 per cent of violent incidents in the home are thought to be witnessed by children, in itself constituting emotional abuse (Abrahams 1994). Leaving a violent home may often have further effects on children's health and well-being. Although children may be removed from the violence, some may grieve for the absent parent, and moving to a refuge or bed and breakfast hostel may well be accompanied by a change in economic resources, plunging the family into poverty. Leaving a family home is stressful and children may miss their friends and neighbourhood; some children, especially from minority ethnic groups, may face bullying (Mullender and Morley 1994). These difficult circumstances may lead to some children showing their distress through emotional or behavioural difficulties, or developing mental health problems such as depression (MHF 1999) (see Chapter 8).

So, although the overall physical health of children in the UK is improving, this masks huge variations and the new patterns of ill health that are emerging. There are variations in health and well-being in different ethnic groups, in different social classes and between different regions of the country (BMA 1999). At the beginning of the twenty-first century, opportunity for a healthy life is still linked to social circumstances and to family income. The next section highlights some specific increased health risks faced by children in the UK living in low-income families. Many of the health and well-being outcomes that are due to the impact of living in relative poverty are discussed in more detail in other chapters and the following summary directs the reader to appropriate chapters.

Diet and nutrition

Having a low income has a direct impact on the type and the quality of food that families consume. People in lower socio-economic groups often shop more carefully to obtain more food for their money, but they are more likely to buy foods with high levels of fat and sugar because these are richer in energy and cheaper than fruit and vegetables (Leather 1996; Acheson 1998). Foods that are high in fat and sugar are linked with poor health outcomes such as obesity, heart disease, diabetes, some cancers, and dental decay. Lack of variety in the diet is linked with iron-deficiency anaemia, which may leave the young child feeling tired and unable to concentrate, and may compromise growth.

Despite the benefits of breastfeeding having been clearly demonstrated by numerous research studies, there is a dramatic contrast in the incidence of breastfeeding, with women in higher socio-economic groups being twice as likely to breastfeed as women in lower socio-economic groups (BMA 1999). Research indicates that the physical, cognitive and emotional benefits of breastfeeding are many, including fewer allergies, fewer infections, less risk of **diabetes**, and the promotion of brain and intestinal development (Jenner 1988; James *et al.* 1997). Issues to do with breastfeeding are covered in more detail in Chapter 5.

Childhood injury

Child accidents are the major cause of death for children aged over 1 year in the UK, and children from the lowest socio-economic groups are four times more likely to die from an accidental injury and nine times more likely to die from a house fire than a child from a more affluent home (OPCS 1994; Roberts 2000). Children in poorer neighbourhoods are also likely to have fewer safe places to play and often face increased danger from traffic. The reasons for such a wide differential in morbidity from accidents between the socio-economic groups have been the cause of much speculation. It is most likely that a wide combination of contributory factors interplay in these outcomes. For example, a smoke alarm may seem an unnecessary expense when struggling financially to provide food for the family, and factors such as depression or lack of awareness of child development may mean that risks to children are evaluated differently from one family to another. Child injuries are discussed further in Chapter 7.

Smoking

Women from the lowest socio-economic group are four times more likely to smoke in pregnancy than women in the highest group (Foster, Lader and Cheesborough 1997), resulting in lower birth weight, an increased risk of sudden infant death syndrome (Leather 1996) and lower levels of educational achievement (Fogelman and Manor 1988). In addition, other research has linked parental smoking in low-income families to less balanced diets. In families where both parents smoked, 26 per cent reported that they were unable to afford essential dietary items such as vegetables and fruit, compared with 9 per cent in low-income families where the parents did not smoke (Marsh and McKay 1994). The prevalence of **asthma** and chest infections is higher where children passively inhale cigarette smoke (Upton *et al.* 1998). Passive smoking is explored in Chapter 7.

Mental health problems

Although at least 10 per cent of all mothers suffer post-natal depression (Cooper 1991, cited in Roberts 2000), studies indicate that the long-term effects of maternal depression on the cognitive and emotional development of children are more marked where there is socio-economic disadvantage (Murray and Cooper 1997; Petterson and Burke Albers 2001). Mental health difficulties are more prevalent in parents who are economically and socially disadvantaged, and this is likely to have an impact on their parenting styles. Spencer (2000: 247) highlights the connection between poverty and depression and the impact on the child: 'Parental depression and loss of self esteem resulting from the privations of poverty have been shown to directly affect the developmental progress of children and the parenting strategies used.' Lack of appropriate stimulation in the early years may result in language delay and, together with inappropriate parenting styles, especially if characterized by neglect or inconsistency, may lead to emotional or behavioural disorders (DoH 2004a) (see Chapter 8). Children living with depressed parents may take on some of the caring roles themselves (Aldridge and Becker 2003; Dearden and Becker 2004) and be constantly worried about the well-being of their parent(s). Children who take on caring responsibilities are often 'invisible' as this is not a role that is associated with the way 'childhood' is perceived by society. This means that young carers are denied a voice because they are considered too young to have a valid view, even though they may be very involved with day-to-day caring tasks. Young carers and their families often do not disclose family roles as they fear a lack of understanding and that interventions by the services may make things worse. Very flexible and responsive services may be required to support whole family needs (Underdown 2002).

Poor accommodation

Housing is a major public health issue affecting the poorest families in countries throughout the world. Living in substandard accommodation in the UK, affected by damp, condensation and mould, takes a toll on physical health, causing increased respiratory infections, triggering asthma in susceptible children (Burridge and Ormandy 1993) and resulting in more accidents in the home. While the physical effects are perhaps most obvious, there is also a wide range of more subtle and pervasive health issues linked with inadequate housing. In the UK, families on low incomes often live in overcrowded, substandard accommodation in areas of high pollution with poor-quality services. Local shops sell limited ranges of lower-quality produce and the transport to better served areas is expensive. Leisure facilities are fewer in deprived areas and high levels of crime and drug use result in a threatening environment for families raising young children (Spencer 2000). Some families will experience a temporary period of financial hardship – for example, if a woman and children leave the family home because of domestic violence. Where domestic violence has occurred children's health may be compromised again by living in an overcrowded temporary refuge (see Chapter 6). Many families on low incomes are housed in flats without accessible, safe play spaces (Gill 1992), which has a direct effect on children's well-being and physical health. Direct links have been found between living in high-rise accommodation and maternal depression (Richman 1974), which is in turn associated with a higher rate of child behaviour problems and poorer cognitive function in children (Sharpe *et al.* 1995; Murray 2001). Families who have faced homelessness have been found to experience high levels of mental health problems, and a study by Vostanis *et al.* (1998) found that symptoms persisted in a substantial minority even after rehousing. Certain groups are particularly likely to face health challenges. In the UK, lone parents – often single mothers (Dorling 1995) – may dip into relative poverty for a time after a relationship breakdown, and experience poor housing or homelessness. Minority ethnic groups often experience some of the worst housing conditions, generally in run-down inner-city areas (Central Statistics Office 1995). Refugee families may find themselves traumatized after fleeing their country of origin only to experience further stress caused by very poor-quality temporary accommodation.

Unemployment
For some children, parental unemployment may mean long-term poverty and poor housing. Parents may be without work because of disability, mental or physical illness, or through lack of suitable local opportunities. In 2005, 1.83 million children (NSO 2006), representing 16 per cent of all children in the UK, lived in workless households. Unemployed parents face obvious tensions about how to pay the bills and provide for the children, but the resulting lack of self-esteem and feelings of being excluded from the mainstream of the community may deepen depression or lead to addictions, all of which directly impact on young children's health and well-being (see Chapter 8).

Educational achievement
Children from disadvantaged backgrounds tend to have lower educational attainments, and research studies (Duncan *et al.* 1994) have shown clear deleterious links between poverty and children's cognitive abilities, from as early as 2 years of age (Smith, Brooks-Gunn and Klebanov 1997). Acheson (1998: 40–1) recommended that more high-quality pre-school education should be developed.

How can these health inequalities be addressed?

The government's Independent Inquiry into Inequalities in Health, chaired by Sir Donald Acheson, produced its report in 1999, highlighting three key areas for health improvement:

1. all policies likely to have an impact on health should be evaluated with regard to their impact on health inequalities
2. a high priority should be given to the health of families with young children
3. further steps should be taken to improve the living standards of poor families.

The pledge to end child poverty

The UK government pledged to tackle health inequalities and to end child poverty within a generation, and has raised the threshold for defining poverty from 50 per cent to 60 per cent of median income (DSS 1999b; Howarth *et al.* 1999). The government policy agenda recognized that increasing benefits alone would not end disadvantage for children living in poor families and that a whole range of initiatives and approaches is required to improve the health and well-being of children and their families. The plans were laid to ensure that a combination of national policy and local action encouraged new and innovative partnerships to tackle inequalities. In particular the government paper *Every Child Matters* emphasized five outcomes for children, as follows.

1. Being healthy: enjoying good physical and mental health and living a healthy lifestyle.
2. Staying safe: being protected from harm and neglect.
3. Enjoying and achieving: getting the most out of life and developing the skills for adulthood.
4. Making a positive contribution: being involved with the community and society and not engaging in antisocial or offending behaviour.
5. Economic well-being: not being prevented by economic disadvantage from achieving their full potential in life.

Every Child Matters (DfES 2003) laid the foundations for the Children Act 2004, which made provision for a Children's Commissioner to act as an independent champion for children, particularly those suffering disadvantage. Children in the UK had often been overlooked in health service provision, and services from one area to another were often fragmented. However, since

1999 there has been a range of policies aimed at improving the health of children, particularly those experiencing disadvantage.

The UK policy agenda includes:

- reducing child poverty by reforming benefits and tax systems
- raising awareness of healthy behaviour through the Healthy Schools programme, where schools get accreditation for ensuring certain health measures are implemented
- setting up the National Family and Parenting Institute to value and support family well-being
- introducing the *National Service Framework* (NSF) *for Children, Young People and Maternity Services* to ensure consistency of health services for children in all areas and that children and families are consulted about services; the NSF focuses on early child-centred interventions with a programme to promote the health of children from conception to adulthood and a remit to tackle health inequalities
- improving the health of children looked after by the local authority through the Quality Protects scheme
- improving access to healthy food through school breakfast clubs in disadvantaged areas and the National School Fruit Scheme, where every child at infant school receives a free piece of fresh fruit every day
- strengthening the support available to families in disadvantaged areas through the Sure Start scheme for families with young children (see below).

Sure Start

Sure start was introduced in England 1999 to:

> work with parents-to-be, parents and children to promote the physical, intellectual and social development of babies and young children – particularly those who are disadvantaged – so that they can flourish at home and when they get to school, and thereby break the cycle of disadvantage for the current generation of young children. (Sure Start 2001: 4)

Sure Start, a bold social experiment, was hailed as the cornerstone of the government's fight against poverty in England and it was the first time that generous ring-fenced resources had been firmly targeted at children under 4 years old and their families. The vision of Sure Start was innovative, and was designed along principles of community capacity and empowerment (see

Chapter 1) that would allow parents to participate in running and deciding on the content of programmes. Sure Start represented a unique approach to early intervention for children in an attempt to change existing services. This consisted of reshaping services to work with parents rather than expecting parents to adjust to what was on offer. It was about 'working with' rather than 'doing to' families, so that services would become flexible to meet need rather than imposing what professionals thought best. Professionals being recruited to Sure Start projects found themselves being interviewed by a team that included well-prepared parents, highlighting equal partnership rather than professional hierarchy. Every family with a new baby in a Sure Start area was offered a home visit to explain the scheme and many families were involved from before the birth. Families were able to access a range of support such as parenting groups, breakfast clubs, infant massage classes, cooking classes, smoking cessation classes, breastfeeding support and advice, and access to services such as health and housing. The aim was for Sure Start staff, from education, health, social services and voluntary sectors, to work in partnership with families to decide what services would be most effective in meeting the needs of young children and families in that area. The vision intended to raise the self-esteem of parents by encouraging active participation and partnership, and to build supportive networks to increase levels of social capital. Sure Start was set up as a ten-year programme, with the main focus on the health and well-being of the child and with an intention to fully evaluate services so that an evidence base of what works in promoting health and well-being could be formulated.

Sure Start evaluation

The first evaluation of Sure Start (NESS 2005) was published in 2005 and was conducted when most programmes had not reached their halfway points. This interim evaluation was not as positive as had been hoped, and did not show any improvement in the behaviour or language skills of the children in the most disadvantaged families. However, there were changes in parenting styles, and it was found that mothers were smacking children less (see Chapter 8) and finding other ways of setting boundaries for behaviour. The evaluation suggested that Sure Start was not engaging with the most disadvantaged and socially excluded families who may have been 'overwhelmed' or 'turned off' by what Sure Start had to offer. In many ways this evaluation raises far more questions than answers. Could major change be expected to have any measurable impact so early in the development of this programme? If staff were entrenched in working in traditional ways, changing the philosophical approach to service delivery would require time and staff training. The political agenda has changed and the original 524 Sure Start programmes situated in areas of disadvantage are being extended to provide a new nationwide network of 3500 children's centres, which will provide a mix of childcare, parental support, health and education services.

The changing Sure Start initiative

A major catalyst for changing the design of Sure Start was the fact that the original projects were able to reach only a small proportion of the disadvantaged children in the UK and there was heavy criticism for not offering support to more families across the UK. The original approach was seen by some as creating innovative elite services for a small number of disadvantaged communities. A community capacity and empowerment approach, however, requires time to build up trust with families who have experienced disadvantage. Responding to pressure, government policy has changed and the few hundred pioneering initial projects are now being rolled out across the country in the form of several thousand Children's Centres. While it is undoubtedly positive that more young children and their families should access services, the fear is that the focus has shifted away from supporting early preventive services to the provision of childcare and supporting parents into employment. The generous funding to Sure Start was intended to enable new ways of working to be developed; the Children's Centres will make services available to more children and families but will now be reliant on local authority funding. Norman Glass, who was one of the creators of Sure Start, argued in the *Guardian* (Glass 2005):

> Something had to give if there were to be 3,500 Children's Centres, if they were to be funded on the same basis as the local Sure Starts and were to expand at the required rate and rolled out in tandem with a general raising of childcare standards ... What gave was the autonomy of the 'local' Sure Starts and their 'generous' funding. The programmes are to be wound up within the next two years and folded back into local government control. No more management boards with local parents and volunteers, a severe cut in funding per head so it can be spread over 3,500 children's centres: and no more ring fencing.

The original Sure Start was a visionary project to create change in all family systems and to build social capital and, as the project has changed course, a rigorous longitudinal evaluation of this may well not now be possible. Coote (2005) argues that 'what is clear however is that one bold social experiment is being transmuted into another rather different one, before anyone has a chance to learn whether the original approach was worthwhile'. Sure Start in 2006 has retained the aim of improving health and emotional development for young children but it also now has a focus on increasing the availability of childcare and supporting parents into employment. Although the pledge to reduce child poverty may be achieved more easily by getting parents into employment, considerations must also be given to whether this is beneficial for young infants.

Conclusion

Child health inequalities will be reduced worldwide only if appropriate economic, health and social policies are able to reduce income disparities and ensure that all families have access to appropriate health services. Acheson's (1998) report into health inequalities recommended that all policies should be evaluated in terms of their impact on child and family health. However, international and national economic policy decisions are frequently made without consideration of the impact on the child health and well-being (Vylder 2000). On the international stage the UN has set global goals to improve health and these will require concerted international efforts if the 2015 targets are to be achieved. On a national level, in the UK, there are also goals set to reduce health inequalities caused by relative poverty. Reducing these health inequalities raises complex issues, some of which Sure Start aimed to address by ensuring that children met the UNCRC's aspirational goals for social and emotional well-being alongside their physical health. Although there will be no long-term evaluation of Sure Start, it is still important that lessons are learnt about what works in supporting children's health and well-being within their families. Early prevention of ill health is much preferable to treating illness once it has occurred, and increased understanding of changing patterns of health makes the sharing of these evaluations important internationally. Nelson Mandela, the South African human rights activist, argues that 'we must move children to the centre of the world's agenda. We must rewrite strategies to reduce poverty so that investments in children are given priority.' Once poverty really is history, resources may be made available to achieve even higher levels of health and well-being for all young children and families.

5 Growth and nutrition

A nutritious balanced diet provides children with the daily energy they need to play, explore, experiment, learn and form relationships with others, while building the foundations for future physical health and well-being. Children's entitlements to nutritious food and a pure water supply are stated in Article 24 of the United Nations Convention on the Rights of the Child, and Article 6 outlines governments' responsibilities for ensuring that children survive and develop healthily. Across the world people are united by their need for food – although, for some, food is much more than just a basic survival need. While in richer countries gastronomic excesses and 'junk food' are leading to children becoming overweight or even obese, in poorer nations some children are regularly facing hunger.

In the UK our fascination with food is reflected by the popularity of television cookery programmes, with 'celebrity chefs' making their fortunes from cookbooks, TV shows and restaurants. However, interest in food does not necessarily lead to healthy balanced diets. While a small minority of people in richer countries buy organic and fresh foods, a large majority buy 'ready meals' and less healthy convenience options. Healthy balanced meals are a foundation for health and well-being yet, within the UK, there are wide disparities caused by what sort of food is affordable and available, and the value placed on children's diets. Recently in the UK there has been growing awareness of the poor quality of children's school meals and a more questioning approach to the traditional two-tier system in restaurants where a varied adult menu sits alongside a cheaper 'kids' menu', typically offering a burger or sausage and chips. Our relationship with food is complicated; it is not only a sign of economic prosperity or deprivation but it also reflects family culture, custom and education levels. Food is often an expression of love and nurture and eating disorders a symptom of a lack of well-being. In this chapter healthy eating and the effects of poor nutrition are considered within a cultural and ecological framework. Starting from conception, the effects of nutrition on the developing infant are considered, reflecting on how culture, class and economics influence decisions about breastfeeding, weaning and what young children eat.

What is a healthy balanced diet?

In the UK people are so bombarded with advice about suitable diets it would be difficult to miss messages about healthy eating. However, while most people have heard the advice to eat 'five portions of fruit and vegetables a day' to avoid obesity and help to prevent some cancers, heart disease and diabetes, it is not always easy to identify what constitutes a healthy dietary balance. Broadly, a healthy balanced diet means eating a range of foods from the five main groups in the correct proportions for that particular individual. Generally, advice suggests that moderate proportions of carbohydrates such bread, pasta, potatoes and cereals, dairy foods, and proteins such as meat, fish, cheese, eggs or vegetarian alternatives (such as pulses) are eaten each day alongside lower proportions of foods containing fats and sugar. Of course proportions vary according to lifestyle and stage of development. Young children, for example, generally need more fat in milk for healthy growth than adults, who may choose almost fat-free skimmed milk. What does make eating a healthy balanced diet more difficult is the fact that modern lifestyles in the UK often mean eating fast convenience foods. Pre-packed ready foods form the central part of many family diets, but 'clever' marketing may mean that the mandatory labelling can be confusing. 'Less than 2 per cent fat' may sound healthy and tempt busy shoppers, but packets are often unclear about the total fat, so the 'less than 2 per cent' can be meaningless and even though the fat may be lower, the sugar level may be very high and only mentioned in the small print. Although there are regulations to ensure dietary labelling is not misleading, information like 'low fat', 'reduced sodium' and 'high fibre' should be viewed with caution as there are no legal definitions for these quantities. The National Diet and Nutrition Survey (Gregory and Lowe 2000) and the Health Promotion Agency (HPA 2001) indicated that children in the UK eat too much fat and sugar and too little fruit, vegetable and high-fibre products. However, these general facts hide a more complicated profile. Younger children aged 18 months to 4 years were more likely to eat cereal (61 per cent) than adolescents (38 per cent) and although younger children were more likely to eat chips and snacks they were also more likely to eat fruit, nuts and seeds. Children from lower-income families are likely to eat a narrower range of poorer-quality foods with higher levels of saturated fats. International comparisons are carried out every four years by the WHO (Currie *et al.* 2004) and the latest report presents data from 35 countries for 11, 13 and 15 year olds only. It would be valuable to have more international comparative data available for the younger age groups and longitudinal data would offer more insight into the long-term impact of influences from the family lifestyle and pressures from peers and the media. As eating habits developed in early childhood influence later adult eating patterns, health and illness patterns and the health of the next generation, this would offer valuable additional evidence.

Diet in pregnancy

The nutritional status of both parents has an impact on the growth and development of the infant. Rapid development of the foetus in the first few weeks means that this is a particularly vulnerable time for damage from lack of specific nutrients or from environmental influences like drugs and alcohol. For example, the infant's neural tube (brain and spinal cord) develops rapidly in the first weeks of pregnancy and it is now known that folic acid, found in green leafy vegetables and in cereals is crucial for healthy development. Babies lacking the vitamin folic acid are at risk of being born with **spina bifida** and many mothers-to-be start taking this vitamin before conception and up until 12 weeks' gestation. Pregnant women are advised to eat a wide range of foods, with a few precautions such as avoiding undercooked eggs, which may cause salmonella food poisoning, and soft cheeses and pates, which carry a risk of listeria infection that is harmful to the unborn child. Having a low birth weight can have serious long-term implications for health in adulthood, including predispositions to heart and kidney disease and diabetes (Barker and Osmond 1987). The causes of infants being of low birth weight are many and include low maternal weight, poor diet during pregnancy, adverse social conditions, smoking and alcohol abuse (Reyes and Manalich 2005).

Alcohol is damaging to the developing nervous system and if drinking is excessive infants are sometimes born with foetal alcohol syndrome. Such infants have some specific characteristics, such as a low birth weight and a very small head (microcephaly), and there is sometimes developmental delay and intellectual impairment alongside specific facial features such as small eyes, a flat upturned nose and external ear malformations. It is difficult to ascertain the incidence of foetal alcohol syndrome as many children who have this condition may either not be diagnosed or may be thought to have a psychological condition such as behaviour problems or conduct disorder. As the diagnosis is complicated it may be that its prevalence is significantly underestimated (Cousins and Wells 2005) and some would argue that foetal alcohol syndrome is the largest preventable cause of intellectual disability. The latest research has shown that even one unit of alcohol makes the foetus 'jumpy' in the uterus and there are strong indications that pregnant women should not drink alcohol at all (Spohr and Steinhausen 1996). It is always important to check on the latest research about diet in pregnancy; for example, expectant mothers were once advised to eat liver because of its high iron content, whereas now the advice is not to eat it, as the high vitamin A levels can be harmful to the developing child.

Breastfeeding

The WHO recommends exclusive breastfeeding until 6 months of age; many health benefits are highlighted, including: fewer diarrhoeal diseases, less child obesity, fewer allergies, closer mother–baby bonding, fewer sudden infant deaths, increased immunity, more effective brain development due to the higher levels of polyunsaturated fatty acids (Wainright 2002), and five times less incidence of being admitted to hospital in the first year of life. When the benefits are listed it seems unlikely that mothers would want to do anything other than breastfeed their infants, and Article 24 of the UNCRC carefully avoids the conflict of infant rights and maternal freedom by emphasizing the woman's right to information and knowledge about breastfeeding. However, these issues are more complicated than a simple decision made on best evidence and it would be very superficial not to explore infant feeding in its social, cultural and commercial contexts. As family and work patterns change, breastfeeding may be viewed as a lifestyle choice. Rates of breastfeeding are declining worldwide and the prevalence in the UK is among the lowest in Europe, with only one in four babies still being breastfed at 4 months (UNICEF 2005) and with a wide differential between socio-economic groups. UNICEF (n.d., accessed 10 May 2005) has promoted breastfeeding in many hospitals through its 'baby-friendly scheme', although it reports limited overall progress since 2000 and lists the following issues around breastfeeding inequalities.

- Mothers in manual social class groups are less likely to breastfeed than those in non-manual groups (63 per cent as opposed to 83 per cent at birth) – only 13 per cent of babies whose mothers were classified in the 'lower status occupations' group are receiving any breast milk at 6 months, compared with 31 per cent in the 'higher occupations' group.
- Mothers who remained in full-time education until they were 18 are more than three times more likely to breastfeed their babies to between 4 and 6 months of age than mothers who left school aged 16 or under.
- More than three-quarters of mothers aged 30 or over breastfeed their babies compared with fewer than half of mothers aged 20 or under.
- With 81 per cent initiating breastfeeding, mothers in the south-east of England are more likely to breastfeed than mothers elsewhere in the UK. The lowest average rates are found in Northern Ireland, where just 54 per cent of babies are breastfed at birth, and the north of England (61 per cent).

Within the UK there is a distinct class and education divide, with middle-class mothers appearing to heed the health advice, which is reflected in their increased breastfeeding rates. A recent systematic review of all the research evidence on breastfeeding (Renfrew *et al.* 2005) identified a gap in knowledge about the reasons why women in lower socio-economic groups breastfeed less and how rates could be improved. Department of Health (DoH) targets have been set with the aim of increasing the rates of breastfeeding by 10 per cent within five years, as a major contribution to reducing health inequalities and improving public health. The DoH aim is to increase the rates of breastfeeding by promoting awareness of the benefits and by stopping the sale of milk formula at health clinics, so that health professionals do not appear to be endorsing artificial feeding. But will a simple awareness-raising exercise be enough? A recent examination of how breastfeeding was portrayed in the media found little positive information presented:

> Media coverage implies that breast feeding is problematic, funny and embarrassing, and that it is associated with middle class or celebrity women. In contrast, bottle feeding is socially integrated, highly visible, unproblematic, and associated with 'ordinary' families. (Henderson *et al.* 2000: 1198)

A qualitative study of reasons why women choose not to breastfeed found that women in the East End of London who were committed to bottle feeding seemed less confident about their bodies, distanced themselves from sexual issues in the decision to bottle feed and were unwilling to talk on the subject (Hoddinott and Pill 1999). Cultural perceptions of breastfeeding are further reflected by many shops and restaurants having baby feeding rooms usually housed in the female toilet area. Gaskin (1987: 200) takes issue with the relegation of breastfeeding: 'It is strange indeed that countries that so pride themselves on their fastidiousness should make social rules which often force their most vulnerable members to eat in places designed for the excretory needs of other members of the society.'

Gaskin makes a valuable point. How can mothers be expected to make a choice for breastfeeding when the cultural norms consider it as something that is private and slightly obscene? Women with new babies are bombarded with contradictory advice and, predictably, the choice of feeding is mainly influenced by immediate family members (Falicov 1995). In comparison, health professionals have had relatively little impact (Jones and Belsey 1977). Significant inequalities in breastfeeding practices therefore are common within the UK and white women in lower socio-economic groups are less likely to breastfeed; for these women, partner and community ethnicity have a major influence on starting and continuing to breastfeed (Griffiths *et al.* 2005).

Unfortunately, the attitudes and behaviour of the minority, richer in-dustrialized countries are often perceived as reflecting what is best for infant health. Many poorer nations have only voluntary codes to prevent the promotion of infant formula milks and these are commonly flouted. Milk formulas are expensive, and sterilizing bottles and making up infant feeds is extremely difficult without the necessary facilities, resulting in higher levels of illness and deaths from diarrhoeal diseases. The Nicaraguan government has responded to infant ill health by restricting sales and placing a health warning on milk formula and, in New Guinea, baby milk is available only on prescription. Other research has shown that prolonging breastfeeding for the whole of the first year has had a positive effect on infant survival in West Africa (Molbak *et al.* 1994). The systematic review (Renfrew *et al.* 2005) suggests that research is needed to compare policy interventions to promote breastfeeding across different countries with diverse health care systems.

The *National Service Framework* (NSF) *for Children, Young People and Maternity Services* (NSF 2004: Standard 11) has an outcome to promote breastfeeding by giving up-to-date information and support to mothers. Although governments can legislate and guide, they might also be well advised to consider cultural perceptions and actions rather than viewing feeding just as an individual choice that can be influenced by offering information and support. Findings from the millennium cohort study (Griffiths *et al.* 2005) suggest that public health strategies to increase breastfeeding need to be focused on mothers who are young at first motherhood, and address support offered by partners and the communities in which women live.

The ideal recommended infant feeding practice is solely breastfeeding until 6 months when other foods are added so that the infant can learn to chew and receive sufficient iron. The next section gives further consideration to the weaning process.

Weaning

Weaning is a process during which the child moves from an all-liquid milk diet to balanced family meals. At 6 months the digestive tract is mature enough to handle more solid food and the infant will require more energy and certain nutrients, particularly iron, protein and vitamins. In the UK, infants have traditionally started weaning earlier than the recommended 6 months and a wider understanding of the cultural context of this practice may be an important step in combating obesity. Early weaning has been associated with increased weight gain and food intolerance, whereas iron-deficiency anaemia occurs when a balanced range of foods is not offered, and is seen more commonly in children from minority ethnic groups (who may be vegetarian) and in lower socio-economic groups who may eat a more restricted diet. A child with anaemia has low levels of iron (haemoglobin) in their bloodstream, often through eating insufficient amounts of meat and fresh vegetables. A child with anaemia will often seem tired, listless and less able to join in with activities and, if left untreated, this may affect growth and development (Marx 1997). Statistics indicating the prevalence of childhood anaemia are inconsistent but it is thought to be relatively common in pre-school children (Hall and Elliman 2003).

Feeding difficulties

The giving and receiving of food is at the heart of caring relationships and is often a metaphor for underlying emotions such as the giving of love or the feeling of rejection. Food is influenced by all areas of the ecological systems (see Figure 1.3), from the sensitivity in turn-taking between carer and child in the microsystem, to macro level issues such as the economic prosperity of the country determining whether the child lives in a society with an abundance of choice or experiences food poverty.

Feeding an infant and young child is an active and reciprocal act. For successful feeding the adult and infant need to 'tune in' to one another's behaviour. The sensitive adult is able to respond to signals about when the infant wants to pause, when she has had enough and when she is eager for more. Synchrony in turn-taking has been described by Isabella and Belsky (1995) as a 'dyadic dance' in which the parent and baby are so sensitively attuned that needs can be anticipated and cues interpreted. Such an attuned parent will know when the infant is reaching the stage where he wants to explore his food, maybe making a big mess, and when he wants to assert his independence by feeding himself with his fingers. Busy lifestyles often mean that these cues are overlooked and there is a mismatch between the carer and the child at mealtimes. For most children these are temporary phases but, for some, mealtimes will become fraught with anxiety (Underdown 2000). Figure 5.1 gives an example of how a cycle of anxiety can affect a child's feeding.

For some parents and children mealtime 'battles' become a regular feature and the cycle of stress compounds the difficulties. Once these patterns are entrenched, parents often need some experienced professional support if they are to break the cycle of anxiety around mealtimes. Parents may become very concerned that their child is failing to gain sufficient weight and may approach medical practitioners for advice. One mother's feelings are quoted in a Children's Society Report into faltering growth:

> 'My own feelings as a mother, it's very hurtful, it feels like a rejection, what a mother gives her child and the child doesn't want it, it feels quite hurtful' (Underdown 2000: 21).

The same report found that 'feeding' difficulties were not taken very seriously unless a child showed that their weight had dropped so that they were considered underweight.

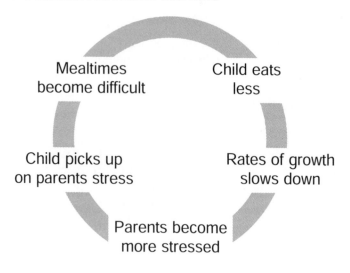

Figure 5.1 Circle of anxiety compounding feeding difficulties

How is growth monitored?

In the UK it has been traditional for infants to be taken to a health clinic where staff will record weight and measurements. In reality, visiting the health clinic may be more important as an opportunity to discuss concerns with health staff and to meet with other parents with similar age children. Hall and Elliman (2003) states that it is good practice to measure and plot on a **centile chart** the height, weight and head circumference of any child causing concern either about growth or other health issues, or where there are child protection concerns.

Feeding difficulties, faltering weight gain and 'failure to thrive'

In the early twentieth century in the UK the term 'failure to thrive' was commonly used to describe children, often brought up in **foundling homes**, who were thought to receive adequate food but still grew poorly. Gradually it became assumed that these children failed to grow because they lacked love and stimulation from their carers. Failure to thrive was divided into two separate categories: organic and non-organic. In organic failure to thrive the reason for the child's poor weight gain was thought to be caused by a medical condition, whereas in the other category, where there was no organic reason for the lack of weight gain, it was thought to be due to neglect or deprivation.

In fact evidence suggests that only about 5 per cent of young children with inexplicable poor growth are found to have a previously undiagnosed illness and only a very small minority have faltering growth because of abuse or neglect (Boddy and Skuse 1994; Wright and Talbot 1996). Historically these two types of failure to thrive were thought to be completely separate, although more recent research has shown that this simplistic cause and effect model is unhelpful. In fact the cycle of anxiety is likely to affect mealtimes whether there is a medical cause for poor eating or not.

Having two separate categories of failure to thrive was particularly unhelpful to parents and children. The usual route for a child who was growing too slowly would be an initial referral to the doctor for tests to diagnose the reasons for the slow growth. The bio-medical model is a powerful one and if an organic condition was diagnosed then parents would not feel blamed as this was usually out of their control. However, most frequently no organic reason would be found for the slow growth and then parents would begin to feel that they had failed and that the slow growth must be due to a 'fault' in their parenting or in how they fed the child. In a study of parents' experiences of having a child with slow growth one mother describes the difficulty as follows:

> It was more of a behavioural problem than a feeding problem. She wasn't eating a lot you know, she was getting down from the table and running around and playing: you know mealtimes are going on and on and she wasn't putting on enough weight. (Underdown 2000: 5)

More recently the term 'failure to thrive' has been replaced by 'faltering weight gain', which really reflects the fact that the child is growing exceptionally slowly and has shown a significant downward movement on the centile chart. In fact 5 out of every 100 children aged 5 years or under in the UK are likely to experience an episode of growth faltering at some stage (Batchelor and Kerslake 1990) because they are taking in too few calories. For most children this will be due to decreased appetite because of an illness, feeding difficulties or dietary misconceptions, such as applying an adult high-fibre, low-fat 'healthy diet' to a child. A few children may have an underlying problem, such as asthma, which causes their appetites to wane. For many children these issues resolve themselves, but for some families the concern about a child's eating becomes so worrying that a cycle of anxiety (see Figure 5.1) builds up and compounds the feeding difficulties.

As children and parents may already be anxious, too frequent weighing or carrying out tests in hospital may actually make the situation worse. As Hall and Elliman (2003: 179) state:

> it is rare that the weight chart is the only clue to a serious abnormality affecting growth in infancy. Other symptoms or signs are nearly

always present as well, and in their absence hospital admission is rarely helpful since the investigation of infants whose only problem is slow weight gain seldom reveals any significant organic disease.

The medical model of trying to diagnose organic causes may therefore compound the difficulties, whereas the social model uses a more child- and family-centred approach. A social model of support takes into account each child and family's unique characteristics and culture and, over a period of time, the family are supported to make changes so that mealtimes are as they would wish them to be. The child's non-verbal interactions at mealtimes can sometimes be overlooked, especially in a tense atmosphere, and parents following some programmes have been effectively supported to tune in to their child's specific communications by watching video observations of their mealtimes (Raynor and Rudolf 2000). If available, enhanced home visiting schemes, usually offered by a specially trained health visitor who is supported by a multi-disciplinary team of dietitians and medical personnel, may offer an effective resolution (Wright et al. 1998).

Varying growth patterns across cultures

One problem with centile charts is that they have not taken into account either cultural differences in growth patterns or the choice of feeding method. Some charts were based on weight standards from artificially fed infants, which may have wrongly indicated that breastfed babies were not gaining weight fast enough. The WHO has recently collected data on children's growth from six centres worldwide (Brazil, Ghana, India, United States of America, Norway and Oman). These six centres reflect richer and poorer countries and the standards have been derived by including infants of non-smoking mothers who breastfed exclusively until 4 months (Wright 2005). Although this may be the simplest way of constructing charts reflecting optimum growth curves there are a number of ethical issues that need to be addressed. For example, in affluent countries the number of obese children is rising and in poorer countries chronic undernutrition means that average growth is suboptimal and charts may not reflect these realities. Whether individual countries will find the new WHO charts an improvement remains to be seen.

In other parts of the world children's growth and development may be greatly affected by poor nutrition and other health threats. For example, China has the largest population in the world, with the majority of families living in poorer rural areas. Over 34 per cent of children under the age of 5 years are reported to show moderate or severe growth stunting (Wang et al. 2005). The reason for this seems to be a lack of exclusive breastfeeding early in life, leaving the infants more at risk from pneumonia and diarrhoea and, as children grow older, they lack variety in foods, particularly high-protein foods, fruits and vegetables. Wang *et al.* (2005) strongly recommend exclusive breastfeeding until infants are 6 months old, but this does of course have implications for ensuring that breastfeeding mothers themselves have a healthy balanced diet.

Childhood obesity

A survey of school-age children (Gregory and Lowe 2000) highlights the fact that school-age children in the UK have become taller and heavier than the previous generations. Increased height, in particular, is associated with healthy nutrition and improved living conditions. Evidence of this height increase across the generations is often apparent in the UK when visiting historic buildings and noticing the height of the doorways! Children's increase in weight, however, causes more of a health concern, with 15.8 per cent of 2 year olds and 18.7 per cent of 5 year olds in the UK being overweight and over 6 per cent being obese (Reilly *et al.* 1999). Children's food intake in the UK has been found to be high in sugars and fats and low in fruit and vegetables (Gregory and Lowe 2000; Bradshaw 2002). The UK is not alone in having an obesity epidemic. The USA perhaps noted these trends first and eastern Europe, Germany and Australia are all seriously affected. Several factors have been identified as possible causes of children's weight increase and these include the following:

- Fast food and portion sizes: foods such as burgers and chips tend to be energy dense (high in calories and fat) and are often marketed in large portion sizes.
- Sugars and sweetened drinks: diets high in free sugars such as those found in fizzy drinks give high energy, low nutrient intake and may contribute to reducing appetite control. In addition, over half of UK 5-year-olds have experienced erosion of dental enamel due to increased consumption of acidic drinks (Hall and Elliman 2003).
- Energy density and hunger satisfaction: fatty foods are energy dense (high in calories low in nutrients) but may not satisfy hunger in the same way as protein or carbohydrate foods. This may encourage snacking and overeating.
- Less physical activity: far fewer children walk to school and parents are cautious about allowing their children to play outside. This may combine with children spending more time watching television or playing computer games.
- Advertising and favourable pricing of energy-dense, nutrient-low foods: the banning of food advertising is a controversial subject.

Food is complex and not usually all 'good' or all 'bad', which leads to much argument from the various stakeholders, such as the companies that market fast food.

- Adverse socio-economic conditions: people in lower socio-economic groups may shop more carefully to obtain more food for their money but they are more likely to buy foods with high levels of fat and sugar because these are richer in energy and cheaper than fruit and vegetables (Leather 1996; Acheson 1998): 'Why do children from poor families consume such a lot of fizzy drinks, milk and white bread? Penny for penny, a chocolate bar provides more calories than carrots, even from a market stall. If the child refuses what is offered there may be no money in the budget for an alternative' (Thurlbeck 2000: 809). In addition, families on a tight budget are less able to bulk buy produce at large supermarkets on the outskirts of towns and may often have to buy more expensive inferior produce at a local shop (Shohaimi *et al.* 2004).

While poorer families are understandably concerned with ensuring that children's stomachs feel full and that they have sufficient calories for energy, repeated studies have shown that coronary heart disease, certain cancers and obesity are linked to nutritionally poor diets in childhood. Type 2 diabetes used to be considered as a disease of middle-aged overweight people but it is also now commonly being seen in obese children. Poor adult health may well be the legacy of nutritionally unbalanced diets in childhood combined with a lack of exercise. Lack of money for iron-rich foods such as red meat and green leafy vegetables has also led to outcomes such as iron-deficiency anaemia, leading to reduced immunity and greater susceptibility to infection (BMA 1999). Long-term iron-deficiency anaemia in children under 5 years has also been linked with a permanent effect on growth rate and cognitive and psychomotor development (Marx 1997).

The emergence of the obesity epidemic in developing countries

With increasing globalization of food markets it is perhaps unsurprising that the obesity epidemic is penetrating some of the poorest countries worldwide. Changes in dietary composition such as increased intake of sugar, more animal fats and oil, and higher-calorie foodstuffs, combined with changes in economic structure from traditional farming practices to industrialization, are leading to a worldwide increase in obesity (Popkin 2001; Prentice 2005). Traditionally children in developing countries have experienced undernutrition and deficiencies in key nutrients but increasingly obesity caused by excess calorie intake is becoming common. Doak *et al.* (2005) describe a phenomenon where large numbers of households in middle-income countries have the 'dual burden' of both underweight and obese individuals within the same family. This needs more investigation and raises interesting questions about whether early malnourishment is a risk for later obesity.

Physical activity

For optimum health a nutritionally balanced diet in childhood should be complemented by an active lifestyle. Many children in the UK have protected childhoods: their parents are afraid of danger from traffic and of abduction. Children are taken to school by car and dropped close to the gate, and are not expected to take part in adult work, as once they might have helped around the farm or collected firewood, for example. In particular, those living in inner cities lack any safe spaces in which to play, resulting in many children becoming inactive, spending most of their time watching television or sitting in front of the computer in their bedrooms. In addition, the national curriculum has reduced the amount of physical exercise taken within the school day.

Some local authorities are launching 'home zone' schemes aimed at ensuring that the local neighbourhood is for people rather than transport. The Northmoor inner-city estate in Manchester based its home zone on a consultation with local people. The area was planted with trees, there were safe play areas and an improved road layout with traffic-calming measures. This scheme was an innovative attempt to try to improve the health and safety of children, but it can have a real impact on health only if it is part of an integrated range of measures. Each initiative needs to add another part to the puzzle of meeting health needs in a holistic way. So, to use the example of developing home zones, this not only provides for safe play in a pleasant environment, it also involves consulting with children, young people and adults to find out what they think will work. By actually participating, people can 'own' the changes and develop personally through meaningful contributions. By actively contributing, children and adults feel valued and competent, whereas those living in deprived situations often feel powerless and unable to influence. Schools have a role to play in ensuring that sufficient time is available in the curriculum for exercise and that there are wide options for activities. Getting children interested in sport will reduce time spent in front of a television or computer but provisions should be affordable and accessible to all.

Psychological effects of childhood obesity

The physical health risks from obesity are alarming, and even more worrying when these risks are considered alongside the social and emotional effects. Overweight children are far more likely to be stigmatized (Must and Strauss

1999) or bullied by their peers (Hill and Waterston 2002), and may develop poor self-esteem, lack confidence or even become clinically depressed (Williams *et al.* 2005). These psychological consequences have been shown to have an impact on children underachieving at school. A publication by the British Medical Association (BMA 2005) on preventing childhood obesity reports a study where children were shown pictures of other children and asked who they would most like to be friends with. Obese children were always the last to be chosen irrespective of children's disabilities, class, gender, race, socio-economic status or living environment. This study was originally carried out in 1961 and conducted again in 2001 when attitudes were found to be even more stigmatizing towards obese children (Latner 2003, cited in BMA 2005).

What can be done to combat childhood obesity?

Bronfenbrenner's ecological systems theory (see Figure 1.3) provides a useful framework for considering the systems that could be influenced to combat childhood obesity. There is much controversy about the most effective way to tackle these issues, from macro level issues involving legislative change to curb advertising and food labelling, through to mesosystem initiatives within school and micro level changes within the family unit. The government has adopted several policies to try to ensure healthier eating and the *Every Child Matters* guidance has set targets to reduce childhood obesity. The government also laid down guidelines for school lunches (DfES 2000), making fruit and vegetables available every day. Interestingly, the greatest effect was recorded when, in a popular television series (*Jamie's School Dinners*), celebrity chef Jamie Oliver exposed the poor quality and lack of funding for school dinners. The result was an announcement of tougher minimum standards for school dinners and new minimum standards for processed foods to limit the amount of fat, salt and sugar in products such as burgers, sausages and cakes.

School-led initiatives

The impact of poor nutrition on concentration, cognition, memory and behaviour has been well established (Doyle 1994; Pollitt and Matthews 1998) but it is only in the last few years that schools have incorporated measures to ensure that children are better nourished. In the UK every child between 4 and 6 years of age receives a piece of fresh fruit every day (DoH 2002) and early evaluations of this are encouraging. Surveys have shown that around 5 per cent of children regularly have no breakfast and 9–13 per cent eat crisps or chocolate to start the day (Lucas and Liabo 2004). Since 1999 a growing number of schools have set up early-morning breakfast clubs where children can eat a healthy meal before starting their school work. Parents often view this as a useful provision where children are safely cared for and have time to eat properly. In addition, children enjoy seeing their friends, and teachers claim that breakfast clubs improve school attendance, cut down on late arrivals and help children to concentrate in class. Provisions of this type are difficult to evaluate because families' needs are diverse and other research has shown that pursuing the healthy eating message too strongly may 'put people off'; as a result some clubs place more emphasis on the social aspects (Shemilt *et al.* 2002). Some would argue that schools should concentrate on educating children and families should ensure adequate nutrition. The links between achievement and being well nourished are clear, but does this mean that the state will take on more and more responsibility for care? Can a few portions of fruit and a healthy breakfast actually impact long term on the types of food consumed by children or do healthy eating patterns have to be established within the family? Diet is important for the child's health now and in the future, so these are important questions about how Article 24 of the UNCRC can best be fulfilled.

Advertising and promotion of foods to children

Children are prime targets for television advertising of sweets, snacks, sweetened breakfast cereals and drinks, and more than 80 per cent of advertisements on children's TV are for these products. In the UK, concerned voluntary groups like Sustain (the alliance for better food and farming) are advocating a children's food bill to set rigorous, legally enforced standards for children's food in order to address diet-related health. The Children's Food Bill proposes:

- protecting children from unhealthy food marketing
- defining good food
- improving the quality of children's food
- improving the quality of food in schools
- ensuring all children have essential food skills and knowledge
- promoting healthy food to children.

Protecting children from the marketing of unhealthy foods remains contentious, and evidence from places like Sweden, Norway and Quebec, which have imposed restrictions, indicates that this has not had a significant impact on obesity levels among children. Sustain (2005) argues that a more comprehensive approach is needed and other countries are adopting different approaches to tackling children's dietary issues. In Australia in 2005, for example, marketing, advertising and media associations launched an 'Eat Well, Play Well, Live Well' initiative, while campaigners in the United States are claiming that self-regulation of the advertising industry is ineffective, and that children's food advertising decreases children's nutritional knowledge and their ability to reason about healthy diets. In England the government has pledged in the *Choosing Health* (DoH 2004a) policy document to have a full strategy in place to control the marketing of unhealthy foods to children. All the countries that have ratified the United Nations Convention on the Rights of the Child have an obligation to fulfil the requirements of Article 17, which states that children have the right to reliable and clear information from the mass media and that products that could harm children should not be promoted.

Conclusion

The diet of the world's children is crucially important to future health and as such is everyone's responsibility. Global food markets are dominated by huge multinational corporations, which should have a corporate responsibility to use their marketing strategies to promote positive health by the consumption of recommended foodstuffs. There is still much work to be done in ensuring accurate labelling of nutritional values and researching into producing healthier foods. Many countries are considering that the marketing of products to children is unethical and should be restricted. In addition, as nations become increasingly industrialized, children are often unaware of the origins of natural food and they lack cooking and budgeting skills. Introducing fresh fruit into nurseries is a start but a more holistic approach is required, ensuring that school meals are nutritionally balanced and that all families have enough money for a healthy shopping basket. The WHO global strategy on diet, physical activity and health should enable nations to learn from the mistakes and successes of others.

6 The impact of family change on children's health and well-being

Family networks are at the heart of communities; they are the 'building blocks' of society and the essential units that protect and nurture the future generation. Without doubt families shoulder the main responsibilities for providing the essential care necessary for children's physical, emotional and social health, laying the foundations for future health and well-being. Yet within the diversity of the twenty-first century the definition of 'family' is very unclear and the question as to whether parenting is a private matter or a public concern is hotly debated (see Chapter 3). In this chapter ideas about how the family may be defined are introduced, family changes are discussed with references for further study, and research into the effect of changing family relationships on children's health and well-being is explored. Policy-level changes in the UK (see Chapter 1) have drawn attention to the importance of listening to children and, wherever possible, research quoting children's opinions is used, as they have first hand experience of the effects that the changing family has upon their health and well-being. In the conclusion there is a reminder about the importance of having social policies that protect and support changing families. Children's health and well-being may be linked more to the associated effects of relative poverty (see Chapter 4) and poor housing than to family change itself (Roberts and Pless 1995).

Definitions of family

Although the majority of people either live or have lived within a family, ideas about what constitutes a family are as complicated and unclear as families themselves. Murdoch's (1949) description of the family reflected his observations within a specific historical timeframe and epitomized a western normative definition of family in the following way:

> the family is a social group characterised by common residence, economic co-operation and reproduction. It includes adults of both sexes at least two of whom maintain a socially approved sexual

relationship, and one or more children, own or adopted, of the sexually co-habiting adults.

This outdated description of the family does not encompass the wide variety of family forms that exist today. Children may be raised in a nuclear family, a single-parent household, a blended family with a combination of step-siblings and step-parents, a gay or lesbian family, an adoptive family, a family where one or both parents are socially, rather than biologically, related to their child because of conception through new reproductive technologies (NRTs), multigenerational families living together, or, in some cultures, children may find themselves being raised in a polygamous family. Family forms are constantly changing as parents and children forge new roles within the family structure. As Pryor and Rodgers (2001: 1) argue, 'families at the beginning of the 21st century are going through a period of change which is bewildering to both observers and family members themselves'. If the aim is to define family, perhaps one effective way is to ask children themselves. Morrow's (1998) study did exactly this and children and young people's de-finitions seem to reflect the nature of family far more clearly. Tara, for ex-ample, defined the family in the following way:

> A family is a group of people which all care about each other. They can all cry together and go through all the emotions together. Some live together as well. Families are for helping each other through life.
> (Tara, 13, cited in Morrow 1998)

This definition encapsulates Tara's experience of caring for one another and supporting each other when facing challenges, especially when living apart from loved ones. One young girl living in a transnational family explained how she felt supported by her father, who lived in another country, when he telephoned once a week and texted a message every day. This meant he re-mained involved in her day-to-day life. The crucial element for children's positive health and well-being is having someone who cares for them sensi-tively and shows warmth and interest. This warmth and care seems more important than whether the adult figures are the biological or social parents. Traditionalists rue the so-called 'breakdown of the family' but others may well view the diversity in family form as a response to modern living that offers the opportunity for children and adults to function in ways that nurture all family members (Pryor and Rodgers 2001).

Family change

Families are dynamic; they are continually evolving and developing within the broader context of technological, political, economic and social influences within the dominant culture. The image of the nuclear family consisting of a 'breadwinning husband' and a 'stay-at-home wife' engaged with her child-rearing and domestic duties was much criticized initially by feminists as the core of women's oppression (Smart and Neale 1999). Later theory has challenged the idea that the family could be experienced as if all women's lived experience was similar and has acknowledged the individuality and diversity of family life. The drivers of family change are many and include the changing role of women and their entry into the workforce (Cherlin 1992; McLanahan and Sandefur 1994), the advent of contraception so that fertility can be controlled, educational opportunities for women in some cultures, and the mobility of the family as work is now increasingly focused away from the home. For many women, particularly in the industrialized countries of the north, their financial independence, combined with changes in divorce laws, makes separation more feasible than in the past. This has been accompanied in some cultures by a shift in attitudes so that women are encouraged to attain career goals in the same way as men, raising questions about who cares for the infant in the early years and what compromises are necessary if all family members are to have optimal health and well-being. The following sections summarize research on the effects of family transitions and diversity on the health and well-being of the child.

Divorce and separation

Within the UK, at least one in four children will experience parental separation or divorce before they reach their 16th birthday (Pryor and Rodgers 2001). Parental separation is not a single event but part of a long-term process, beginning with disharmony within the family, leading to varying degrees of acrimonious or cooperative relationships afterwards. This process may be supplemented with other transitions, such as one parent taking a new partner, meeting new step-siblings or having to move house. Traditionally questions have been asked about whether divorce was harmful to children's well-being and development, but more recent research shows an altogether more complicated and individual picture. Most children will experience deep sadness and a loss of confidence and self-esteem when a parent leaves, although most will settle back into their normal routine, especially if they are able to keep good communication with both parents (Pryor and Rodgers 2001). The crucial elements that seem to ensure healthier outcomes for children include whether parents can keep a reasonably positive relationship after separation and if children have been appropriately involved throughout the whole process. In the past it was often thought beneficial to hide the situation from children, but later research clearly shows that health and well-being outcomes are better when children are able to participate appropriately in discussions and decisions, especially about contact with the non-resident parent (Dunn and Deater-Deckard 2001; Hawthorne *et al.* 2003). Children's lives also change rapidly as they grow and develop, and discussion about contact issues, for example, should be ongoing so that changes can be negotiated according to children's needs and activities. One study (McLaughlin 2004) revealed that a quarter of children had not had any discussion at the time of parental separation and only 5 per cent were given a full explanation and offered the chance to ask questions. Parents may feel that children are protected by being less involved, but excluding children adds to their pain, confusion and feelings of powerlessness. As Pryor and Rodgers state: 'in all situations where children are involved there is a need for balance between the right to be informed and heard, and burdening them with undue responsibility for decisions made' (2001: 275). Parents should be offered support and information about how children can be sensitively and appropriately involved. As one 10-year-old recalls:

> I can't remember the very day but I can remember a couple of weeks later when he came to visit me and I didn't know where he had gone or anything. So he kept on visiting and he kept on driving off in the car. I had a rocking horse by the window when I was little, and I used to sit on the rocking horse and watch his car until I could see it nowhere else, and watch it into the distance. I used to cry my eyes out all night and most of the day. I'd cry and cry and cry. (Dunn and Deater-Deckard 2001: 11).

Often the focus of attention may be on the actual separation, whereas keeping the child's perspective in mind and ensuring that grandparents and friends are accessible for support is associated with better outcomes for children's well-being (Dunn and Deater-Deckard 2001).

Risk factors

Research (McClean 2004) has shown that children whose parents divorce or separate are more at risk from some adverse outcomes than children from intact families. However, the adverse outcomes for children after divorce apply to only a minority of children and certain conditions may make children more at risk. Risk factors are increased for children who have been in a family where there is a very hostile separation, where there has been domestic violence or serial re-partnering, or where the child's needs have not been recognized – for example, by not keeping in touch with extended family networks. Family conflict can contribute to behavioural problems and young children may become very confused if one parent openly criticizes the other. This atmosphere will diminish the quality of contact with the non-resident parent and have a negative impact on the child's well-being. For many children parental separation will entail living in a one-parent family with a resulting loss of income and financial hardship (see Chapter 4), which has many impacts on children's health and well-being. In addition, the change in circumstances may mean a change of address and perhaps a parent struggling with relative poverty and depression over the relationship breakdown. If a parent re-partners this may caused added stress to children but there is little recognition, at either policy or practice level, of the support needs of step-families who are expecting children to live harmoniously together in newly blended families.

Single-parent households

It is commonly believed that growing up in a single-parent household is less good for children's well-being than having two resident parents. But what does it mean to grow up in a single-parent household? Is it better or worse to grow up in a family with one parent due to death or to divorce? Is it better for children to be in a calm atmosphere with one parent or living in conflict with two? Do outcomes vary for children who have always lived in a one-parent family compared with those whose families change due to parental separation? As over 30 per cent of children in the UK will find themselves in a single-parent family at some time these are important questions, but can research actually give any answers to these dilemmas when individual circumstances are all so unique? As single-parent families are now so commonplace, there is also a growing realization that the type of family is far less important to health and well-being than the actual interactions, interest and environment that the child experiences. The reasons for families having only one parent are many: there are women who have well-paid jobs who choose to become single mothers, sometimes conceiving through using the techniques of new reproductive technologies (see below); there are women who choose to go it alone from the start because of an unsatisfactory relationship; there are widows and widowers, and the majority who become single parents through relationship breakdown. Many single-parent families experience severe financial hardship and many parents, in order to fit around childcare times, take on several, often low-paid, part-time jobs to make ends meet. Either way, time or money, or often both, are likely to be more stretched in a single-parent household and outcomes will vary directly according to the amount of support from networks and whether there is adequate finance (McCormick *et al.* 1981). This may be balanced by the amount of support received from family and friends but outcomes for children are likely to be less good where there are adverse circumstances such as poverty, conflict or parental depression.

Step-families and the 'unclear' family

In most countries the majority of children remain with their mothers after separation, not as passive victims but as active family members experiencing their own change processes. Siblings, facing what would appear to be identical circumstances, have to forge and make sense of both new relationships and the possible loss of established ones in their own way (Smart *et al.* 2001). Although children's responses will be individual there are some common threads that can usefully be explored when examining how children's health and well-being can be promoted during family transitions. Bronfenbrenner's ecological systems theory (1979; see Figure 1.3) shows the child at the centre with reciprocal influences from all systems. Some have criticized this as being too static and suggested that children may not be at the centre as relationships break down and reform, and they might be pushed to the side as adult relationships take centre stage. The complicated and ever changing web of influencing relationships is usefully considered in a much more fluid way, rather like a rhizome or root sending out a whole network of interconnecting shoots. 'Rhizoanalysis' (Deleuze and Guattar; 1987; MacNaugton 2005) offers a conceptual framework that challenges ideas of cause and effect by considering how children continually reshape their shifting, complex and contradictory understandings of themselves and others:

> Children may have to learn to live with strangers in the form of their parents' new partners and their children, or even new half siblings. Their expectations of their parents may have to be revised, and they may see them behaving in new and unaccustomed ways; perhaps distressed or lonely, or perhaps loving a new sexual partner, or step parenting 'strange' children. (Smart *et al.* 2001: 68–9)

Children's experiences will be unique and changing but it is important to recognize that this is not necessarily a deficit model – indeed, there may be positive benefits for children's well-being from living in complex families. All children whose families change will have to deal with loss, since the child generally has contact with parents on an individual basis after separation. Most research has explored children's continuing relationships with absent fathers and loss of this contact was often cited as the worst aspect of separation (Kurdek and Siesky 1980). Dealing with the loss of some family relationships and having to accept new ones is often accompanied by a powerful mix of emotions. Some children may find this too hard to manage and express this with difficult behaviour, whereas others may repress feelings knowing that parents and teachers do not like it when children are upset (Dwivedi and Harper 2004). Denying or repressing feelings can lead to deep sadness, and enabling children to have appropriate time and opportunities to express their emotions allows feelings to be processed and is crucial to mental well-being (Dwivedi and Harper 2004) (see Chapter 8). Children who have unreliable contact with a parent may well feel less valued, with a resulting loss of emotional well-being (although this is not necessarily the case). One child, for example, felt his relationship with his father improved after a family breakdown because he received telephone calls, emailed pictures and messages, and a daily text message. Whether children should keep contact with a parent who has been violent can be decided only on an individual basis and needs regular review as the child grows and develops. In the UK, courts are now more open to finding ways of listening to children's views and many countries have set up supervised contact centres as an impartial 'space' for children to see a parent with whom they do not live. Parents in distress may be emotionally unavailable, and many children and a number of studies have reported that children felt that they had to cope alone (Wallerstein and Kelly 1980; Neugebauer 1989; Smith *et al.* 1997). Some children will experience a loss of social networks when parents separate; in particular if, for example, the mother has custody, the children may lose contact with paternal grandparents and other members of the extended family. Parents need to be aware that grandparents and other extended family members are most often cited by children as significant sources of support (Pryor and Rodgers 2001) and older children cite friends as a source of support. Every child's lived experience will be individual but the degree to which children cope is heavily influenced by how much their views are heard and responded to in times of transition.

Family change when domestic violence is involved

Domestic violence is not a new issue, but increasingly acts as a catalyst for family change. Historically, divorce was uncommon and women had no means of financial support outside of the family. In many cultures the changing role of women, legislative change, provision of safe refuges coupled with shifting attitudes and reducing levels of stigma have enabled women to leave violent partnerships. In addition, domestic violence was considered a 'women's issue', whereas current research shows that this is a family concern that has a major impact on children's health and well-being (Hester *et al.* 2000). Domestic violence is known to be prevalent across all socio-economic groups irrespective of race or religion (Women's Aid 1995) but the actual extent of the problem is difficult to estimate as it is often hidden because of stigma. In 90–95 per cent of recorded cases women are the victims and males

perpetrate the violence (Dobash and Dobash 1980). Domestic violence includes: 'any form of physical, sexual or emotional abuse which takes places
within the context of a close relationship. In most cases, the relationship will
be between partners (married, co-habiting or otherwise) or ex-partners' (DoH
1997).

Many victims of domestic violence have low self-esteem and self-
confidence, and may also live in fear of a controlling partner, making it more
difficult for them to seek help. One study recorded that only one in three
women victims had told anyone about the violence (Dominey and Radford
1996) so statistics are likely to offer an underestimate of the problem. A
sample of 1000 women in London (Mooney 1994) found that 25 per cent had
experienced domestic violence at some time, and a much larger Canadian
study (Statistics Canada 1993) found similar levels. There are few figures for
women's violence towards men as there is even less likelihood of this being
reported, and the effects on the children and partner are under-researched
(Cleaver *et al.* 1999). In summary, domestic violence is commonplace and,
regardless of the gender of the perpetrator, seeing a parent that they love
being pushed, hit or belittled may give children the message that this is
acceptable behaviour (Cleaver *et al.* 1999).

Between 75 and 90 per cent of violent incidents in the home are thought
to be witnessed by children, in itself constituting emotional abuse. Studies
have indicated that in homes where there is violence towards women, there is
also violence towards one or more children in 40–60 per cent of cases (Hughes
et al. 1989). Domestic violence has major effects on children's health and
well-being which include the following.

- Pre-school children living in violent situations may present with
  behavioural problems or physical responses such as headaches, stomach aches or diarrhoea, erratic nursery attendance and poor concentration. Abrahams (1994) also found a range of emotional health
  problems, from being frightened and withdrawn to being angry and
  aggressive.
- Primary school children living in violent households may exhibit
  behavioural and emotional difficulties. They may also experience
  erratic attendance at school, be angry and find it difficult to trust
  people (Hester *et al.* 2000).
- Exposure to domestic violence is damaging to children and may lead
  to negative outcomes such as aggression, anxiety, difficulties at
  school and behavioural problems (Holden *et al.* 1998), and may be a
  factor in the development of mental health problems.

Leaving a violent relationship increases the danger of an escalation in violence and children also face further challenges to their health and well-being.

Living in a refuge or bed and breakfast hostel usually means that children will have to leave their friends and family and change nursery or school. One 8-year-old boy explained how the school he attended provided 'emergency' uniforms for children who came from the refuge, so that they would 'fit in'. He also added that his uniform never fitted and all the other children knew why he had joined in the middle of a term. Children's emotional well-being may be fragile after an abusive home life; it is important that they are protected from bullying at school (Mullender and Morley 1994) and that domestic violence is considered when children exhibit emotional or behavioural difficulties (see Chapter 8).

Many countries are developing methods of working with children who have witnessed domestic violence; evidence suggests that children do not 'just forget' these painful experiences and that they benefit from an open attitude and being respectfully listened to and believed (Hester *et al.* 2000). Children report that they often feel that they are the only ones living in a violent family, and research in several countries has shown that appropriate therapeutic group work has been found to aid children's resilience and recovery in some instances (Hester *et al.* 2000). Creating a more open attitude with regard to family violence by, for example, discussing within PSHE (personal, social, health and education) sessions at school, may help to remove the stigma and allow children to seek help. This has implications for appropriate staff training.

At policy level in the UK there was insufficient focus and awareness of domestic violence in the Children Act 1989. For example, it was not recognized how dangerous contact time between perpetrators of domestic violence and their children could be, and this led to changes in policy and practice. Contact may now take place in supervised settings and the family courts have a responsibility to ascertain the views and wishes of the children.

New reproductive technologies

Article 7 of the UNCRC concerns the child's right to identity, to having a legally registered name, the right to a nationality and the right to know and, as far as possible, be cared for by their parents. The rapid increase in new reproductive technologies (NRTs) includes in-vitro fertilization, using donor eggs or sperm for conception, surrogacy and even cloning, and this has raised many ethical issues. For example, a recent court case involved a couple who had stored frozen embryos because the woman was infertile after cancer treatment. The couple had subsequently split up and the woman was asking for custody of the frozen embryos; however, her ex-partner did not wish a child to be born. Edwards *et al.* (1993) argue that procreation is not just about how humans come into being, it is also 'about how relationships come into being, and relationships that have an influence not just on early life but throughout a lifetime'. As Strathern (1992) argues, most people in Britain fear the technology less than how it will actually be used. She makes a strong case for the fact that many people see NRTs as 'against nature'. This is an important distinction as it may mean that any difficulties the child experiences are blamed on unknown biological genes. Edwards *et al.*'s (1993) study reports that an interviewee had used the term 'bloodline' when explaining family relationships. Real kinship relations were thought to be blood-related kin and others described difficulties in relationships because of feelings of difference. Golombok (2000: 33) describes an interview with a mother who had conceived through donor insemination and felt that there was no need to tell her daughter about her origins: 'We just feel like she's ours. It's like it was done, but it's forgotten about. From the day I conceived, it was just like she was my husband's. She has never been thought of as anything else.' Such a case does pose ethical dilemmas: for example, the child might hear about her origins by chance from another family member with a possibly devastating effect on her trust and confidence in her own identity. As NRTs become more embedded in cultures, models of recommended 'best practice' will become known. In the UK the law has recently been changed so that children conceived after April 2006 through donor insemination will be able to trace their biological parent when they are 18 or over. Therefore, the way children who are conceived as a result of NRTs are perceived and perceive themselves will be very much to do with the individual circumstances and attitudes at the time. Being honest with children about their origins and roots has been found to be central to their developing sense of identity and mental health, and the timing and sensitivity with which the information is gradually shared is also important.

Gay and lesbian parenting

The wide publicity that surrounds new reproductive technologies and changes in fostering and adoption laws in the UK has heightened the public's awareness that some children are being raised in families with parents of the same sex. In reality, same-sex parenting is not a new phenomenon, with many people having children before they had openly acknowledged their sexual orientation. Until relatively recently, homosexuality was illegal in the UK, so a shift in public opinion is required before gay and lesbian families become widely accepted. Some people argue that homosexual parenting is 'unnatural' and may have detrimental effects on children's well-being, although others argue that two committed parents of the same sex must make 'better' parents than some heterosexual couples. The way in which the child is conceived may have health consequences for the child, which are identical to those discussed above in the section on new reproductive technologies, as whether a child knows their biological mother or father is a fundamental part of their developing identity. Research in both the UK and the USA (Kirkpatrick *et al.* 1981; Golombok *et al.* 1983; Green *et al.* 1986) shows that children brought up in a lesbian household have been found, by both parents and teachers, to be just as well adjusted as children from heterosexual families. Less research has been conducted on the effects of having two male parents, as traditionally being in a gay relationship precluded fathers from gaining custody of their children. However, gay men are more likely now to gain custody or be able to father children using NRTs. Early studies indicate that the gender development of children of gay fathers is no different from that of the general population and most are heterosexually orientated when they grow up (Golombok and Tasker 1994). The main area of concern for children's health and well-being does not lie in the fact that they have same-sex parents but that children may face prejudice and bullying because they come from a family perceived to be different from the norm. Golombok (2000) argues that this depends on the type of neighbourhood and the prevailing attitudes, and quotes one young person's experience:

> School was one big nightmare really, because I got picked on so much. I had cigarettes stubbed out on the back of my neck, and high heeled shoes thrown at me, and bits of hair cut off, and my head chucked down the loo and that sort of thing. They would say to everyone 'oh your mum's a lesbian.' They were doing it just for a laugh. But by the final year people thought it was really cool. They would say 'It's great! Your mum's a lesbian! Wow!' It was almost respected by the end of year. Everyone thought my mum was cool 'cos she was a lesbian, so it worked out all right. (Golombok 2000: 56)

It is important that education staff are aware from the outset of such discrimination so that these issues can be fully addressed within the class and the whole school.

Children 'looked after' by the local authority

Some children can no longer be cared for at home by their families and may need to be 'looked after' by the local authority. There are many reasons why children cannot be cared for by their own families. Two of the most common are:

1. parents or families needing relief from caring – parents may need support for a whole variety of reasons, such as being unable to manage a child with disabilities or, perhaps, the parents have health problems, preventing them from caring for their child; this would mean that the child was 'accommodated' on a voluntary basis

2. children may be suffering abuse or neglect and a court order may be
    sought to ensure their safety.

The Children Act 1989 states that a child is 'looked after' by the local authority
if he or she is placed in its care by a court order or accommodated by the local
social services department for more than 24 hours. (A care order might be
sought by the local social services if, for example, they assessed a child as being
neglected or abused.) In March 2004 in England, 61,100 children had been
'looked after' continuously for the previous year by local authorities (ONS
2005). About 90,000 children pass through the care system in any one year;
many will be accommodated for a very short time, perhaps during a family
crisis, but other children may stay in care until they are 16. The largest category of need for looked-after children was 'abuse or neglect', with an estimated
38,200 children at 31 March 2004 (62 per cent of the total). The second largest
category was 'family dysfunction' (10 per cent, or 6100 children).

Children who have been in the care of the local authority have had very
poor health and education outcomes. A large proportion of care-leavers have
serious health issues and many underachieve at school. In 2003 only 9 per
cent had five or more General Certificate of Secondary Education (GCSE)
passes at grades A–C compared with 53 per cent nationally. The reasons for
this are twofold:

1. children coming into care are likely to have more health problems
2. the care received from the local authority was not as good as that
    offered by committed caring parents.

The government recognized that 'looked after' children had greater health
needs and were receiving some of the least effective care, so in 1998 the
Quality Protects programme (DoH 1998) was launched, setting standards to
improve the health and life chances of the most vulnerable and disadvantaged children. The Quality Protects scheme has many targets, including ensuring that children have fewer placements so they can form
attachments; making sure that children have appropriate health checks and
immunizations; that specific groups, such as those from minority ethnic
backgrounds and those with disabilities, have their needs met more effectively; and, crucially, that young people can have their views listened to and
receive a response. The importance of **children in need** receiving a full
assessment is also emphasized; the common assessment framework is reviewed in Chapter 8.

Young carers

Children who take on significant caring tasks and assume a level of responsibility usually carried out by an adult are sometimes referred to as 'young

carers' (Aldridge and Becker 1993). The caring role may be physical or emotional, or both. Young carers are children and young people under 18 years old whose lives are in some way restricted because of the need to take responsibility for other family members, usually because of disability, mental illness or addiction. Taking on the responsibilities of caring at an inappropriate age may take an enormous toll on the mental and physical health of the young carers. Children may feel a deep sense of commitment and responsibility, and parents may feel guilt because their child is carrying such a burden. Both parent and child may feel that the authorities' knowledge of the situation might result in a harmful separation. Research by Frank *et al.* (1999: 30) shows that 'caring as a child has a range of concealed and long-term consequences' affecting both their mental and physical health. Further research is required in this area but it would appear that young carers have relatively greater mental and physical health needs than their peers, yet they have poorer access to health care services, perhaps because in some cases the parent/child caring roles have been reversed. Health workers must recognize this and actively offer appropriate health care.

Two young carers from a study in a UK South Asian community describe graphically how they felt that their role was stigmatized:

> 'No, I don't tell them about my Dad. If I tell them they might start making fun out of him' (Sajid, 12).

and

> 'They make fun, if we are going to the shop and we meet someone who goes to my school as well, then they start telling everyone that I've got a sister who hasn't got any hair or can't walk properly. They make fun of her and I don't like it' (Hina, 10). (Shah and Hatton 1999)

Young carers describe a number of effects on their lives:

- feeling different and being isolated from their peer group
- lack of time for homework, play, sport or leisure activities
- conflict between their own needs and those of the person for whom they are caring, leading to feelings of guilt and resentment
- feeling that no one understands and that no one listens
- lack of understanding or acknowledgement of their role
- problems with relationships
- underachievement at school, leading to difficulties moving into adulthood.

Teachers may not recognize that the reason for a particular young person being late for school is because he or she is having to organize younger siblings. Doctors and other primary health care staff often treat adults with mental illness, yet they do not always enquire how the burdens of care are distributed at home.

Similarly many young carers have reported that they and their families were too frightened to ask for help because they feared being taken into the care of the local authority. Young carers were often facing challenges within loving families and needed to be offered flexible help so that they could enjoy family life and their childhood. Article 12 of the UNCRC states that children's opinions should be heard in matters that affect them. Children and young people living in families where other members have health problems have intimate knowledge of their own circumstances. They understand the day-to-day pressures in a way that no professional can. One young carer described how each day is different: 'My mum gets very depressed sometimes and she just can't function at all and I have to look after my brother. Sometimes though she has good days and things can be okay.'

The same young carer described how he cared for his mother when she was poorly, yet when the doctor visited the house to discuss future care he was sent from the room because he was too young to hear or take part.

Often, primary health teams will be treating a parent for a mental illness and there is a now a requirement to identify dependent children who are taking on adult caring roles. Yet identifying the physical circumstances of caring is only the start. Caring takes place within the context of family relationships, and meeting the needs of individual children may mean designing very flexible care packages. Children who are young carers have an important role to play in influencing this service design.

Refugee and asylum-seeking families

Refugees are recognized as having left their own country because of a real risk of being persecuted for reasons of racial origin, religion, membership of a particular social group, nationality or for holding a particular political opinion. In the UK refugees become asylum seekers when they apply for refugee status. Young children in refugee families may have a whole range of health and well-being needs, for example:

- children and parents may be experiencing **post-traumatic stress disorder**
- families may experience the effects of poverty and lack of resources
- adjustment to a different culture may cause depression
- children from some countries (e.g. within Africa) may have chronic conditions not usually seen in the north, such as recurrent fevers from malaria

- children from eastern Europe may be at increased risk from tuberculosis or diphtheria.
- children who have lived in orphanages or had blood transfusions may have a greater risk of **hepatitis** or being HIV positive (Hall and Elliman 2003).

In the UK refugee children are entitled to use the health services, but this may be difficult as staff may not be aware of their specific health needs, and there may be language and cultural barriers. For example, parents may have a different cultural perception about mental health needs and well-being. A group of young asylum seekers in London were asked about their health concerns and they raised issues about family loss, loneliness, depression, lack of resources, language barriers and bullying (Hall and Elliman 2003). The rates of mental health problems in refugee children are uncertain, but one study (Fazel and Stein 2003) indicates that more than a quarter had a significant psychological disturbance, showing particular difficulties with emotional symptoms. Article 22 of the United Nations Convention on the Rights of the Child states that children who come into a country as refugees should have the same rights as children born in that country. Children who are refugees have specific health and well-being needs, and Article 3 reminds us that the best interests of the child should always come first and Article 2 that they should not face discrimination.

Family group conferences

Where there are many difficult family issues to resolve and decisions have to be made concerning children, some authorities or voluntary projects may offer a family group conference facility. At a family group conference the family invites everyone concerned to a discussion to try to reach the best decisions. Although professional staff may coordinate the meeting, the family group and close friends that they have invited are given private time when they can focus on effective plans (Lawrence and Wiffen 2002). Young children will usually have an advocate to listen to and represent their views. Although this approach has been used widely in New Zealand and Australia, the reasons why it has been slower to develop in the UK are debatable and may include the difficulty of professionals sharing 'power' in situations where there could be a risk to children (Brown 2003).

Conclusion

Family transitions pose real challenges to children's health and well-being. Adverse conditions related to family change, such as family violence or poverty, are likely to have the most damaging effects on children; *Every Child Matters* (DfES 2004) states that children should be protected from violence and experience economic well-being. Policies could also usefully reflect on the process and the risks to children at times of family change so that proactive help might be available. How these transitions are experienced will dictate whether outcomes are positive, and research indicates the health benefits of having an open attitude to discussion that enables children to express their views and influence what support is available. When parents are too distressed to provide this, a supportive network is important and others, such as grandparents, may take on this role. The *Every Child Matters* guidance paper (DfES 2004) suggests strengthening support from universal services such as schools and the **primary health care team**, as well as targeting specialist services. Some children like to have support at school whereas others prefer to keep a clear separation between home and school matters (Hawthorne *et al.* 2003; Wilson and Edwards 2003) this indicates the need for sensitivity in offering help. Individual children make sense of family inter-actions in their own way and some children will be more resilient than others, but it is perhaps unsurprising that research (Dunn and Deater-Deckard 2001; Hawthorne *et al.* 2003) indicates that even young children who are appropriately involved, listened to and who experience 'warmth' from their parent(s) are likely to experience a higher degree of well-being even when circumstances are difficult. The challenge is to ensure a balance of young children's appropriate involvement without overburdening them with undue responsibility, and to identify ways of supporting the quality and consistency of relationships in changing family structures.

7   Child public health

Child public health is concerned with improving quality and length of life, through health promotion and disease prevention, within the population. Acheson (1998) described public health as 'the science and art of promoting health, preventing disease and prolonging life through the organized efforts of society'. This definition highlights the fact that organized proactive strategies aimed at preventing ill health and promoting positive health are crucial if quality of life is to improve for communities and whole nations.

The World Health Organization (WHO) was established in 1948 and is the United Nations specialist agency for health, with the central objective of the attainment 'by all peoples' of the highest possible level of health. The WHO adheres to the definition of health as 'a state of complete physical, mental and social well-being and not merely the absence of disease or infirmity' (see Chapter 1), and holds that the enjoyment of the highest attainable standard of health is one of the basic rights of every human being without distinction of race, religion, political belief, economic or social condition. The WHO's constitution highlights the health of all people worldwide as fundamental to the attainment of peace and security, and states that this is not only dependent upon the fullest cooperation of individuals but also on the sharing of knowledge and expertise from one country to another. The WHO views the healthy development of the child as crucially important and holds governments responsible for the provision of adequate health and social measures.

Prevention of ill health and the promotion of positive health and well-being

Disease prevention through immunization programmes and the early screening, detection and treatment of ill health has been one of the major public health success stories of the last century, along with improved sanitation and housing (see Chapter 4). New developments, such as the universal hearing test for infants and **meningitis** vaccines, continue to be added to the range of effective public health measures. This chapter reflects initially on early health screening and then considers the scope and importance of childhood immunizations. Nutbeam (1998) identified a 'new' contemporary public health agenda, which views a significantly different area of public health by distinguishing the ways in which lifestyles and living conditions (housing and social capital) impact on health. Many aspects of the 'new' public health agenda have already been discussed in this book – for example, childhood obesity in Chapter 5, and the possible effects of family change in Chapters 2 and 6. The rapid increase in children's emotional difficulties is a major public health concern and aspects of this are covered in most chapters and especially in Chapter 8. In this chapter further important children's public health issues are explored and questions raised about how health messages can most effectively be communicated to children and families. Considering that child injury is a major cause of ill health and disability in the UK, it has received proportionally little attention from researchers. Childhood injury, dental decay, passive smoking and sudden infant deaths are all more frequent in lower socio-economic groups and the importance of finding ways of reducing their incidence is discussed with reference to theoretical approaches to health promotion. Finally, aspects of public health that have emerged as a direct result of the interface between health and well-being and the changing environment are explored. Ecological public health issues are diverse and include risks that have increased because of environmental change. For example, damage to the ozone layer has led to an increased risk of skin cancer particularly for susceptible children who have experienced doses of sunburn before puberty. Not all health promotion is equally effective at achieving its goals, and health belief models are discussed within an ecological interactive approach. Consideration of these dimensions of child public health leads to a concluding debate about the need for more research evidence about what works in encouraging families to make healthy choices to promote health and prevent disease.

Early detection and disease prevention

Screening involves the early detection of possible disease or ill health through the use of tests, examinations and other procedures that can be applied rapidly (Hall and Elliman 2003). Screening tests are not diagnostic; they are a way of identifying people who are more likely to have a particular condition. Testing begins early in the UK. Shortly after birth an infant's physical health is assessed by scoring the five components below on a scale of 0–2 (with 2 indicating optimum condition):

1. heart rate
2. respiration
3. colour
4. muscle tone
5. cry.

This 'Apgar test' – named after the pioneering paediatrician who devised it, Dr Virginia Apgar – is usually administered twice: once at one minute after birth and again at five minutes after birth. The test gives trained staff a clear indication of whether an infant needs more oxygenation or life support. If an infant in poor physical condition at birth is not treated quickly this could have long-term health implications, such as disability caused by lack of oxygen. Screening tests aim to reduce ill health by detecting conditions at an early stage when treatment can be most effective and the Apgar test fulfils the criteria for a screening test, which (according to Hall and Elliman 2003: 137) include:

- simple, quick, easy to interpret
- acceptable
- accurate
- repeatable
- specific
- good yield (ability to detect new, previously undetected cases).

The Apgar screening test is the first of many; it is very acceptable as it is non-invasive and there are no real ethical concerns about its administration.

In the first week of life the new infant will have had a general physical examination with particular emphasis on the eyes, heart and checking for congenital problems such as **congenital dislocation of the hips**. A spot of blood is taken from a heel prick to test for **phenylketonuria** (PKU) and **hypothyroidism, sickle cell disorders** and **cystic fibrosis**. In addition, it is envisaged that all newborn infants in the UK will be able to have a hearing test. The neonatal universal hearing test is replacing the dated distraction hearing test, which was administered at 7 months. This distraction test involved observing whether infants turned to soft high- and low-pitched sounds. It was criticized for being costly because two staff were required to administer it, and it was considered unreliable because many children who could hear effectively were referred for further tests. There is some concern now that children who develop impaired hearing due to fluid or thick mucous 'glue' in the middle ear will no longer be detected at 7 months. Glue ear affects around 20 per cent of 2-year-olds (Zeilhuis *et al.* 1990), and if left untreated can affect hearing and language development and be a factor in behaviour problems (see Chapter 8). In fact, a Cochrane systematic review (Butler *et al.* 2003) showed that a routine screening programme to detect glue ear would not significantly improve children's language development. It could also be argued that increasing parental awareness of the signs of glue ear may be more appropriate than a single screening test that may be administered at a time when the infant does not have a problem with fluid in the middle ear. This example is useful in demonstrating the need to constantly evaluate screening procedures alongside the vital role that **epidemiologists** play in monitoring the spread and control of disease.

Screening: issues and concerns

When screening is undertaken families should be confident that treatment will be available for any detected conditions as it would clearly be unethical to offer screening if there were insufficient services in place. Screening tests play a major role in the early detection of problems and the minimizing of disability and disease. In order for all infants globally to benefit from early screening the infrastructure must be in place to support these tests, which includes:

- trained health staff
- science laboratories with skilled technicians
- accessible expert treatment centres to treat conditions when they are detected in the early stages
- continuing research into disease patterns and the effectiveness of screening
- sharing of knowledge and expertise to ensure that continuing health improvement is sustainable.

Screening can cause anxiety for parents and this has to be balanced with the benefits of early detection. A test that gives too many false positives might be considered harmful in terms of the amount of stress that is caused to families. The distraction hearing test, for example, did give many false positives, making it essential that parents were well informed about the limitations of the procedure. Parents should be made aware of the benefits and limitations of screening tests so that when necessary they can make an informed choice.

Public health theories

Some health promotion approaches are much more successful than others. For example, the benefits of breastfeeding (see Chapter 5) are clear, yet the fact that many women choose to bottle feed their infants indicates that there are more complex beliefs and behaviours involved. A theoretical approach to health promotion offers a systematic way of understanding the issues and the influences on behaviour. Two related theories are presented here; the health belief model (HBM) is described and then considered as a detailed representation of the individual level of the ecological model.

The HBM was developed to aid understanding of why people accept or reject health screening or health promotion advice. The HBM consists of several concepts representing the perceived threat, perceived susceptibility,

INDIVIDUAL PERCEPTIONS   MODIFYING FACTORS   LIKELIHOOD OF ACTION

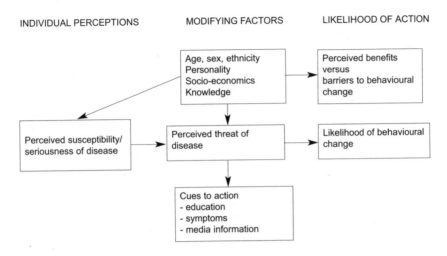

Figure 7.1 The health belief model: using immunization as an example

Source: Glanz *et al.* (2002:52)

perceived severity, perceived benefits and perceived barriers. These factors are thought to underpin an individual's likelihood of changing their behaviour. The 'cues for action' concept interacts with the perceived threat and may result in behaviour change. To take immunization, for example, 'cues for action' might be health education about the benefits or, as discussed later in this chapter, sensational media reporting about immunization. Figure 7.1 indicates how the variables may influence behaviour.

Self-efficacy has been added to HBM and relates to the confidence an individual has in being able to take action. The HBM enables an assessment of health beliefs and related influences to be considered in relation to the wider ecological context.

An ecological interactive approach

Although it is crucial to understand individual perceptions and health beliefs, the HBM is considered here within a wider ecological perspective. Promoting health and preventing ill health is complicated and involves understanding the multiple contexts of influence, which include individual, interpersonal, organizational, community and public policy factors (McLeroy *et al.* 1988). Each level of influence interacts with the other levels in a dynamic model. Behaviour both influences, and is influenced by, all other levels. This is known as reciprocal causation and is characteristic of ecological models. Taking smoking as an example, Table 7.1 uses some examples of smoking behaviour to illustrate the ecological approach. A child with a strong personal

Table 7.1   The ecological context: using smoking as an example

Concept	Definition	Example
Individual level	Personality traits, knowledge attitudes and beliefs; may be deep-seated beliefs that are still believed instead of accepting newer research	Believing that smoking is not harmful
Interpersonal level	Family and friends influence and are influenced by those around them	Partner or social group may reinforce smoking behaviour as part of social identity
Institutional factors	Rules, regulations and policies that may constrain or promote healthy behaviours	Banning smoking in the workplace – so social group forms to smoke outside
Community factors	Informal or formal social networks and norms of behaviour	Peer group pressure to smoke
Public policy	Laws and policies that support disease prevention, health-promoting behaviours and early detection	Banning smoking in public places; smoking cessation classes; anti-smoking campaigns; chest X-rays (screening)

belief in the dangers of smoking might well resist later peer pressure to smoke, for example.

Six examples of child public health issues

An effective health promotion strategy usually considers every level of the ecological context and employs multiple interventions. This section considers six crucial areas of child public health:

1.   immunization
2.   safety
3.   passive smoking
4.   sudden infant death syndrome
5.   dental health
6.   sun exposure and skin cancer.

A brief description of how each area impacts on child health is followed by issues and concerns about the influences on promoting health. The theoretical models are useful in encouraging exploration of the wide range of factors that must be considered when designing and evaluating health promotion interventions.

Immunization

Protecting children from disease by raising their immunity levels, through giving **vaccines** at key ages, has been one of the biggest health success stories of the last century. The body's natural immune system generates **antibodies** after fighting a particular disease. Vaccines stimulate the immune system to produce antibodies, which destroy or neutralize pathogens (organisms that are harmful), which means that children can gain protection without having the actual disease. Scientists around the world are researching to try to develop new vaccines against dangerous diseases; this is increasingly important as disease patterns change and new threats to health develop. Many countries, like the UK, already offer an impressive package of immunizations. Immunization begins at 2 months at present and the list below gives an indication of the diseases against which children are protected:

- diphtheria
- **tetanus**
- pertussis (whooping cough)
- polio
- Hib (*Haemophilus influenzae* type B – a bacterial meningitis infection)
- meningitis C
- pneumococcus (a bacterial infection that causes diseases including ear infections and, occasionally, meningitis).

Immunization against pneumococcus is a recent addition and illustrates the importance of checking the Department of Health website as immunization patterns are regularly changed and updated as new research becomes available.

Disease patterns are dynamic: a century ago many children died from an acute respiratory disease called diphtheria but fortunately in the twenty-first century this is largely controlled by immunization. Parents in the UK are much more likely to be concerned about dangers from the various viral and bacterial strains of meningitis (see the glossary for details). Over the past ten years immunization schedules have included vaccines to combat more strains of meningitis. Bacterial meningitis is a serious disease worldwide, and Molyneux *et al.* (2006) studied the outcomes of 197 UK and 175 Malawian children who had the disease before vaccinations were introduced. They found that mortality from bacterial meningitis in Malawian children was five times higher than in British children, even when infected with the same organisms. This might be owing to delay in presentation, malnutrition or prevailing HIV infections. This research is of value not only in showing how crucial it is to offer the appropriate vaccines to all children but also as a reminder of all the different factors that contribute to health and the ability to fight disease.

Immunization issues and concerns: the case of measles

Measles is one of the most contagious diseases and can have devastating complications for some children, causing inflammation of the brain, blindness or even death. Although an effective and cheap vaccine has been available for over 40 years, many children in the newly industrializing countries in the south, who are less well nourished, still die from measles every year. Figures from the WHO (2006) show that, worldwide, annual deaths from measles have been reduced by 48 per cent, from 871,000 in 1999 to 454,000 in 2004, due to immunization programmes. Children in the UK are offered the MMR (measles, mumps and rubella) immunization at 13 months and, by receiving a small dose of live measles vaccine, positive protection against the disease is conferred. However, although this programme has been in place for many years there are still constant needs to ensure the safety of vaccines so that families are confident to take up the offer of immunization. The need for research evidence of what works safely to raise children's immunity is clear, and threats to children's protection can be caused by acceptance of poor research or sensationalized media reporting. In 1998 Dr Andrew Wakefield (Wakefield *et al.* 1998) published an article in prestigious medical journal the *Lancet*, suggesting a link between MMR, autism and bowel disease. The popular press reported the story widely, often using very emotive headlines and, although Wakefield's original sample included only 12 children, the media gave it equal weighting to other studies (Peltola *et al.* 1998) with very large samples that showed no connection between MMR immunization and autism. Parents responded with confusion and fear, not knowing whether to have their infants immunized, and some health professionals' responses to parents were unclear, as they too were affected by the media outcry. Some parents felt unable to trust the information they were receiving and, bizarrely, whether or not the prime minister's infant son had been immunized became of deep national interest.

If immunization rates fall below the level needed for population protection, epidemics of that disease may occur. Therefore, it was important for the Department of Health to undertake a huge information campaign to inform health professionals of the relevant research showing that there was no link between MMR vaccine and autism or bowel disease. There are many lessons to be learnt from this event; the need for a rigorous research evidence base is clear, and although the media did not start this panic they certainly reported in a way that maintained high levels of fear. The role of the media has been examined in two separate articles in the *British Medical Journal* (Jackson 2002; Fitzpatrick 2005) and these serve to highlight the sensitivity of public health information dissemination.

Child safety

Injury is the leading cause of death and disability in childhood in the UK (UNICEF 2001a) and is second only to infectious diseases in the developing world (Murray and Lopez 1996). Road accidents, drowning, fires, falls and poisoning are the main causes of death (WHO 1997) in all countries of the European Union (EU). Although child injuries in developing countries are 5 times higher than in richer nations (Bartlett 2002) and affect millions of children, these issues tend to be given a lower priority than infectious diseases and malnutrition. Children living in poverty or relative poverty are more at risk from injury because of poor living conditions, lack of safe places to play and inadequate childcare (Bartlett 2002). Therefore, as with many other aspects of ill health, there is an unequal distribution of child accidents with a higher incidence in lower socio-economic groups (Hapgood *et al.* 2000; Roberts 2000) with house fires demonstrating the greatest social gradient. In the UK, child death from a house fire is 15 times more frequent in lower socio-economic groups (Towner, cited in Horton 2005), and with the highest risk in multiple occupancy or temporary housing or accommodation that is in a poor state of repair (Bradshaw 2002). The number of children killed or injured in road traffic accidents accounts for 46 per cent of child deaths in children aged under 14 years in the UK (UNICEF 2001a). Most traffic accidents involving children occur on the way to and from school. Parents' attempts to protect children by driving them to school may create greater hazards. This 'unhealthy' practice increases the risk of accidents for pedestrians, lessens children's exercise rates and increases pollution from car emissions.

Child safety: issues and concerns

The UNCRC clearly outlines nations' social responsibilities to ensure that children have safe environments in which to live and play. Protecting children from injury should be a major concern but Vincenten and Michalsen (2002) argue that it has only relatively recently been acknowledged as a preventable public health problem. Some argue that the reason for this is that accidents are viewed by many as random events that embody the idea of unavoidable chance and inevitability (Bartlett 2002). Influencing individual health belief models is just one of many factors affecting the whole area of accident prevention. For example, Roberts (2000) warns against simply thinking that the answer to reducing house fires lies in providing smoke alarms, and urges more in-depth analysis of which alarms will work and why people fail to use them. The way in which children and caregivers view risk is important in discovering which preventive strategies are most effective. Munro *et al.* (2006) investigated caregiver perceptions of childhood injury risks in disadvantaged South African communities. This study indicated that parents living in low-income communities attribute most risk to the environment rather than to individual action. The author found that, until the environment was changed to reduce risk factors, parents viewed individual action to reduce injury as 'futile'. Researching parents' views in this way is crucial to understanding and perhaps gives an indication of why some common interventions in the prevention of child injury, such as leaflets, posters and health education campaigns, are not effective. Roberts *et al.* (1993) claim that there is little research to prove the effectiveness of this type of campaign and some to suggest that such approaches merely raise parental anxiety without reducing risks. Understanding how to reduce childhood injury requires strategies at every level of the ecological model, including government policies and practice, and influencing and promoting individual and community action. Vincenten and Michalson highlight the factors involved in child injury reduction:

> Reducing child injuries efficiently usually requires a combined approach of healthy public policies, supported by well-designed products and environments, a variety of educational methods, engineering improvements and well enforced regulations and guidelines. (Vincenten and Michalsen 2002: 2)

Mullen and Smithson (2000) suggest that the whole area of injury prevention in deprived areas is still in its infancy and although UK (DfES 2004) policy and European policy (Vincenten and Michalson 2002) is placing a high priority on preventing morbidity and mortality, there is much scope for high-quality research into effective accident prevention. That said, there are many emerging success stories. Here are some examples.

- Reducing speed limits in some zones to 20 miles per hour in the UK has decreased child road accidents by 70 per cent (BMA 2001).
- Smoke detectors are an effective and an inexpensive method of reducing fires in the home (Harbourview Injury and Prevention Research Center 2001).
- Child-resistant packaging has led to a marked reduction in hospital admissions for poisoning (Towner *et al.* 2001).
- Stair gates have been shown to reduce the number of serious falls by young children (Towner *et al.* 2001).

- Flame-retardant fabrics have reduced hospital admissions for burns by 75 per cent in the USA (Harbourview Injury and Prevention Research Center 2001).

The diversity of these effective strategies is an indication of the breadth of knowledge needed to reduce child injury in any specific area. Other research has explored how safety benefits can be conveyed to individual families. An innovative family safety scheme is described by Carr (2005), who looked at the case of three local mothers employed in an inner-city, multi-ethnic community in the north of England as peer educators. Using peer educators appeared more acceptable to local families and seemed, in part, to address the problem of how to develop trust between a service provider and disadvantaged groups. While the study does not make any claims of injury reduction it does report increased parental knowledge about accident prevention and is, perhaps, a good example of how services must become creative in order to tackle the diversity of issues that result in child injury. Families living in hazardous communities have often developed a wealth of knowledge about balancing risks, and effective prevention policies need to take this into account.

Young children can be encouraged to identify hazards and to suggest practical solutions. In one project young children monitored traffic at a school crossing for an hour and noted that 31 drivers went through on a red light and 73 at amber (McNeish 1995). Individual community knowledge combined with locally appropriate environmental change, such as developing 'home zones' where pedestrians have precedence over cars and putting traffic calming measures in place, may be the most effective way to tackle injury rates. Clearly there is a need for more research into families' perceptions of risk and safety and into what preventive measures would be effective and acceptable.

Passive smoking

Inhaling other people's smoke is called passive, involuntary or secondhand smoking. Cigarette smoke contains literally thousands of different chemicals and some 60 are either known or suspected carcinogens (cancer-causing substances) (ASH 2005). While adults are banned from smoking in most workplaces to protect colleagues, children are not offered the same consideration. Article 24 of the UNCRC states that all children are entitled to a clean environment, so this should include protection from the harmful effects of smoke, a study of 250 primary school children (Woods et al. 2005) revealed that children as young as 4 were very articulate about passive smoking. Their views ranged from negative feelings about the smell, feeling sick, coughing and smoke acting as an **allergen** triggering asthma, to real concerns that a parent might die from smoking. Children have a right to protection from tobacco smoke, yet despite awareness-raising campaigns, 70 per cent of UK parents who smoke do not acknowledge the harmful effect passive smoking has on their child (ASH 2001). Passive smoking is associated with a number of adverse health outcomes for children, although Hall and Elliman (2003) argue that it is difficult to estimate whether the impact is greater before or after birth. Pregnant women who smoke have a higher incidence of pre-term births and babies who are smaller, due to restricted nutrient and oxygen levels. Babies who inhale smoke passively after they are born have a much higher chance of sudden infant death syndrome and suffer more middle ear and respiratory tract infections. The Royal College of Physicians (2003) estimates that 17,000 pre-school children are admitted to hospital annually due to illnesses resulting from passive smoking, and risk possible long-term health implications. Forty-two per cent of UK children live in a household with at least one smoker. The high smoking prevalence among people facing social and economic deprivation suggests that smoking may be used as a stress coping mechanism (Jarvis and Wardle 1999).

Passive smoking: issues and concerns

Discovering the most effective ways of preventing ill health and premature death through smoking is a major issue globally. The World Health Organization (2006) has the commitment of more than 75 per cent of countries worldwide to implement effective measures to curb tobacco use, including strong legislation and graphic warning labels, supported by smoking cessation assistance and advertising bans. UK government policies have shown a demonstrable shift over the last decade. In 1999 the government produced standards for children's day care that permitted childminders to smoke when caring for children if parents gave consent. Fortunately, five years later, the rights of the child to health were upheld when this was revised to ban childminders from smoking in the workplace (Ofsted 2004). Much of this pressure for change came from childminders themselves, who felt that their professionalism was compromised by the original standards. Other macro level policies include Ireland being the first country in 2004 to ban smoking in all workplaces, and in 2006 the Scottish law banning smoking in enclosed public spaces like pubs and restaurants came into force. The government has funded smoking cessation programmes but there is also a need for research to discover more about what would motivate individuals to stop smoking. Health promotion strategists are reporting some success where initiatives accept the adult's decision to smoke and concentrate on the practical tasks of protecting children by asking questions such as 'What can you change about where you smoke to protect your baby?' (Percival 2002: 165). Recent campaigns have emotively targeted the parental conscience by featuring children grieving because a much loved parent has died prematurely through smoking-related diseases. An American **randomized control trial** (Eammons 2001) showed that motivational strategies often led parents to make changes for the benefit of their children and that parents may then go on to contemplate effects on their own health. Appropriate strategies need to be thoroughly researched to ensure that infants and children have a solid foundation for their own health and can be cared for by healthy parents.

Sudden infant death syndrome

Sudden infant death syndrome (SIDS), sometimes known as cot death, is the term used when a baby or young child dies unexpectedly and the post-mortem does not show any obvious cause. In 1989 the number of recorded sudden infant deaths in the UK was 1,545, but by 1999 this figure had dropped to 419 (HMSO 2001). The reduction was not gradual: there was more than a 50 per cent fall in the number of deaths between 1991 and 1992, which coincided with a public health campaign to 'reduce the risk' by sleeping babies in the supine position (on their backs). Previously, medical advice had advised sleeping infants in the prone position, but research from a number of countries showed that babies are safer in the supine position (Dwyer and Ponsonby 1996). Other health-related issues, such as ensuring that infants do not get too cold or overheated, putting babies' feet against the bottom of cots so that they can't wriggle down under covers, avoiding bed sharing, especially if the parents have been drinking alcohol, and seeking prompt medical advice if an infant is unwell, have all been the subject of health campaigns. These campaigns have been effective in reducing the numbers of SIDS, but although parental smoking is still a major risk factor in SIDS (Blair *et al.* 1996) smoking behaviour seems to have been less influenced.

SIDS: issues and concerns
An evaluation of the UK government's campaign to reduce SIDS found that there was very little effect on the prevalence of smoking by mothers or other household members, although more mothers claimed that no smoking was allowed close to the baby (Hiley and Morley 1994). Blackburn *et al.* (2005) found in a study of 314 smoking households with young infants that families were more likely to have a father who smoked than a mother, and tobacco use was higher for fathers if the mother also smoked. Although anti-smoking campaigns have often been directed at mothers, protecting infants from fathers' as well as mothers' smoking is key to reducing environmental tobacco exposure in early infancy, when the risk of SIDS is highest. Blackburn *et al.* (2005) suggest that attention needs to focus on the interactive smoking behaviour within the household rather than focusing on mothers and fathers in isolation. In addition this study found that a parent's smoking behaviour was influenced by their partner; for example, cigarettes were readily available and

part of social interaction where both partners smoked. Doherty and White-head (1986) argue that the social dynamics of smoking behaviour should be examined within the context of family systems. Other studies have shown more success with long-term smoking cessation when partners encouraged each other to give up smoking (Waterston *et al.* 1990).

Dental health

Fluoride (in toothpastes and some water supplies), regular tooth cleaning, avoidance of prolonged oral contact with sugar, and regular dental check-ups should mean that dental caries (decay) is largely preventable. Yet dental caries remains one of the most common chronic diseases of early childhood, causing pain and infection, and sometimes requiring the risk of anaesthetics for treatment (Gussy *et al.* 2006). There is a strong social gradient associated with dental caries, particularly with young children who may have had ad-ditional sweeteners added to bottles (Gussy *et al.* 2006). In Scotland, for ex-ample, levels of decay are strongly related to deprivation: the poorest 10 per cent of children have over 50 per cent of the decay (Scottish Office 1999). The Scottish Office is prioritizing dental health and aims to ensure that, by 2010, 60 per cent of 5-year-olds should have no experience of dental disease. In Scotland the government is to commission, and fund, the development of a prevention programme from birth, involving registration with a dentist, dental education for all new parents, tooth brushing with a fluoride tooth-paste for infants and advice on how to reduce sugar in the diet of infants.

Dental health: issues and concerns

Methods of reducing dental caries are clear, but what works in promoting dental health in disadvantaged communities is less so. Andrews (2004) re-ports an innovative public health campaign in which families and carers were invited to bring their infants' feeding bottles to the local health centre and exchange them for a new beaker, toothbrush and toothpaste. In addition, advice on tooth brushing, low-sugar drinks and information about local dental practices was available. This project started with profiling the local population so that specific health criteria were identified. In particular the staff ensured that posters and leaflets were available in English, Punjabi and Urdu, and that interpreters were available. Evaluation was positive, with mothers commenting 'This is a brilliant idea. Lots of Asian women don't brush their children's teeth, this is a great idea ... more people need to know' (Andrews 2004: 22). Comments like this give an important insight into pos-sible health belief models and indicate how further research may help target health promotion. More innovative interventions are needed that clearly involve the community in the identification and resolution of health inequalities such as dental caries.

Sun exposure

Young children are especially vulnerable to solar radiation, and repeated excessive exposure can lead to an increased risk of skin cancer in later life (Stinco *et al.* 2005). While skin cancer is the most common malignancy, it is also the most preventable (Weinstein *et al.* 2001). Despite increased public education on the importance of sun protection, national surveys of parents in the USA showed that almost half of all children under the age of 12 years had experienced sunburn within the previous year (Hall *et al.* 2001; O'Riordan *et al.* 2003). Pre-school children and their parents are an important target group for skin cancer prevention campaigns but Gritz *et al.* (2005) argue that further studies need to identify the most effective methods for disseminating sun protection interventions.

Sun exposure: issues and concerns

Australia has the highest incidence of skin cancer in the world (Stanton *et al.* 2004) and has campaigned to reduce the incidence of this disease by encouraging children to wear hats and long-sleeved swimming suits that cover most of the body. Preventive measures have also included behavioural modification by getting children to stay in the shade, rescheduling the times of sports activities, and environmental change such as planting trees and providing shade canopies (Stanton *et al.* 2004). These levels of change, aimed at all ecological systems levels, have been augmented by huge publicity campaigns to increase knowledge and change attitudes to sun exposure. However, a number of studies of parental health beliefs have shown that the use of sunscreen is more linked to concern about children burning than to prevention of skin cancer (Butler and Borland 1998; McLean and Gallagher 1998). Children usually play outside more in the sunshine: some studies show that they are likely to absorb three times more UVB rays than adults and are often outside in the peak sunshine hours (Stinco *et al.* 2005). Most of the studies referenced here have been conducted in Australia and the USA, although Stinco *et al.*'s (2005) research claims to be the first study of sun exposure in children in Italy. Some of the research appears to ignore the colour of the child's skin and perhaps parents vary their concern according to whether or not their child is very fair skinned. Although darker skinned children need protecting from sunburn the risk of skin cancer is less. Questions may also be asked about how research relates generally to cooler climates, such as the UK and Scandinavia. One difficulty in these countries is perhaps that parents feel that children should make the most of the sun while it is shining, and children can be overexposed very quickly. In addition, hot days on summer holidays can often mean that children have prolonged exposure. Schools in the UK are much more aware nowadays and practices of making children attend sports days without sunscreen, shade or water should no longer happen. It is important that young children and families living in cooler climates are fully aware of the risks of sun exposure and how to take adequate protective measures.

Public health practice involves influencing healthy behaviours and the understanding of health belief models, and considering these in the light of other influencing factors may be an effective way to approach this. The 'stages of change' model may also be useful when considering readiness to accept health advice.

The stages of change model

This model is based on the realization that every individual is at a different point of readiness to take action to change their behaviour. Health promotion interventions should be targeted at the appropriate stage of the change model. Prochaska and DiClements (1983) define five stages where differing approaches of health promotion can focus:

1. precontemplation – unaware, no intention to change
2. contemplation – intention to act, open to information
3. preparation – beginning to act and setting goals
4. action – making change and using will power
5. maintenance – resisting cues to relapse.

This model proposes that change progresses through each stage and that health promotion is most effective if it matches the stage appropriately. For example, in the early stages awareness raising is required, whereas in the later stages social support and rewards for goals achieved may be more effective. For young children, awareness raising by participation can be especially useful. As discussed earlier, children involved in counting the number of cars jumping red lights on crossings were likely to be more conscious of this in the future. Active participation is an excellent way to increase awareness and informed action.

Conclusion

> Child public health is potentially the most important and the most effective activity in improving outcomes for children, encompassing as it does work in health, welfare, education, housing and public policy. In terms of the public policy agenda in the UK and internationally, child health is a key part of public investment in improving current well-being and later outcomes. (Petticrew and Roberts 2004: 667)

Child public health encompasses a wide range of factors and only a few have been selected for discussion in this chapter. Health screening and immunization have had huge impacts on reducing child mortality and morbidity and social justice dictates that every child, wherever they live in the world, should benefit from the best practice available. The Wanless Report (2002) into securing future health in the UK recommends that investment should be made in public health information accessed through the media, such as the internet and digital television. The increasing use of technology highlights the global nature of public health, and information, combined with resources, is part of the UNCRC commitment that richer countries should help poorer countries to achieve improved health.

Wanless (2002) recommends that people should be 'fully engaged' in public health, and the issues raised in this chapter indicate the complexity of achieving healthy behaviour changes, involving so much more than simply giving information about healthy practices. Health promotion programmes can be targeted at the individual level, the social or community level, or the policy level (Blair *et al.* 2003). At any level, programmes are more effective if they are underpinned by research evidence of health beliefs and behaviours. Application of theoretical models can offer a scientific approach to analysing which interventions are more likely to promote healthy behaviours. Interventions must be thoroughly evaluated using rigorous methodologies so that knowledge about what works in particular situations can be shared. Finally, there is much scope for encouraging more participation of young children in discovering healthy behaviours for themselves and their families.

8 Children under stress

Children experiencing positive mental health have a foundation for emotional, social, intellectual and spiritual development. This 'resource of mental health' acts as a foundation for children to be able to initiate and sustain satisfying friendships and, as young adults, to develop respectful intimate relationships with future partners. Children who are experiencing positive mental health are aware of other people and are more able to develop empathy so that joy and fun can be shared and feelings of distress processed. The concept of mental health was reviewed in the first chapter, and how caregivers support and protect early infant mental health was discussed in Chapter 3. These themes are further explored in this chapter, which considers why many young children are experiencing high levels of distress, sometimes leading to mental ill health.

Young children's distress is usually communicated through particular behaviours, and questions are raised about how adults listen and interpret. Traditionally young children's behaviour has often been dismissed by comments such 'they all have tantrums at this age; it's just the terrible two's'. While it is true that many children of this age experience frustration as they become more independent, to dismiss this may deny the intensity of feelings and does not help the child to regulate his or her emotional well-being.

In this chapter children's behaviour is considered in the broadest context of the child's genetically determined characteristics, families' competencies and challenges, the physical environment in which children are raised, networks of support and the services that are available, and the extent to which government policies are family friendly. Considering children's distress in an ecological systems context explicitly acknowledges the interaction of multiple factors that influence children's behaviour. This chapter starts by exploring the ways in which young children may communicate that they are experiencing distress. It is suggested that how children are perceived and parents are socialized to act within their own cultures shapes the way that behaviour is considered. In the UK and the USA, for example, there are rising numbers of children being diagnosed with attention deficit hyperactivity disorder (ADHD), and questions are raised about the qualities that these societies expect and value in young children. Setting boundaries for children's behaviour also varies, and parenting styles and corporal punishment are explored in their cultural contexts.

Families are the greatest protective factor for children experiencing distress but, for some children, the roots of distress originate in family circumstances or functioning. Child abuse, early prevention, identification and intervention are discussed. Universal support services were described in Chapter 3, and targeted parenting support and specialist services are discussed in this chapter. It is argued that developing a culture of listening to young children may lessen difficulties and lead to earlier appropriate support.

What are emotional and behavioural difficulties?

Most young children, at some point in their development, experience some behaviour 'problems' such as tantrums, sleeping or feeding disorders. For many children these difficulties are fairly transient as parents 'tune in' to their child's communications and find effective ways to support him or her. However, there is increasing concern about children in the UK who are experiencing established emotional and behavioural problems that interfere with daily living and are more extreme in comparison with their peer group (BMA 2006). Children with emotional and behavioural problems are troubled; their behaviour is often unpredictable and outside of their own control. Children experiencing emotional difficulties may appear quiet, preoccupied, tearful and anxious, and they may withdraw from the everyday activities enjoyed by others. Emotional difficulties include phobias, anxiety states and deep sadness, and some children may express these with related physical symptoms such as chronic aches and pains. Carers of children with behavioural difficulties may not be able to manage the externalizing behaviour (which may, for example, include tantrums, defiance and aggression) and the resulting negative atmosphere may impact further on the child's self-esteem and feelings of failure. The term 'behaviour problem' may also include frequent sleep disturbance, soiling, excessive fears or worries, impulsivity and overactivity (Campbell 1995). Rising numbers of children are also being diagnosed with hyperkinetic disorders; these include ADHD, which affects activity and attention.

How many children have emotional and behavioural difficulties?

Meltzer et al. (2000) state in a government report that emotional and behavioural difficulties are the most important cause of functional disability, and studies (Stallard 1993; Charlton et al. 1995) indicate that the extent of the problem is high with between 7 and 10 per cent of children aged under 3 years experiencing emotional and behavioural problems. Campbell's (1995) study found that 7 per cent of 3-year-olds had moderate to severe behaviour difficulties and a further 15 per cent had mild problems. Many studies link early emotional and behavioural disorders with later mental health problems and the number of young people experiencing difficulties in the UK is generally accepted as approximately 20 per cent 'there are approximately 14.9 million children and young people under twenty living in the UK, representing 25 per cent of the population. It is calculated that at any one time, 20 per cent of children and adolescents experience psychological problems' (MHF 1999: 6).

Certain groups of children and young people face an increased risk of experiencing mental health problems. Children whose families live in deprived circumstances or face homelessness or live in temporary accommodation, for example, have a much higher incidence of mental health problems (BMA 2006). Children in minority ethnic groups, and particularly refugees and asylum seekers, are also at greater risk as they have:

> often suffered traumatic experiences prior to reaching the UK, and can face discrimination once here. They are likely to have come from countries with poor human rights records, may have witnessed acts of violence, and will need to cope with new social and cultural experiences of living in the UK. (BMA 2006: 13)

In addition, refugee and asylum-seeker children are more likely to be living in deprived circumstances, further increasing the risk of mental and physical ill health.

Whether the incidence of young children experiencing emotional and behavioural problems is increasing is difficult to assess accurately. Blair *et al.* (2003) argue that most professionals working with young children feel that the difficulties are becoming more common, but this may need to be balanced with raised awareness and possibly earlier recognition within changing cultural expectations. Earlier recognition and support may in some cases prevent mental health problems developing.

What are the long-term outcomes for children with emotional and behavioural difficulties?

A number of longitudinal research studies have demonstrated that there are strong links between emotional and behavioural problems in young children and later mental health difficulties. There is evidence from a New Zealand study that very withdrawn, inhibited young children have a much higher rate of depression as young adults (Caspi *et al.* 1996) and other studies have linked early behavioural problems with an increased likelihood of later mental health difficulties (Robins 1991; Caspi *et al.* 1996). For some children, behavioural difficulties may develop into a continuous pattern of antisocial behaviour from middle childhood through to young adulthood (Patterson *et al.* 1992; Moffitt 1993). Children who are psychologically distressed are more likely to be bullied or become bullies themselves. Glew (2005: 1026) defines bullying as: 'any repeated negative activity or aggression intended to harm or bother someone who is perceived by peers as being less physically or psychologically powerful than the aggressor'.

Glew's (2005) study of elementary school children found that both bullies and their victims were more likely than others to feel sad most days and to have lower school achievement. Children with behavioural problems are less able to recognize what they or others are feeling, and less able to use social cues to guide their behaviour in relation to others. Children whose emotional and social development is compromised are often unable to manage conflict effectively and are more likely to use aggression to express distress. Those with emotional and behavioural difficulties are less able to concentrate, and therefore cannot take advantage of the learning opportunities available to them (Audit Commission 1999). Many will go on to underachieve at school and have difficulties making friends, or may later develop relationships with other disaffected children who form antisocial peer groups. There is an increased likelihood of poor later relationships, poor employment prospects and poor health (Audit Commission 1999).

Why do children develop emotional and behavioural disorders?

A traditional 'medical model' approach might have tried to find a single cause to remedy; this is sometimes called a deficit model because it assumes that there is a problem within the child. This is not a useful approach as there are no simple lines of causality. Emotional and behavioural problems in children can be influenced by interrelationships between factors in all systems. For example: the child's inherited characteristics, disability, brain irritation from birth trauma, the parenting style, the type of day care or education establishment, the economic situation of the family, challenges facing the family, kinship and neighbourhood networks, the government's family policies, and so on. All these factors are situated within a culture that has developed expectations about the way children behave. The reasons, therefore, why children experience emotional disequilibrium are very individual and affected by the interaction of many dynamic factors. There is no doubt that inherited conditions such as autism or other disabilities, environmental adversities, such as brain trauma during the birth process, allergies to food additives, or the frustration of a speech and language disorder may predispose some children to have externalizing behavioural difficulties, but even these are heavily influenced by other factors. Most importantly, seeking a simple cause and effect model without considering all the contextual factors may lead to problematizing the child and possibly the parents, and offering medical treatment without consideration of the social and cultural factors. Examining the case of ADHD is useful in illustrating this argument as there is much debate about the possible causes and, although diagnosis rates are soaring in some cultures, it is rarely identified in others.

Attention deficit hyperactivity disorder

Many young children have periods when their behaviour is characterized by restlessness, inattention and impulsiveness. While for many children this behaviour would be thought to be within the norms of development, for some, particularly boys, the level and extent of hyperactivity is considered so extreme that it is thought to be a disorder. Efron (2005), a paediatrician, states that ADHD is now a mainstream paediatric condition and the primary diagnosis in a quarter of paediatric consultations in Australia. In the USA the rate of diagnosed ADHD is around 7.5 per cent, with 6 per cent of school-age boys taking medication to control their behaviour (Olfson *et al.* 2002), and is reported as being five to ten times higher than in other countries. The rate of ADHD diagnosis in the UK, still quite high at approximately 1 per cent (Meltzer *et al.* 2000), is said to be rising and is markedly higher than in other European countries, with Norway and Sweden rarely diagnosing the condition (Breggin and Breggin 1995). There has been much research into why children exhibit behaviour that is considered outside the mainstream. On the one hand there is a biological interpretation in which it is suggested that ADHD is an inherited genetic trait, classified as a mental health disorder, requiring psychiatric, psychological and educational assessment and possibly pharmacological treatment. Biological explanations consider that there may be a chemical imbalance that affects the functioning of the frontal lobe of the brain, preventing the child from concentrating and sitting still. Neurodevelopmental impairment in brain maturation caused by pre-term birth has been cited as increasing the incidence of behaviour that is restless, solitary and inattentive, with poor concentration (Minde and Minde 1977). Babies seek active communication right from the start, but fragile infants, such as those who are born very pre-term, may struggle more to build early social relationships (Wocadlo and Rieger 2006). The possible causes of ADHD that have been researched are diverse and include reactions to food additives, dietary deficits, pre-natal exposure to nicotine (Linnet *et al.* 2003) and alcohol, excessive television watching in the early years (Christakis *et al.* 2004), iron-deficiency anaemia (Konofal *et al.* 2004) and early deprivation (Kreppner *et al.* 2001).

The UK starts formal education early and children who fidget, are easily distracted, talk excessively and interrupt do not fit into the social and cultural expectations of highly self-regulated behaviour at a relatively early age. Perhaps it is unsurprising that there are few children being diagnosed with ADHD in Norway and Sweden, where young children experience an increased emphasis on outdoor play and less on formal learning. What is interesting is that ADHD is almost certainly the result of the interplay of a multiplicity of factors consisting of individual predispositions, environmental factors and cultural influences. What is concerning is that the rapid increase in the number of children diagnosed with ADHD in some countries means that many more are being prescribed drug treatments to heighten alertness and subdue behaviour. Those in favour of drug treatment for ADHD would argue that it is the child's right to have stimulants like Ritalin (one of the most common treatment drugs) so that he or she can be calmer and concentrate on learning. Others would argue that Ritalin is little more than a 'chemical cosh' aimed at making children conform to an adult-centred society.

What is clearly missing from the debate about ADHD is how children feel about the condition and their perspectives about the use of drugs to control their behaviour. Breggin (1998) argues that the drugging of children should raise profound ethical questions about how the adult world views children and often fails to elicit their views: 'The feelings and attitudes of children themselves have been systematically excluded from all studies ... with a few exceptions, the literature doesn't even comment on what children themselves feel about any aspect of being diagnosed and drugged' (Breggin 1998: 82).

As more and more children are diagnosed with ADHD there is a need to learn from their personal experiences so that parents and society can help the child to manage difficult feelings. Timimi (2005) argues that children should be understood within the context of what is happening in their lives and alongside an examination of the prevailing cultural expectations of children's behaviour. In the UK the emphasis on school achievement has led to tests and targets even for the youngest children, who may leave nursery to enter a more formal learning situation even before their fifth birthday. Given the lower rates of ADHD diagnosis in countries starting education later, it would appear that there is a clear reason for examining the appropriateness of the prevailing cultural expectations of children. Prout (2005) argues that children are 'systematically ranked' according to the cultural expectations of the education system and that, when a child is 'failing' or problematic, parents may seek many solutions before accepting a diagnosis of ADHD. Cultural expectations exert a powerful influence on how a child's behaviour is considered and whether the approach follows a medical or social model.

The next section considers some of the social and cultural factors that may either increase or decrease the incidence of children developing emotional and behaviour difficulties.

Family functioning

Research from industrialized countries such as the USA and the UK has highlighted the crucial impact of parenting on children's well-being and mental health. Sensitivity, warmth, setting consistent boundaries for behaviour and being responsive to the child's needs are characteristics of authoritative parenting and associated with children who are higher in self-esteem, more independent and cooperative, and more likely to show altruistic behaviour (Lamborn *et al.* 1991). When children face challenges, such as parental separation (Chapter 5) or bereavement (Chapter 9), a parenting style that encourages discussion and explanation has been shown to be linked to the best outcomes for children's emotional health. This style of parenting may be difficult to achieve. For example, when parents themselves have only experienced negative, indifferent or hostile styles, it may be more difficult for them to discover a new approach. Also young children play an active part in constructing the styles of parenting adopted. For example, a study by Woolfson and Grant (2006) indicated that some parents of children with disabilities found that the amount of repetition required, the limited success and the constant demands on parenting time and energy made authoritative parenting more difficult and stressful. In addition, Woolfson (2004) argues that some cultures have more negative views of children with disabilities when they exhibit behaviour difficulties, and this may influence how some parents view their role. It should also be added that many parents whose children have very challenging behaviour minimize this by patient, consistent, warm and sensitive parenting.

It is not the structure of the family that plays a part in determining children's mental health but the way in which it functions. There may be associated risk factors that impact upon family functioning, such as alcohol or drug abuse, mental health problems or poverty, and there is a very strong association between domestic violence and children's emotional and behavioural difficulties (see Chapter 5). It is devastating for young children to see or hear violence towards a loved parent or sibling, and researchers (Hughes 1988; Stagg *et al.* 1989; Fantuzzo *et al.* 1997) have found that exposure to family violence during early childhood, when the capacity for emotional regulation is emerging, has a particularly negative effect on infants and pre-schoolers. (Domestic violence is often linked with child abuse, and being witness to this is in itself emotional abuse, which is discussed later in this chapter.) Jaffe *et al.* (1990) note that domestic violence may be in the backgrounds of many children who attend mental health services for treatment and yet, in some cases, this may not be discussed at all: 'the presence of violence in the family is often overlooked. At times, "the family secret" is kept from mental health professionals or more commonly, the issue is never raised or actively pursued' (Jaffe *et al.* 1990: 468).

Hester *et al.* (2000) point out that concentrating on strategies for changing children's externalizing behaviour not only fails to meet children's needs but also serves to 'condone' the violence. Traditionally, concentration on the 'patient's' individual signs or symptoms of ill health has been encouraged in the UK by the narrow focus of specialist training. In the past this has led paediatric workers to focus on the child's externalizing behaviour in isolation, rather than the context in which it occurs. Similarly, a mental health worker treating an adult family member might give little consideration to the effects on the child unless he or she begins to present with some signs of ill health. This narrow specialist focus not only causes much psychological distress but also impedes effective preventive services. For example, the unpredictability of living with a parent with a mental health problem may also impact on children's emotional well-being, as one mother describes in her own behaviour:

> even the expression in my voice, he'll look and he doesn't know how to take me because one minute I can be stressed, not actually at him or any of the children, but at myself and then the next I'll pick him up and swing him round. It must be so confusing for him, mustn't it? (Gopfert *et al.* 1999: 12)

These subtle changes in demeanour that the mother describes could affect a child's developing security and she indicates an awareness of the health implications for her son. Secure attachments (see Chapter 3) are an important part of the stability that children need for their emotional well-being and mental health, and are less easy to build if a child receives inconsistent or hostile parenting.

Setting boundaries for behaviour

When parents are experiencing problems such as mental ill health, drug addiction or alcohol abuse this is likely to impact on the consistency of their parenting, making the setting of safe boundaries problematic.

The *authoritative* parent (Lamborn *et al.* 1991) is typified as demonstrating high levels of both control and warmth, which results in children feeling valued but also knowing what the limits are for their behaviour; whereas *authoritarian* parenting (Patterson *et al.* 1992) is characterized as being very low in warmth and high on control, resulting in children feeling more anxious and less confident. Forty-two parent–child dyads from Dunedin, New Zealand (Rodriguez 2003), with no known history of child abuse were studied to examine whether there were any links between children's emotional functioning and parental discipline procedures. The research provided evidence that children growing up in families with severe discipline practices experienced more anxiety symptoms. In addition, the study reported that parents who had physically abusive attitudes were more likely to have children who reported signs of depression.

Physical punishment is the most questionable technique for reducing undesirable behaviour. In both the UK (Nobes and Smith 1997) and the USA

(Gallup Organization 1995) most parents use it, yet it has significant adverse effects. Although a child might be likely to comply with parental demands immediately after being hit, he or she will not learn the desired behaviour (Gershoff 1997); its use also teaches that violence is a solution to inter-personal conflict and can therefore increase aggression (Strassberg *et al.* 1994). Article 19 of the UNCRC states that children have the right to be protected from violence and although the UK ratified the UNCRC in 1991, it has fallen short of meeting its responsibilities in some areas (Payne 2003). In 1999 the UK became the last country in western Europe to ban corporal punishment in schools and, until 2004, parents were able to claim a defence of 'reasonable chastisement' if they smacked or assaulted their child. The law did not define 'reasonable chastisement', thus leaving it open to interpretation, while giving the message that it was acceptable to hit children.

Proverbs such as 'spare the rod and spoil the child' are deeply embedded in UK culture and this has led to many people having an unquestioning approach to child discipline. Indeed, to raise the debate about smacking children was tantamount to criticizing the deeply held values and customs of one's own parents.

Europe and the physical discipline of children

In the following countries, children are protected by law from being hit: Germany, Finland, Sweden, Denmark, Austria, Norway, Croatia, Cyprus, Latvia, Hungary, Bulgaria, Romania, Iceland, Ukraine and Israel. Italy, Belgium and Portugal have also taken steps towards complete prohibition. It is worth noting that in every country that has changed the law, except Finland, the government has led, not followed, public opinion on, and cultural attitudes to, the issue. The first country to legislate against the physical punishment of children was Sweden in 1979, and it was recognized that a cultural shift in attitudes would be needed. The Swedish government organized a campaign to inform parents about child development and how appropriate boundaries for behaviour could be implemented without resorting to physical punishment. This was highly successful, and parents found information on child development and behaviour management in leaflets and even on the side of milk cartons. Children's views about corporal punishment have been absent from this debate until recently and their perspective adds a powerful dimension to the effects of discipline.

Children's views on corporal punishment

The UK government funded research to explore the views of 250 children aged 5 to 11 (Willow and Hyder 1998, cited in Lyons 2000). The results showed that children had strong views about smacking; one 5-year-old stated: 'A smack is when people hit you and it stings and I cry' (Willow and Dugdale 1998: 26). Children did not consider physical punishment to be light or gentle, and described smacking as a 'hard hit'. One child explained that a smack is parents hitting you, but 'instead of calling it a hit they call it a smack' (Willow and Dugdale 1998: 27). Children also described the psychological impact of physical punishment and one 5-year-old told how it made him feel 'sick inside and it breaks your heart'. Willow and Hyder (1998, cited in Lyons 2000: 24) also importantly highlight research which suggests that young children's attitudes towards physical punishment are affected by their own experiences of being hit: the more children are hit, the more they expect that others are hit. A study of 403 families (Nobes and Smith 1997) found that children who were frequently aggressive with siblings were more likely to have been severely punished at some time. These studies raise important lessons for working towards a non-violent society – clearly, the more children experience violence, the more legitimate violence becomes. The use of physical punishment has led to many controversial phrases such as 'a loving smack' – the ultimate contradiction in terms – and definitions of 'reasonable chastisement' were very subjective and open to individual interpretation, as can be seen in the following case.

Case study

In 1994 a child who had been beaten with a garden cane by his step-father had the case reported to the police by his natural father. The step-father was charged with causing actual bodily harm, but the case was dismissed by a jury who judged the beating to be 'reasonable chastisement'. Following this, in 1998 the European Court presented a direct challenge to the UK government, which it claimed had failed to protect a boy from severe beatings with a cane by his step-father. In the case, A vs UK (cited in Lyons 2000), the European Court said that the UK had failed to give adequate protection to the boy and it deemed that the beatings constituted 'inhuman and degrading treatment'.

This is a highly significant case because it clearly demonstrates that the definition of 'reasonable chastisement' was open to debate and what may be deemed reasonable discipline to one person may be deemed child abuse by another. The judgement also required the UK government to change its legislation, which led to a government consultation on the use of physical punishment (DoH 2000) but, significantly, the consultation paper did not include complete prohibition of parental use of physical punishment as an option.

After sustained campaigning by organizations and individuals, the law has now been modified and Section 58 of the Children Act 2004 states that parents may use 'reasonable punishment', although this defence may not be used in cases of serious assault. It remains to be seen how this will affect the response to reports of parental use of physical punishment, as the new law came into effect in England and Wales in 2005. It is due to come into effect in Northern Ireland during 2006 (see http://www.opsi.gov.uk/si/si2006/draft/20060039.htm). In Scotland, however, the law is different. Section 51 of the Criminal Justice (Scotland) Act 2003 (see http://www.opsi.gov.uk/legislation/scotland/acts2003/30007–h.htm#51) introduces the concept of 'justifiable assault', and defines shaking, blows to the head and use of an implement as unjustifiable. So far, no UK country has taken the lead and prohibited all physical punishment of children. UK law therefore still fails to give children equal protection with adults under the law on assault, and children remain the one group in our society who can legally be hit. Section 58 is as open to subjective interpretation as its predecessor. These discussions are important. While the majority of UK parents have used an occasional 'smack' as part of setting secure boundaries for behaviour, this arguably contributes to the way that society perceives children and childhood. The fact that it has been culturally acceptable to 'smack' children may mean that a minority interpret this much more severely. Gibbons *et al.* (1995: 12) argue that child maltreatment 'is a socially constructed phenomenon which reflects [the] values and opinions of a particular culture at a particular time'. It has long been accepted that the concept of childhood is socially constructed and therefore culturally specific. Ariès (1962), in his historical study of children and childhood, first noted that although children are present in all cultures, they are very differently regarded. Childhood is, in effect, a temporary state or a transition between being born and adulthood, often perceived as a prelude to adulthood rather than a worthwhile time in its own right (Alderson 1993). Gittens (1998) differentiates between the 'child' and 'childhood'. She defines the child as being a non-adult, conveying dependency and lack of power, or other attributes given by a specific culture, whereas childhood is not only a category but is a social and cultural concept.

It is important to consider how the dependency of children is linked with powerlessness and a sense of ownership. Lansdown and Lancaster (2001: 40) argue that there is a need to re-examine the welfare model of the child, which assumes that:

- adults can be relied upon to act in the child's best interests
- children lack the competence to act in their own lives
- adults have the monopoly in determining outcomes in children's lives.

This welfare model, therefore, assumes that children's well-being will always be promoted by adults and that children are too inexperienced to participate or affect their own well-being. Respecting children's human rights places a value on their individual feelings and experiences, and encourages adults to acknowledge children's individual characteristics right from start. Sadly many children in the world do need safeguarding from abuse, both from adults and from bullying peers. In the next section there is a definition of child abuse and a brief synopsis of how services in England are changing.

Child abuse

Young children who have been abused are much more likely to experience a range of emotional and behavioural difficulties, such as depression, lack of interest in learning, disturbed relationships or aggressive behaviour. Article 19 of the UNCRC defines abuse as 'All forms of physical or mental violence, injury or abuse, neglect or negligent treatment, maltreatment or exploitation, including sexual abuse.' In the UK child abuse has been defined within 'four categories of abuse', described simply by the charity 'Kidscape' (in Elliot 1988) as:

1. emotional abuse – making a child feel unwanted, ugly, guilty, unloved
2. physical abuse – being physically violent to a child
3. sexual abuse – exploiting a child sexually
4. neglect – failing to provide the things needed for a child to grow.

Inevitably there is a cross-over between all forms of abuse and, sadly, it is often the case that children experience more than one form of harm. Young children who have been physically, sexually or emotionally abused may appear extra vigilant but also unresponsive; this is sometimes known as 'frozen watchfulness', as if they are waiting for further assaults. Sexually abused young children may engage in sexually explicit play, become withdrawn or anxious, or present physical symptoms such as headaches, stomach aches or regression with toilet training (Trickett and Putnam 1998). Children who are neglected will not have had their physical or emotional care needs met and may exhibit a range of signs and behaviours, such as appearing constantly hungry, being generally unkempt and inappropriately dressed, and being prone to accidents, due to lack of supervision.

Although some abused children may not appear to show any behavioural signs, all forms of child abuse impair emotional health, and sustained abuse is likely to have a deep impact on the child's self-image and self-esteem. Emotional abuse, therefore, is present in all the other categories of abuse and is recognized as being experienced by children who witness domestic violence:

Difficulties may extend into adulthood: the experiences of long-term abuse may lead to difficulties in forming or sustaining close relationships, establishing oneself in the workforce, and to extra difficulties in developing the attitudes and skills needed to be an effective parent. (DoH/HO/DfEE 1999: 6)

Intervening in family life

Child protection social workers have a sensitive and difficult role to weigh up when deciding whether and when to intervene in family life. The Children Act 1989 introduced the concept of **significant harm** as the threshold that justifies compulsory intervention in family life in the best interests of the child, and the Children Act 2004 places a duty on all agencies involved with children to safeguard and promote their welfare. The term safeguarding is wider than child protection and aims 'not to just minimise the danger to children but to maximise their welfare' (Munro 2002: 2). The government (DfES 2003) has introduced a common assessment framework (CAF) to aid understanding of the range of needs of individual children. Parents are asked to help with the assessment as soon as there are any concerns about a child so, where appropriate, early supportive interventions can be offered to the family to protect the child from harm. With one lead professional worker co-ordinating assessment and support, multi-agency working should be enhanced and the amount of bureaucracy faced by families reduced. The CAF assesses three key areas in a child's life:

1. child's developmental needs
2. parenting capacity
3. family and environmental factors.

This assessment aims to give a comprehensive view of the child's needs; the intention is to build on a family's strengths and offer support to maximize the child's care and development (HM Government 2006). Children were once perceived as passive and powerless within this process but the UNCRC has underlined the importance of ensuring that children's views are taken into account and this is reflected in policy. The UNCRC divides children's rights into three areas, sometimes known as the 'three Ps':

1. protection
2. provisions
3. participation.

The UNCRC is clear that children must be protected from any form of abuse or discrimination, and if it should occur that they have an entitlement to treatment to aid recovery. The CAF discussed above is part of the attempt to reorganize services to ensure that children are better protected. The safety of the child is paramount and services aim to ensure this while respecting the inherent worth and dignity of the family unit. This is no easy task as it challenges traditional hierarchies where 'expert professionals' have more power than parents. Adults who abuse children exert power and control inappropriately; Smith *et al.* (1995) found links with poor couple relationships, domestic violence and sibling aggression. Power in society is weighted against children, especially if they are very young, disabled, from an immigrant black minority group, from a traveller family or if children are taking caring responsibilities. The third 'P', participation, challenges states to find respectful ways of enabling children to participate, to be more visible, and to ensure their voices are heard (Laming 2003). Very young children, those with intellectual disabilities, speech and language difficulties or those who have a different first language, will need skilled support to ensure that they are able to express themselves.

Support services

The traditional ways of perceiving children, combined with the challenges of power differentials and the sensitivity of family life make ensuring children's protection and participation a complex business. Clearly some families need extra help; Howe (2005) argues that the earlier support is given the greater the likelihood of children experiencing healthy socio-emotional development. In this last part of the chapter there is an overview of some services that aim to work with parents and young children when they are facing challenges. Three examples of targeted support services are discussed: the 'watch, wait and wonder' programme; home visiting and parenting programmes; and, finally, specialist child, adolescent and mental health services (CAMHS) (see Figure 3.2).

The 'watch, wait and wonder' programme

The 'watch, wait and wonder' programme (Cohen *et al.* 1999) aims to enable the caregiver to interpret the young child's communications. The main carer is encouraged to observe (watch) and follow the infant's spontaneous play activity, see what happens (wait) and reflect on what the infant may be thinking and feeling (wonder) (Muir 1999). The carer is asked to notice and respond to the infant's cues and signals but not to instruct or guide the play. Carers who are able to 'read' cues and signals are more able to understand their infants' emotional states and to help them to regulate their feelings.

This technique aims to encourage the carer's reflective function (Fonagy *et al.* 2004) in which an empathetic understanding develops. In a typical session the mother will play for about half an hour with their child (usually aged between about 1 and 2½ years old). Cohen et al. describe the role of the therapist as follows:

> The therapist does not instruct, give advice or interpret the infant's activity or play but provides a safe supportive environment so that the mother can express her own observations, thoughts, feelings and interpretations of her infant's activity and their relationship. The mother and the therapist discuss the mother's observations of her infant's activity and attempt to understand themes and relational issues that the infant is trying to master, focussing on inevitable problems that emerge as the mother begins to struggle with following her infant's lead. (Cohen *et al.* 1999: 434)

An evaluation of this programme showed an increase in parenting satisfaction and competence, a shift towards more secure attachment patterns, and improved cognitive and emotional regulation in the infants (Cohen *et al.* 1999).

Home visiting programmes

Home visiting programmes usually consist of a professional or volunteer visiting the home with the aim of supporting the carer and improving outcomes for the child. In the UK there is a tradition of universal home visiting to families with young children by midwives and health visitors. When families are facing extra challenges there are examples of home visiting programmes that have used specially trained health visitors (Percy and Barker 1986) or community mothers as volunteer visitors (Johnson *et al.* 1993; Johnson *et al.* 2000).

While the results of these studies have been variable, there is increasing consensus that home visiting programmes are able to improve a number of important outcomes for both parents and children. Home visiting programmes have been shown to be associated with improvements in parenting and child behavioural outcomes, improved cognitive development and reduced accidental injury (Bull *et al.* 2004). One home visiting programme aimed to support families with a pre-school child with ADHD. This programme of eight structured one-hour sessions was found to be effective in raising awareness of ADHD, introducing behaviour management strategies and improving the mother's sense of well-being (Sonuga-Barke *et al.* 2000).

Parenting programmes

The voluntary and statutory sectors have developed many parenting programmes in the UK over the last few decades (universal preventive services are described in Chapter 3). Programmes are also available to help improve emotional and behavioural outcomes for children by supporting parents to explore new parenting techniques that promote prosocial behaviour. Behavioural programmes aim to help parents recognize the triggers for children's behaviours and focus on changing behaviour by using social learning techniques such as positive reinforcement, negotiation and alternatives to physical punishment.

An American programme by Webster-Stratton (1999) consistently showed effective results using video-tape modelling of structured play, learning praise/ignore techniques and positive reinforcement of 'good' behaviour. The group sessions usually run weekly over a period of about 20 weeks, with the aim of supporting parenting skills to enable parents to cope with difficult or challenging behaviour. A UK evaluation of this technique (Manby 2005) indicated that the programme was effective in relieving the stress associated with parenting and showed moderate improvements in the way that parents perceived children's 'problem' behaviour. The study highlighted the need for more research into programmes for minority ethnic parents and into the role and influence of fathers who did not attend the course.

Relationships-based programmes focus on developing communication and understanding behaviour in the context of relationships. Parents are encouraged to reflect on their own attitudes and behaviour in order to promote family relationships and develop skills in listening. Some would argue that the group leader's skills are more important than, or at least as important as, the theoretical base. Barlow and Parsons (2004) found in a systematic review that programmes are effective in enabling change in parenting practices and improving behaviour problems in young children, and suggest that combination programmes using both behavioural and relationship approaches may be most effective.

Further research indicated that parenting programmes effectively supported maternal mental health and helped to raise self-esteem and improve couple relationships (Barlow *et al.* 2002). However, this approach does not suit everyone and drop-out rates are greater for families experiencing high levels of stress and relative poverty (Liabo *et al.* 2004). Jack and Jordan (1999) agree that parenting programmes play a role in supporting families where children's behaviour demonstrates their distress, but they feel that this is a small part of promoting social capital:

> We will not argue that legal and professional protective systems, services for children in need and parenting skills are not relevant

factors in promoting children's well-being. Indeed, both some local services and all parenting skills are part of what we mean by social capital – but only a small part. Our argument will be that the prevention of harm to children and the optimisation of their development are best secured by an environment in which adults interact as relatively equal members of a community which fosters trust, co-operation and individual initiative, and promotes strong associations and voluntary organisations for the common good. (Jack and Jordan 1999: 242)

Social capital is clearly an important element and may be instrumental in preventing families from suffering social exclusion and failing to take up services. However, Korbin (1989) found that social networks failed to challenge abusive families because of the difficult circumstances in which they were raising their children. Clearly there are many factors involved in each system if children are to be effectively supported and protected.

Child and adolescent mental health services (CAMHS)

Child and adolescent mental health services (CAMHS) are a comprehensive range of statutory services that provide help and treatment for children and young people who are experiencing emotional or behavioural difficulties, or mental health problems, disorders and illnesses. Services are usually provided by child and adolescent psychologists, psychiatrists, family therapists, and/or nursing and social work specialists. Young children and families are usually referred to the CAMHS service when difficulties are established, so clearly it is preferable if early recognition of children's distress leads to early support before difficulties are more developed. Unfortunately services are often oversubscribed, resulting in children and families being seen at a later stage when problems are more established. Some CAMHS teams offer specialist advice to community staff at health centres or in schools and this would seem a positive way of ensuring some early support for families. Young children who feel different because of a disability or are frustrated because of language difficulties may be more likely to suffer distress, and early specialist advice and support might help avoid some difficulties. Children who have emotional and behavioural problems are more likely to have communication difficulties (Benasich et al. 1993) and other research indicates that these problems have often gone unnoticed (Cohen et al. 1998).

Conclusion

Over 60 years ago Dorothy Gardner, head of child development at the Institute of Education in London, argued that:

> we cannot educate a very unhappy child, or one who is even temporarily in the throes of jealousy, anger or mourning. We are also coming to realise that emotional satisfactions lie at the root of all intellectual interests and that feelings are the driving force between all intellectual effort. (Gardner 1956: 11)

Young children can only communicate their distress through specific behavioural patterns, and unresolved stress impacts on every aspect of child development. Traditionally, children's distress has often remained hidden because the contextual reasons have not always been explored, due in part to the way in which childhood is constructed within many countries. Communities may readily accept the rights of children to be protected and to have provisions, but adults may struggle more with the third 'P', participation, which involves listening to young children and interpreting their behaviour. Parenting programmes may encourage better communication between adults and young children:

> the way the course was done – getting us to spend more time and attention on them, playing with them more in the beginning – it works really well. I'd say 80% of the bad behaviour to get attention has just disappeared. (Manby 2005: 324)

In England and Wales, new policy and legislation, *Every Child Matters* (DfES 2003), the Children Act 2004 and the Childcare Bill (2005) are moving towards making children more 'visible' and fulfilling the 'three Ps' of the UNCRC. Children's Commissioners are now in place in England, Northern Ireland, Scotland and Wales, with a remit to represent children's views. Cultures that value and respect children and families, so that there are not wide social inequalities tend to have the lowest rates of child harm (Briggs and Cutright 1994). The impact of parenting is felt throughout life and in succeeding generations, and Bavolek (1990) argues that 'no other form of human interaction can boast such power and longevity' – a strong reason for finding the most appropriate ways to value and support families.

9 Children's involvement in health

The social study of children and childhood has played a key role in questioning how adults regard children and in stressing the active part that children play in creating and making sense of their daily worlds (James and Prout 1997; James *et al.* 1998; Alanen 2001; Mayall 2002; Hallett and Prout 2003; Alderson *et al.* 2005; Prout 2005). These **discourses** and the ratification of the UNCRC are linked with recent policy and practice developments in the UK in relation to children's participatory rights and have a specific relevance to children's health and well-being. Policy has also been driven by the public outrage and subsequent public inquiry, chaired by Lord Laming (Laming 2003), into the tragic death from abuse and neglect of 8-year-old Victoria Climbie. The Laming report highlighted the missed opportunities for asking Victoria herself how she had sustained such terrible injuries. The ramifications of the Laming report were therefore timely: it encouraged reflection on the way children and childhood are perceived, and the resulting *Every Child Matters* consultation paper and Children Act 2004 acknowledged that children have entitlements not only to protection but also to participation.

This chapter begins by discussing perceptions of infancy and childhood, and linking this with perceptions of children's participation in health matters. Research (Alderson *et al.* 2005) that considers the participatory rights of the youngest infants is explored in relation to whether children are too young to have their views considered. Children with disabilities often have extra health requirements, and the social and medical models of disability are explored. Research into the participation of children who have chronic conditions is reviewed, and the difficult and painful subjects of bereavement and life-limiting conditions are discussed.

The historical context

In many cultures young infants are often perceived more as 'human becomings' than as human beings in their own right. Mayall (2002) argues that young children are seen as pre-social beings, to be socialized by adults; this may have strong historical roots. An anthropologist, Nancy Scheper-Hughes (1993), wrote very movingly about her observations of mother–infant interactions in a poor shanty town in Brazil. The mortality rate in the first year of life was so high that mothers were noticeably detached and indifferent to infants considered too weak to survive. It was suggested that perceiving infants as pre-social when families were large and death rates high was a protective coping factor. As birth control and health improvements enable families to plan a smaller number of children, who are likely to have increased lifespans, parents can concentrate on wider issues than just survival and, increasingly, parents and researchers are discussing the importance of the active social nature of infants and young children. Families with fewer children can concentrate more on individual children and consider wider issues than survival. There is increasing awareness of the social nature of infancy and early childhood (Murray and Andrews 2000), and recognition that young children actively seek communication with others. This increasing awareness (see Chapter 3) has challenged the view of children as objects to be acted upon. Traditionally, young children have been thought too young to have any part in important health matters, which are the domain of adults and experts; this is questioned in the next section by considering research with the very youngest infants.

Children's participation in heath

Alderson *et al.* (2005) explored the participation rights of premature babies. This important study highlights the fact that the smallest pre-term infants being nursed in intensive care units, who might be considered by some to be the least likely to be rights holders or participants, can be seen as collaborators in their care. Alderson *et al.* (2005: 46) argue that:

> countless observed and reported examples in the four NICUs [neonatal intensive care units] showed that many adults were convinced that they were not mechanically caring for the unconscious organisms that some philosophers allege babies to be. Instead, they were interacting with human relationships influenced by the babies' views.

Alderson *et al.* (2005) explore how parents and staff were able to describe in detail the likes and dislikes of small pre-term babies. For example, one mother sensitively outlines her baby's individual characteristics (see the section on reflective function in Chapter 3):

> Yes, I see him as a person, sitting and watching him for hours, learning about what he likes. He likes lying on his left side and on his

> tummy, not on his right side, and he's also like his father, he dislikes
> anyone playing with his feet, even if he's sedated he'll squiggle but
> he likes his head and chin and forehead and his back being stroked.
> (Alderson *et al.* 2005: 40)

It was noted that care that was consistently responsive to infants' individual
signals and cues helped to prevent them becoming stressed, which would
have made their condition less stable. Alderson *et al.*'s (2005) work with such
young pre-term infants contests the way in which infants are perceived as
passive receivers of adult care and challenges views about the whether the
youngest children can participate in matters that concern them. Neonatal
intensive care units are highly technological, with expert staff often needing
to carry out painful life-saving procedures. The status of staff is likely to be
higher in NICUs, and programmes such as NBAS (see Chapter 3), which enable staff to demonstrate the characteristics and individual preferences of
each infant may be used to support practitioners and parents in discovering
the unique characteristics of small infants. Sadly this status is not reflected in
the way society views the care of young children in the community. Elfer
(2005: 116) argues that the work for practitioners caring for the youngest
children in nurseries is often seen 'as the least challenging and skilled: it's all
feeding and changing and they don't do much'. Perhaps lack of support for
practitioners carrying out their complex and emotionally demanding work
sometimes leaves them feeling detached or with a fear of getting too involved.

Young children and 'self-maintenance' health activities

Changing cultural perceptions of infants' abilities to participate may take
some time, especially when older children may be rendered invisible by virtue
of the fact that they are young. Mayall (1994) describes how young children
need to carry out 'self-maintenance' health activities within schools. They
need food, access to the toilets, drinks, exercise and a balance between play
and work. Most children have a say in the order of these at home, but within
the confines of school these activities are bound by timetables, customs and
the power structure of the establishment. Children are often expected to accept the adult-orientated regime without question (Mayall 1994). One mother
describes her concern for her daughter thus:

> It all started with a battle against my daughter's junior school. I had
> assumed that my daughter could drink at school – but very quickly
> realised that she was getting headaches, was far more tired than usual
> and even had early symptoms of a urinary tract infection. The school
> only had two old drinking fountains between 500 children and they

were in the upper years' loos, so the younger ones didn't go in there. I thought drinking water had just been overlooked. (Brander 2004)

'Overlooking' such a fundamental physical need may seem surprising, although until recent publicity raised awareness, many young children in the UK had very little access to drinking water during the school day (Croghan 2002). School routines may be deeply rooted in the way children are perceived within a culture that vests power in adults, assuming that they will always know what is best for the child and will act in his or her best interests. This welfare model of adult–child relationships (Lansdown and Lancaster 2001) considers the child as a passive recipient, often assuming that children lack the competence to decide for themselves and, perhaps unwittingly, has 'allowed' adults to construct routines that are often more about adults' best interests than children's health needs. In the regimentation of the school setting it would have been unusual to have asked for children's opinions about basic health routines. More recently, with heightened awareness, healthy schools standards and school councils, and the influence of the UNCRC, attitudes are beginning to change.

Children's competence

The mother's account of her concern about her daughter's lack of drinking water is useful in exploring ideas about how children are often considered as 'objects' to be acted on by others rather than as social individuals who construct meanings from their own experiences. Article 12 of the UNCRC and an underpinning principle of the Children Act 1989 state that children should have their views taken into account in matters that affect them, and there is research to indicate that children who have some control over their own lives show greater emotional well-being. Taking the time to explain things to children and offering opportunities where they can influence what is happening gives an opportunity for young children to share in decisions about their health. Young children's cooperation is likely to be greater when it is based on insights and knowledge rather than on passive compliance (Alderson 1993, 1995; Mayall 1994; Alderson and Montgomery 1996). Consider the following case study.

Case study

A mother told the story of attending a hospital outpatients clinic with her 4-year-old daughter, Maria, prior to hospital admission for removal of her tonsils. The mother had explained all the procedures to Maria so that she could understand. The last part of the appointment involved getting a ticket and queuing to have blood taken. Maria said that she didn't want to have blood taken because it would hurt. Her mother carefully explained that there would be a prick, which would hurt for a short time, but that it was important for the doctors to know what type Maria's blood was before the operation. Maria asked more questions about this and her mother answered honestly and in a way that Maria could understand. Maria still didn't want to have blood taken and said she wanted to go home. Her mother was worried because the appointment had taken over two hours and she had left her baby with a friend. The mother suggested to Maria that they leave to fetch her baby brother. To her amazement, Maria didn't want to leave the queue and said they should wait and have it done. Maria's blood was taken quickly and efficiently because she was cooperative, after having made her own decision. (Underdown 1999, unpublished research)

Maria's mother had effectively kept her daughter informed about what was happening. She didn't pressurize Maria, she merely gave a factual account at an appropriate level. This resulted in Maria making a positive decision about her own health care. The balance between the child's and the adults' interests and ensuring that the child feels informed and included, but not pressurized, is delicate and needs to be managed with sensitivity: 'In all situations where children are involved, however, there is a need for balance between their rights to be informed and heard, and burdening them with undue responsibility for decisions made' (Pryor and Rodgers 2001: 275).

Foley *et al.* (2001) highlight the ways in which mothers (or main carers within the home) enable young children to explore, negotiate and define their competence about health issues. Some parents, like Maria's mother, are often very 'attuned' to their own children but other parents may struggle with accepting their child's competence. Alderson and Montgomery (1996: 89) suggest defining competence as when a child understands the type and purpose of his treatment, the general nature and effects of treatment, the benefits and risks and the consequences of not receiving treatment. While assessing children's competence may superficially seem straightforward, it involves one of the most controversial areas of ethics and rights, which is open to many different interpretations and beliefs. Many individual examples of children's understanding indicate that there can be no fixed age for developing competence or logic, and that developing awareness is an invisible and personal process. Trying to force Maria to have the blood test would have almost certainly had a very different result, and young children's competence is explored further in the next section.

Children with chronic conditions

Some children have to cope with the demands of a specific chronic illness, such as diabetes or asthma, and research evidence indicates the benefits of the appropriate involvement of young children in managing their own health (Eiser 1993). One study investigated different methods of educating children between 2 and 5 years old about asthma (Holzheimer *et al.* 1998: 96). It concluded that children in the experimental groups who had received asthma education had better medication compliance, experienced fewer delays with asthma symptoms and required fewer medical consultations. Asthma, affecting one in five children in the UK, is potentially less threatening if children know how to recognize their symptoms and have easy access to their medication. Yet there have been reports of children in school having their inhaler 'drugs' locked away 'for safety' so that they have been unable to access them quickly when needed (Seipp 2002). It is to be hoped that health education campaigns in schools (McGhan *et al.* 2002) have raised awareness about asthma, but it is useful to reflect on how this practice came about. Generally, young children are considered incompetent to interpret bodily symptoms (Foley *et al.* 2001) and in knowing when to take medication. Parents at home may be sensitively aware of their young child's growing independence and competence, and feel confident enough to gradually share responsibility. However, this is more difficult for education professionals, working in a culture where children are generally thought unable to participate in important health matters and where any risk to the child is unacceptable. The paradox is that by removing the risk (the inhaler) from the child the risk was actually increased.

Young children develop their competence gradually through everyday experience and conversations, and assessing a young child's competence requires knowing them well and building up a level of trust. Staff who work with hospitalized children often develop intimate knowledge about young children's competence and this is demonstrated by many studies. For example, in one study at Great Ormond Street Hospital in London (Llewellyn 1993), doctors allowed children to control their own pain relief. Children decided how much pain relief they needed, with safeguards to ensure that they were not able to exceed a safe dosage. Doctors found that children asked for the same amount or less than they would have been prescribed and they deduced that even young children could make safe choices.

When young children are appropriately encouraged to take part in decision making about their own health there can be both immediate and long-term benefits. However, this is not reflected commonly. For example, Lowes *et al.* (2004) carried out a small survey into the responses of parents of 20 children newly diagnosed with the acute type 1 form of diabetes, requiring insulin injections. This study examined the grief responses of parents as they negotiated their child's newly diagnosed chronic condition. However, this study, like many others, completely omits the child's transition to coping with the illness, a factor that surely must impact on the parents' coping mechanisms and that possibly predicts how well the child manages his or her condition in the future. Many children worldwide suffer from the chronic skin condition eczema, and in a large German study, Staab (2006) evaluated the long-term outcomes of educational interventions to improve compliance with treatment. Poor adherence to medically advised eczema treatments is an important factor in the unpleasant recurrence of this condition. However, although Staab's outcomes were positive with tailored education programmes for differing age groups, the intervention for the youngest group (children with eczema of 7 years and younger) was aimed solely at the parents. Traditional stage theories of development have been dominated by evidence of cognitive immaturity, with a focus on identifying the young child's limitations rather than his or her potential to understand (Piaget and Inhelder 1969; Bibace and Walsh 1980). As a consequence, decisions may be made, based on evidence from age stage development theories, deeming it inappropriate to attempt to involve a young child because of cognitive immaturity. This approach overlooks the way in which young children continually attempt to make sense of their experiences and that acquisition of knowledge is a more effective determinant of children's understanding of health than age stage theories of cognitive development (Eiser 1989). Vygotsky (1978), while recognizing that there may be a limit to what a child can understand at a specific point in time, also acknowledged the value of skilled instruction in extending knowledge and that sensitive support should build on the individual child's understanding.

Presenting treatment interventions to young children and to children with some disabilities does require a different set of skills and approaches but children will gain confidence and become more competent if their opinions are valued, and ultimately are more likely to be able to manage their condition (Holaday *et al.* 1994). For example, only the child with diabetes can feel the onset of a **hypoglycaemic** event and discussing this with the young child is important in managing treatment and care. Qvortrup (cited in James and Prout 1997) argues that perceiving children as dependants, best served by adults who know what is in their best interests, leads to 'protective exclusion' of children. Perhaps this sheds light on the fact that researchers have only just begun to investigate the feelings of parents when their child develops a chronic disease; a new generation must expand this work so that children's views are routinely sought. Unless this happens, children may continue to experience less optimal care because they cannot be active partners in their own care.

Children with disabilities

Traditionally, children with disabilities were perceived as being different, with an impairment that was the focus of attention. The main emphasis often concentrated only on trying to 'cure' the disability so that the child could be part of the 'able-bodied world', rather than accepting the child as an individual within a diverse world. This approach is often labelled the 'medical model'; it is sometimes thought of as harmful to a child's 'sense of self' because it views him or her as 'faulty' and concentrates on weaknesses rather than strengths. The 'social model' is considered by many to be a more effective and positive way of viewing disability. This model celebrates and values every individual for who they are and focuses more on adapting the environment and encouraging positive attitudes to ensure that the child with a disability is included. The social model acknowledges the problem in the way that society responds to disability and considers that the child may be dis-abled by societal attitudes, prejudice and discrimination, which create barriers. Micheline Mason (1992) campaigns for the rights of people with disabilities. She argues that: 'although we do of course have medical conditions which may hamper us, the major disability we face is that caused by social and environmental barriers placed upon us by the structures of our societies' (Mason 1992: 223).

In the past, people used to talk about integrating children with disabilities into mainstream schools. In reality, this meant trying to make the child fit into the existing provision. Inclusive education requires many more resources because it means changing the environment and the curriculum so that it can fully meet the needs of all children. Children who feel valued in this way should develop a healthier self-image and increased emotional well-being. However, Marchant reminds us that children with disabilities are frequently devalued and excluded:

> Acts of omission are fairly common in children's everyday lives: disabled children may not be asked around to play at other children's houses, they may experience being left out by other children in the park and playground, and they may not be included in outings or gatherings. Acts of omission also happen within services. Policies may be written as if all children are non-disabled, buildings built as if all children can walk, communication carried out as if all children can talk, literature produced as if all children can see and procedures in place assuming that disabled children do not share any needs with other children. (Marchant, cited in Foley *et al.* 2001: 216)

Marchant demonstrates how the self-concept of children with disabilities can be affected by the attitudes of others and the way that society erects 'barriers' that prevent communities from being truly inclusive. Young children with disabilities may experience a lack of well-being, which is heightened by a growing sense of feeling different. A healthy sense of self requires acceptance, and part of this means young children having ongoing relevant information that focuses on what they want to know about their disability. Middleton's (1999) study found that young people lacked information about the most basic issues to do with their own conditions. Support for young children with disabilities and their families may concentrate more on receiving physical support than on developing emotionally and socially, and there may be relatively few opportunities for participation. Priestly (2001: 158) argues that the voices of children with disabilities are 'submerged in a quagmire of ignorance, fear, and extreme negative attitudes, while policy makers hide behind the contingencies of article 23 of the UNCRC, that enforcement of the rights of disabled children is "subject to available resources".' Sadly, 55 per cent of families with a disabled child live in or on the margins of poverty, and minority ethnic families face further barriers and disadvantage, especially if English is an additional language (BMA 1999).

Children with disabilities often have increased experience of health services and can be a valuable resource when planning service provision and development. However, their first-hand experience may receive little recognition (Davis and Watson 2000). Medical models have often marginalized children by labelling the child's disability and, by focusing on label stereotypes, overlooking the child's individual competencies and understanding. Davis and Watson (2000) argue that children with disabilities are able to participate when adults make the effort to learn the individual ways in which they communicate. Young children with disabilities are a very diverse group, needing a wide range of approaches to ensure that they can participate in health matters. Having some control over events is not only positive in promoting individual mental health; it would also benefit all children who may need to use the health services.

In the next section children's participation is further explored by considering young children who face bereavement.

The bereaved child

It is so emotionally painful to think about a child's loved one dying that as a subject it is relatively rarely discussed openly. Yet in many places, like sub-Saharan Africa, many young children have lost one or maybe both of their parents through AIDS or some other disease (Foster 1997). The death of a parent is much less common in the richer industrialized countries, although it is estimated that 40 children a day across the UK experience the death of a parent and many more will lose a grandparent. Concern about how to approach bereavement issues, combined with a perception that children may be too young to understand, may result in feelings not being 'worked through' or processed (Worden 1996). Young children need to make sense of their loss, as the case study of Jonathan shows.

Case study

Aisha and Tom had moved to South Africa from the UK shortly before their son Jonathan was born. Tom worked as a mining engineer and Aisha was busy caring for their son and seeing groups of other mothers around their township. Two years later Tom was suddenly killed in a mining accident, leaving Aisha devastated. She made plans to return to the UK and three months later she was living in a small house near her parents. Every time she thought of Tom she cried and she decided that she must pull herself together for Jonathan's sake, so she put all pictures of Tom away and told her parents not to speak of him. As Jonathan approached his third birthday his behaviour was causing concern: he was alternately clinging and aggressive towards Aisha, he had a very poor appetite, and he would sleep restlessly and often awake screaming with fear. Fortunately, through the Childhood Bereavement Project, Aisha and Jonathan were put in touch with a counsellor who worked with them over a period of the next year. Gradually Aisha got out the photographs of Tom and sometimes she and Jonathan cried together as they looked at them. Aisha also made a memory box with Jonathan, containing precious items like the picture of Tom with Jonathan at his second birthday and a Mother's Day card they had made together. Aisha had not realized that, at such a young age, Jonathan would need to work through his feelings and that the denial of his grief had been reflected in his lack of well-being.

Grieving children's behaviour may seem contradictory in that periods of sadness seem short and may be followed by the child enthusiastically joining in play with peers. This often misleads adults into thinking that the child does not understand or has forgotten. In fact children and young people will often revisit their loss regularly at different stages within their lives, especially at transition times like going to school or away on holiday or, as adults, when they partner or have their own children. Supporting bereaved children in nursery or school can also be very challenging, and questions are best answered honestly and directly and using the correct language. 'We lost him' is confusing and may make the child wonder if she will become lost too. Young children often wrestle with questions about whether they caused the death, whether it is going to happen to them and who will look after them if a parent has died (Worden 1996). Planning and participation are an important part of the process of coming to terms with death, and children benefit from sensitive explanations focusing on what they want to know at that time.

Although there are wide variations in cultural rituals (Helman 2000), consideration of whether the children can be appropriately involved may help them make sense of what is happening and offer a chance for them to take part in saying goodbye and in respecting the memory of their loved one. Children will continue to try to make sense of happenings, and will benefit from the attentions of a sensitive adult who can answer questions as they arise. **Circle time** is sometimes used for discussion of sensitive issues, or a book appropriate for stage and culture can be used. Some useful titles and details of a training pack, *Not too Young to Grieve*, are included at the end of this chapter. Several studies (Van Eederwegh *et al.* 1982, 1985; Chieftaz *et al.* 1989) report childhood dysphoria (generalized feelings of being ill or depressed) in parentally bereaved children and one in five children is likely to develop a mental health problem, often presenting itself in the form of fears, angry outbursts or behavioural difficulties (Dowdney 2000). The death of a loved one has been recognized as a factor that precipitates depression for some young people so helping children express their feelings and come to an understanding about death is an important mediating factor in the promotion of well-being and future mental health. The Child Bereavement Trust, based at the National Children's Bureau in London, and the charity Winston's Wish are involved in promoting children's well-being by setting up network of bereavement services to help children understand and acknowledge loss. Services for bereaved children are still developing in the UK, and Kmietowicz argues that 'research on the effects of bereavement in childhood is scant, and because of the haphazard manner in which services have developed they are often uncoordinated, unpublicised, underfunded and unmonitored' (2000: 893).

Bereavement has a major impact on the well-being of many children worldwide and differing initiatives are attempting to offer support. For example, Killian (n.d.) set up a structured group therapy programme in South Africa to support the psychosocial needs of children living in a community where many families are affected by HIV/AIDS and other adversities. Cross-cultural research, reflecting on what children, their siblings and families find helpful should underpin the development of accessible bereavement support.

The child with a life-limiting condition

The realization that a child's illness is life limiting presents a crisis for all family members, and parents may feel that their expected roles of nurture and protection are challenged (Sloper 1996). The uncertainty, often combined with invasive treatments, results in high levels of parental stress (Eiser 1993). Each parent, grandparent, sibling, nurse or doctor will have different capacities and expectations of what they can accept and believe, and what they can speak about. This tension between recognizing how the young child needs to make sense of what is happening and protecting them from distress raises ongoing issues for parents and staff. Even very young children are usually aware of their parents' emotional pain, and their reactions and involvement will often focus on shielding parents from further anguish. Parents, in turn, may wish to protect their child from knowing about his or her illness. Bluebond-Langner's (1978) study of children with leukaemia clearly shows how children built up their understanding of their illnesses in a number of ways, such as discussion with other children on the ward, overhearing adults talking and making sense of atmospheres, moods and non-verbal communication. Older children may gain information from reading labels such as those on drug packaging.

While a young child's ability to understand may be recognized, it may also be difficult to acknowledge because it is too painful and contradicts how young children are perceived. Alderson (1993: 102) records a psychologist speaking of an 'exceptional, brilliant 3 year old' who understood his haemophilia, and a doctor speaking of another 3-year-old who understood his liver biopsy as well as some adults did. Janusz Korczak argues that, 'if we are constantly astonished at the child's perceptiveness, it means that we do not take them seriously' (Korczak, cited in Clark and Moss 2001). Children's understanding is individually constructed, and adult responses that are sensitive to this will enable children to process difficult feelings as they arise over time.

Increasingly, health practitioners are training in palliative care and counsellors and therapists are able to offer more in-depth support for families. Concerns have been raised that there are few provisions for training in transcultural medicine, and that staff may not be always be aware of the specific rituals and spiritual needs of minority ethnic groups (Gatrad *et al.* 2003). Some children may have respite or 'end of life' care in a specially designed children's hospice that caters for the psychosocial needs of the family as well as offering physical care. Hospices aim to create a positive atmosphere, ensuring that the young child and family's wishes are valued and respected, and that any religious or cultural needs are recognized. Part of this holistic family support may involve working with siblings, who are trying to make sense of what is happening during a time when they feel that all the parental attention is directed towards their brother or sister.

Conclusion

New research evidence is emerging that provides a deeper understanding of children's participation in health matters. Children of all ages have often been perceived as innocent and unaware of medical procedures, yet research indicates that infants can be observed to have individual preferences and that young children are making sense of the world through constant interactions and observations. The process of listening to children's views involves respectful discussion and negotiation. When adults and children are communicating effectively on a day-to-day basis about health issues and are 'in tune' with one another, decisions may be arrived at by a process of 'mutual consensus'. There can be no generalized account of how to approach each situation as each child's understanding and wishes for involvement in their health care will be unique. Yet professionals' views in the past were often dominated by age/stage theories of child development and by concepts that see the child as 'having rights to protection and training but not to autonomy' (Ennew 1986: 21). Changing these perceptions requires an awareness of how children are often routinely excluded and a belief in children as competent active participants. Respectful listening, using appropriate play materials, leads to a process of negotiation and shared understandings, achieving a balance so that the child is empowered but not overwhelmed. When this balance is found, children are enabled to develop a responsible and knowledgeable attitude to their own health.

Resources dealing with bereavement, for use with children

Books

Alborough, J. (1994) *Where's my Teddy?* Walker.
Baum, L. (1986) *Are we Nearly There?* Bodley Head.
Burningham, J. (1988) *Grandpa*. Picture Puffin.
Dupasquier, P. (2002) *Dear Daddy*. Anderson Press.
Durant, A. (2003) *Always and Forever*. Doubleday.
Fox, M.J. (1984) *Wilfred Gordon MacDonald Partridge*. Picture Puffins.
Gould, G. (1987) *Grandpa's Slide Show*. Puffin.
Hathorn, L. (1995) *Grandma's Shoes*. Viking.
Hoffman, M. and Binch, C. (1995) *Grace and Family*. Frances Lincoln.
Hughes, S. (1977) *Dogger*. Picture Lions.
Limb, S. and Munoz, C. (1995) *Come Back Grandma*. Red Fox.
McAfee, A. (1984) *Visitors Who Came to Stay*. Hamish Hamilton.
Robinson, C. and Broadley, S. (1994) *Leaving Mrs Ellis*. Bodley Head.
Selway, M. (1993) *Don't Forget to Write*. Red Fox.
Simonds, P. (1989) *Fred*. Penguin.
Varley, S. (1992) *Badger's Parting Gifts*. Julia McRae.
Waddell, M. (1990) *Grandma's Bill*. Simon & Schuster.
Waddell, M. (1991) *Once There Were Giants*. Walker.
Weninger, B. and Marks, A. (1995) *Goodbye Daddy!* North-South.
Wilhelm, H. (1985) *I'll Always Love You*. Hodder & Stoughton.

Training materials

Not too Young to Grieve (2006) Available from www.childhoodbereavement network.org.uk.

10 Listening to young children

Angela Underdown and Jane Barlow, Reader in Public Health Medicine, University of Warwick

There is increasing recognition of the need to transcend some of the theoretical, philosophical and methodological dichotomies that have beset the study of childhood to date (Prout 2005). Such dichotomies have resulted, on the one hand, in a sociology of childhood that addresses the 'large-scale patterning' that shapes children's lives while simultaneously ignoring the voice of the child and, on the other, in a sociology of children that focuses on children as individuals who are 'diversely and locally constructed through iterative interaction with human agents' (Prout 2005: 64), at the expense of the macro social context in which the child is located.

The task of this final chapter, then, will be to pull together some of the themes that have been developed throughout this book by exploring reasons why the voice of the child should be heard and how infants who are too young to speak may still participate. The chapter will then examine why we need to move forward in terms of the way in which childhood is conceptualized, and what the implications of this are in terms of the way in which we explore childhood and 'what works' for children. It will be argued that only by moving beyond the 'social construction of childhood' will it be possible to acknowledge the commonalities of childhood, alongside the voice that this provides to young children in particular. It will also be argued that such an approach would improve the ability of researchers to adopt the type of mixed-methods research that is capable of reflecting not only the child's agency and voice, but also their location within existing social structures.

The voice of the child

There is increasing acknowledgment of the importance of recognizing the agency of children and, more specifically, permitting them the opportunity to have their voices heard. This reflects, in part, an increased understanding that children's health and well-being is compromised if their views are not heard, as is explained by one young person who reflects on being raised by a mother with mental health problems:

People tend to protect children and young people. For me, this translated into ignoring my need to be informed and involved. My life was affected anyway and if I had guidance it might have made the experience more positive. I needed good, age-specific information about my mother's condition and its consequences. And I needed someone to talk to who would listen in confidence and help me explore the complex feelings and situations I was dealing with. (Marlowe 1996, cited in Gorin 2004)

There are many examples where children's health and well-being is affected because they are isolated by being perceived as too young to understand; Chapter 9 reflects on the tragic consequences of failing to listen to Victoria Climbie and the possible effects when bereaved children are not able to process their grief. The same chapter also references the groundbreaking research that Priscilla Alderson (2005) has conducted with pre-term infants, clearly identifying them as human beings rather than 'becomings' and already able to demonstrate characteristics and preferences. Young children and infants may be perceived as voiceless because they have not yet acquired the formal language with which to express themselves. Discovering the many languages or ways that babies express themselves and respecting their individuality should, however, be the foundation for ensuring that all children are valued. Recent studies (Murray and Andrews 2000; Alderson 2005) with infants and young children indicate that the question is not whether children can demonstrate preferences and opinions but how these can be interpreted in the best interests of the child.

Infant behavioural signals

The recognition that even the youngest babies are able to use expressive facial gestures, body movements, crying and vocalization as cues or signals to guide sensitive responses to their needs (Murray and Andrews 2000) means that young children and infants are dependent on adults (both parents and professionals) to recognize and interpret such signals in order to be heard. So, for example, recent research based on close examination of video-taped interaction between mothers and infants shows that very young infants look away when the interaction with a carer is being experienced by the baby as either overwhelming or intrusive (Beebe 2000). There is no evidence to date of social or cultural differences influencing this aspect of early infant behaviour, and looking away may be one of the few mechanisms that an infant has for managing overwhelming feelings. Infants who are parented by carers who are continually unable to recognize their signals indicating the need for a break in interaction, or who engage in overwhelmingly intrusive interaction with the infant, often develop permanently defensive behaviours to protect themselves. For example, some babies become uncooperative, while others who experience extremely overwhelming or threatening interaction become compulsively compliant in order to diminish the perceived threat (Crittenden 1988; Crittenden and DiLalla 1988). Both of these defensive positions compromise the infant's later emotional health.

While such communication may not be 'intentional' in the sense of it being motivated by conscious thought, it does have a meaning and should be treated as intentional, particularly because it is an accurate guide to the emotional state of the infant. Furthermore, there is an increasing body of research which indicates that having emotional states understood by our carers is important in enabling young infants to learn about emotions and mental states in themselves and others. Elizabeth Meins (Neins *et al.* 2001), a UK-based psychologist, has suggested that carer 'sensitivity' refers to the ability to 'read' the young child's mental states rather than just responding to physical and emotional needs. Meins (1997) uses the term 'mind-mindedness' to describe a parent's inclination to treat the infant as an individual with a mind rather than as a creature with needs that must be satisfied. This capacity to 'read' things from the baby's point of view leads adults to be attuned to the infant (see Chapter 3) so, for example, the tempo at which the infant wishes to feed is recognized and the baby is not fed when trying to initiate social interaction (Meins *et al.* 2001).

Research has shown that early parental 'mind-mindedness' and exposing children to language about emotions early on encourages children to understand their own and others' mental states (Fonagy *et al.* 1994; Meins *et al.* 2001), and predicts children's development in terms of language and play abilities by age 2 better, irrespective of background, social support or maternal depression (Meins 2006). This research demonstrates that by responding to infants not as helpless dependants, but as intentional interaction-seeking individuals, by attempting to accurately 'read' what is being communicated, is good for their long-term development. This is probably not very surprising.

The next section examines the broader implications of a social constructionist perspective, in terms of the way in which research may be conducted with children.

The social construction of children: implications for research

As was suggested earlier, the sociological study of *childhood* has focused on childhood as a 'structural form', or a socially constructed and permanent category that determines what happens to children within any given historical period (Corsaro 2005: 4). The sociological study of *children*, on the other hand, has tended to focus on children themselves as active agents (Corsaro

2005: 4). The latter approach has provided a welcome challenge to the type of theorizing about children in which they were treated as passive agents of the socialization process (Corsaro 2005: 4). It has also involved the adoption of research methodologies in which the voice of children could be heard – including, for example, ethnomethodology (the study of the ways people make sense of their social worlds) and a range of techniques specifically adapted to meet the needs of children (the Mosaic technique, for example) (Clark and Moss 2001).

There is, however, increasing recognition that individualistic approaches of this nature, in which most aspects of childhood are thought to be 'interpreted, debated and defined in processes of social action' (Corsaro 2005: 344), fail to take into account the larger-scale social structures and contexts that form the basis of individual children's lives. This has led one sociologist to call for a break from such 'individualistic doctrines' and a movement towards a new perspective which recognizes that socialization is not only about adaptation and internalization but also a process of 'appropriation', 'reinvention' and, perhaps most importantly, 'reproduction' (Corsaro 2005: 18), something that Corsaro calls 'interpretive reproduction'. Such interpretive reproduction recognizes that children are 'constrained by the existing social structure and by societal reproduction' (Corsaro 2005: 19). The fact that children are located within different social and cultural structures – such as, for example, living in socially disadvantaged or war-torn areas – that constrain how they behave and what they experience, needs to be recognized. So, for example, when observing children and interpreting their behaviour in naturalistic settings, or when talking with them about their experiences, or encouraging them to use other mediums to express their thoughts and feelings, it is important to ensure that all opportunities are used to explore the impact of the broader social and cultural context on the beliefs or experiences to which they are giving voice. This might involve ensuring that children within different social or cultural groups are listened to or observed. Or it might involve us using larger-scale research methods, such as surveys or cohort studies, in which large groups of children from different social and cultural groups are followed up over extended periods of time in order to explore the impact of social and cultural factors on their behaviour and experiences. This points to the importance of recognizing that larger-scale research approaches of this nature also provide a voice to children by identifying the social and cultural factors that influence their lives, and also that methods that are regarded as providing the optimum opportunity to hear children's voices and recognize their agency (such as the Mosaic technique and interviewing) must also take into account the fact that children are not just 'interpreted, debated and defined in processes of social action' but also constrained through their location within different social and cultural contexts.

Research methods

Observations

While there are a range of methods available to researchers wishing to explore children's lives, and indeed childhood, observations of children are increasingly being recognized as a powerful 'tool' for research, particularly in the case of young children, who are not yet able to articulate their thoughts and feelings. Methods of observation have traditionally been divided into two general groupings: naturalistic observations, where the researcher employs a free-flowing narrative style of recording, and those that use standardized procedures that can be analysed using a rating scale. Naturalistic observation is a powerful medium for understanding child health and well-being within the complex network of relationships in which children live their lives. A key advantage of naturalistic observation is that an 'independent' researcher can see how children construct their worlds without having to rely on the 'filter of the accounts and perceptions of others' (Dunn 2005: 99). Patterson's detailed naturalistic observations (1986) in the home showed how children's behaviour was 'shaped' by aggressive siblings and how the quality of these relationships impacted on later adjustment.

Observations can be conducted in a variety of ways. Judy Dunn (1988) observed children within their families in Cambridge. Using a narrative method of handwritten notes and tape-recorded conversations, rich data was collected showing young children's developing understanding of their social and emotional worlds. Dunn (1988) chose this method as she felt video-recording was too intrusive for the families. However, the power of the visual medium is clearly demonstrated in the longitudinal observations made by Robertson and Robertson (1989). As described in Chapter 3, the Robertsons made a series of films documenting young children's distress when separated from their parents by hospitalization or being admitted to a residential nursery. The strength of these films lay in the fact that adults could not dispute that the children's behaviour showed high levels of stress when separated from their parents. These films probably had one of the most significant impacts on child care practice in the last century (Barrett 2006) by ensuring that parents are welcomed to stay with their children in hospitals, and that children in the care of local authorities are no longer placed in residential nurseries. However, watching films of children in such distress is emotionally painful and some would argue that, ethically, the Robertsons should have ceased filming and tried to comfort the children. It seems very unlikely, however, that the sort of policy changes that have ensued would have occurred without their powerful visual evidence.

Another method of naturalistic observation is the Tavistock method, which is described on a video called *Observation Observed* (Miller *et al.* 1999).

This method of naturalistic observation not only utilizes seeing and hearing what is happening, but also encourages researchers to 'feel' the emotion in the behaviour. Observers do not make notes at the time as this would detract from full concentration on the smallest details of interaction within the observation. Detailed notes are written after each observation, which are part of a longitudinal study over a period of one to two years. This type of longitudinal observation is often carried out in the home and follows a baby's development during the first two years (Rustin 1989). The focus of the observation is not the infant or carer but the actual interaction between them (Elfer 2005). This may seem very subjective research but the researcher confidentially discusses the meanings that have been identified within a seminar group and makes sense of the observations.

Entering the privacy of someone's home is a privilege and it may seem surprising that families agree to this 'intrusion'. The researcher's 'stance' is that of a professional observer: friendly but not involved with the family. Miller (2002) comments that families may be pleased to find someone as interested in their infant as they are and that as the weekly pattern of observations takes place an individual relationship is built with the researcher.

The CARE Index

A different type of observation, which is used in research and sometimes in clinical work, is known as the CARE Index (Crittenden 1997, 1998). This involves a short clip of video interaction of the carer and infant or toddler 'playing as they normally would'. This interaction is coded by researchers who have had intensive training in the technique. What is interesting about this method is that behaviour is coded on 14 different dimensions for both the adult and the child, and includes details such as facial and vocal expressions and turn-taking contingencies.

The CARE Index is an effective tool in aiding researchers to learn more about adult–infant interactions. (It has also been used as an element in clinical work in the Sunderland Sure Start Infant Programme (Svanberg 2005), where parents watch the video clips with a health visitor or psychologist and discuss their infant's communicative cues and signals.) The benefit of video is that there is a record that can be reviewed from different perspectives, although it may be deemed more intrusive than naturalistic observations and can raise increased ethical concerns.

Ethical concerns

Research with young children and their carers raises many ethical issues. While there is no doubt that close relationships are crucial to young children's health and well-being, the furthering of knowledge in this way means that researchers have to observe intimate and private relationships between family members or childcarers and infants. It may also raise other ethical issues. This is demonstrated by a body of research that has actually developed understanding about the social nature of infancy. Mary Ainsworth (Ainsworth *et al.* 1978), a student of John Bowlby, designed a situation to measure young children's attachment patterns to their main carers (see Chapter 3). The 'strange situation' involves a young child being briefly left by a parent, in a laboratory playroom. A stranger enters the room and tries to comfort the infant; then the parent returns, and researchers 'measure' the child's distress and the reunion behaviour. How can deceiving a young child into believing that his or her parent has just left and then measuring his or her distress be considered in any way ethical? Clearly the child who expresses the expected distress is also not consenting to the research. Psychologists have often justified this procedure by saying that the stress is very brief and that parents have consented and can quickly comfort the child. This defence cannot justify the child's wishes being ignored, and Woodhead and Faulkner (2000) draw an interesting parallel by asking readers to consider an imaginary reversal of the strange situation. In this imagined reverse scenario the child would inexplicably leave the parent and a stranger would then try to comfort the parent. To contrive a situation, even for a few moments, which causes panic in a parent is unthinkable, but it does serve to raise an interesting perspective about why such a procedure should be thought acceptable for young children.

The British Psychological Society's Code of Ethics (BPS 1991) prohibits any research that may do harm and researchers have in the main shifted focus from laboratories to real-life settings such as the home and the nursery. Other ethical considerations are paramount, such as issues of informed consent. Are parents or carers totally aware of all the implications of the research and how can assent be obtained from young children? In fact, the naturalistic research that has demonstrated the social nature of infants should also allow researchers to respectfully 'read' whether babies wish to be observed.

A rigorous national ethical committee has to approve any research that involves Health Service staff or families contacted using National Health Service information. Usually committees convene monthly and examine in detail the ethical aspects of any research before giving approval. This procedure is necessarily detailed as it is important to protect families from any harmful or time-wasting research. The points that committees consider would include topics such as the following:

- What is the purpose of the research? Will the findings provide valuable information that is not already available elsewhere? How will the research findings be disseminated to young children, families, involved health staff and wider audiences?

- How will parents and children become fully aware of all the implications of the research, including the amount of time required?
- Are children and families given a reasonable amount of time to consider whether they want to be involved after they have received the information?
- How will informed consent be obtained from the parents or carers, and assent from young children? How will the researcher ensure that children and families do not feel any pressure to take part and that they know that their usual health services will not be affected in any way? Is signed consent required from both parents?
- How will confidentiality be assured?
- How will parents be made aware that they can leave the research at any time and without giving a reason if they so wish? How will the researcher ensure a sensitive withdrawal if a young child indicates that they do not wish to take part?
- Have parents, carers and young children been able to comment on the proposed research?

Although research with young infants may mainly involve observations and reports from main carers, an increasing body of research demonstrates that children have been underestimated and much greater insights can be gained when they can be actively involved. Article 12 of the UNCRC refers to the rights of children who are capable of forming their own views to be entitled to express those views freely in matters affecting them, and states that these should be given due weight in accordance with the maturity of the child. Young children have often been underestimated because they lack a level of adult language. Books like *The Mosaic Approach* (Clark and Moss 2001) indicate that there are many more creative ways of engaging with young children, through mediums such as art, music and discovery walks. To include young children as participants in research recognizes them as active participants rather than passive objects, and accepts that children may communicate in a many different ways, such as touch, expressive body language, sign language and sounds.

> To involve all children more directly in research can therefore rescue them from silence and exclusion, and from being represented by default, as passive objects, while respect for their informed and voluntary consent helps to protect them from covert, invasive exploitative or abusive research. (Alderson 2000: 243, cited in Christensen 2000)

Conclusion

Perceiving children as active participants rather than passive objects has major implications for their health and well-being, and exploring the ways in which the youngest children show their likes and dislikes should add to the development of a culture of respectfully 'tuning in' to children. While this is something many parents do in day-to-day interaction (see Chapter 3), more research focusing on the 'many languages of children' should raise awareness of the need for listening to children when they are experiencing stress (see Chapters 8 and 9). This is timely as the focus of children's health in the UK moves to include emotional well-being and mental health rather than just physical health. Further research into the many ways young children communicate will enable young children to be more 'visible' in their everyday settings, such as nurseries, the home, at the childminders, playgroups, crèches, hospitals, health centres, homeless families' units, supervised contact centres, and so on.

Really listening to young children is about respectful and appropriate involvement that enhances well-being by enabling young children to express their views and feelings. Some people may argue that supporting children's rights is about giving 'power' to young children when adults should know what is best for them. In fact the power in listening is shared as the adult can only really 'know what is best' by tuning in to a child's individual preferences and giving these consideration. Research into mind-mindedness and reflective function has important implications for children's well-being and mental health. The last century saw huge advances in industrialized countries promoting children's physical health with the use of immunizations, health screening and improved living conditions (see Chapter 7), and children across the world should benefit more quickly from these developments. In the UK there have also been significant advances in understanding children's mental health. The research is clear in stating that children's well-being and mental health is promoted when they are able to participate appropriately in a listening culture that values well-being and mental health equally with physical health. Public health specialists have long known the impact of poor housing, living in poverty, parental depression or family violence on young children's physical health. In order to promote children's well-being and mental health new research methodologies are needed so that more can be learnt about how young children can participate in their everyday settings. This is the challenge that lies ahead.

Glossary

AIDS (acquired immune deficiency syndrome) A collection of symptoms that may develop after being infected with HIV (human immunodeficiency virus). HIV is transmitted through bodily fluids such as semen, vaginal fluid, blood and breast milk. HIV/AIDS is now a pandemic, with millions of people estimated to be either HIV positive or to have developed AIDS worldwide. There is no cure for the disease, which leaves untreated patients weak and prone to infections and tumours in the late stages. Although antiretroviral drugs are able to significantly slow the progress of the disease, routine access to these drugs is not available in every country. The disease is widespread in sub-Saharan Africa where access to medical care is limited, resulting in high mortality rates and many children being orphaned. There is a risk of the virus being transmitted from mother to child during pregnancy and childbirth, but if the mother takes antiretroviral drugs and gives birth by Caesarean section the risk is much reduced. Resources are needed for prevention campaigns, health care and therapies to slow the progress of the disease. Scientists are researching to discover vaccines to prevent infection.

Allergen An allergen is an antigen that causes an allergic response in a hypersensitive person. Common allergens that affect the respiratory tract include pollen, fur, feathers, mould and house dust mites. Allergens can affect any bodily organs in susceptible individuals. Common chemicals found in everyday products are sometimes linked with skin rashes, dermatitis or eczema. Some common foodstuffs, such as nuts, may also trigger allergic responses in susceptible people.

Antibody Protein produced by the body to neutralize or destroy toxins and disease-carrying organisms.

Asthma Asthma affects the respiratory tract and, during an attack, there is widespread narrowing of the bronchial airways, causing coughing, wheezing and difficulty in breathing. Asthma attacks may be triggered by a wide range of allergens, such as the house dust mite, animal fur or stress. Treatment varies but young children will commonly have two inhalers: one that is used routinely to prevent an attack occurring and one to relieve an attack.

Autism Autism is a disability that affects understanding and communication with others. Autism has a very broad spectrum so children are differently affected but most experience some difficulties with:

- *developing imagination* – children may be very literal and become focused on repetitive details like spinning the wheel of a toy car over and over again
- *verbal and non-verbal communication* – children with autism may interpret language literally and find it difficult to recognize social cues such as facial expressions, gestures, eye contact and speech tones
- *social relationships* – young children with autism often appear aloof and indifferent to other people.

Autism also includes the condition known as Asperger's syndrome, which describes children who show the characteristics of autism, but are of average or above average intelligence and have better communication skills. Autism affects four times as many boys as girls.

Specialized teaching strategies and structured support can help maximize a child's skills and minimize any behaviour problems.

Centile chart A centile chart is used to plot a child's growth curve: weight, height and head circumference are usually recorded. A centile chart is based on the 'norms' of growth across a wide cross-section of the population. An 'average'-size child might follow the 50th centile, whereas a naturally smaller child might follow the 25th centile and a larger child may follow the 90th centile growth curve. Health staff note particularly whether a child deviates from her or his growth curve – for example, by gaining excess weight or too little weight.

Children in need Under Section 17 (10) of the UK Children Act 1989, a child is considered in need if:

- he/she is unlikely to achieve or maintain, or have the opportunity of achieving or maintaining, a reasonable standard of health or development without the provision for him/her of services by a local authority
- his/her health or development is likely to be significantly impaired, or further impaired, without the provision for him/her of such services
- he/she is disabled.

Circle time A space within the nursery or school curriculum that offers an opportunity for young children to feel unconditionally accepted so that they may explore feelings through the discussion of their experiences. The group leader will usually encourage the children to sit round in a circle and a toy may be passed so that the child who chooses to hold it speaks and is listened to by the rest of the group Any coercion to speak or judgemental attitudes are avoided. Effective circle times may help children make sense of their feelings and also improve their communication and conflict resolution skills. An increase in emotional literacy may help support peer relationships and assist in avoiding bullying situations.

Congenital A condition that is present at birth.

Congenital dislocation of the hips (CDH) An abnormality present at birth in which there is a dislocation of the hip joint (a ball and socket joint). CDH is thought to occur in about 1.5 of every 1000 live births and is more common in girls, breech deliveries and where there is a family history of the condition. The name CDH is sometimes replaced by developmental dysplasia of the hip (DDH) in recognition of the fact that it is not always detectable at birth.

Cystic fibrosis (CF) An inherited condition that particularly affects the lungs and digestive system, which become blocked with thick sticky mucus. This results in a deficiency of pancreatic enzymes, and blocked airways leading to possible lung damage and repeated respiratory tract infections. Treatment aims to minimize the disease by regular physiotherapy, combating infection. Digestive problems are treated by administering pancreatic enzymes. CF is the most common inherited disease in white children, affecting about 1 in every 2500 children born. It is much less common in people of African or Asian descent.

Diabetes A condition in which carbohydrates are not metabolized into energy due to the lack of the pancreatic hormone, insulin. The signs and symptoms of the disease include rapid weight loss, excessive thirst, and high levels of glucose in the blood and urine. There are two types of diabetes.

1. Type 1 is more severe and the child requires insulin injections balanced with carefully controlled amounts of carbohydrate in the diet.
2. Type 2 is less severe as the pancreas usually retains some insulin-producing function; it can be managed with oral drugs and dietary measures.

Type 1 is more common in children and, traditionally, type 2 diabetes affected middle-aged people. As obesity levels rise in children, however, there has also been an increase in type 2 diabetes in younger age groups.

If left untreated, the use of fats as an alternative energy source leads to disturbances in the amount of ketones (acid balance) in the body and can result in diabetic coma. A child who is being treated for diabetes needs regular meals to balance the insulin administered. If there is too much insulin in the bloodstream, the child may feel weak, sweaty and disorientated and this is known as hypoglycaemia (low glucose levels). Children whose diabetes is well balanced should not experience 'hypos' often, but illness or extra exercise may unbalance the condition. Children need to recognize how they are feeling and treat a hypoglycaemic episode promptly by eating some glucose.

Diphtheria A bacterial disease that affects the respiratory tract and produces powerful toxins that can be life threatening. Routine immunization has made diphtheria rare in many parts of the world. Cases still occur if immunization levels drop.

Discourse A set of interconnected ideas or beliefs that draws on its own particular knowledge base. Individual groups will have different views of reality and build discourses accordingly. As people share their discourses this not only reflects their beliefs but also actively builds on this.

Eczema A common form of dermatitis or inflammation of the upper layers of the skin. The term eczema is applied broadly to a range of persistent or recurring skin rashes characterized by redness, swollen skin, irritation and dryness, with blistering skin that oozes, forms crusts, flakes and bleeds. Infants with eczema often develop an irritant red rash on their cheeks, which may spread across the body. Toddlers often have eczema patches behind their knees, in the bends of their arms, and/or on their wrists, ankles and neck. Treatment includes avoiding allergens such as perfumes, moisturizing the skin well, washing with non-soap-based cleansers such as aqueous cream, and following medical advice.

Epidemiologists Scientists who study the factors affecting health and disease in individuals and in populations. By monitoring the spread and control of disease, epidemiologists provide the scientific evidence to support decisions in public health medicine.

Foundling home Orphanage.

Hepatitis Inflammation of the liver. There are a number of types of hepatitis and a wide range of causes. Hepatitis A occurs when sanitation is poor; it may be transmitted through contaminated food or drink. The child may develop jaundice (yellow discoloration of the skin), fever, tiredness, abdominal pain and sickness. Hepatitis B and C are transmitted through infected blood products and other bodily fluids. All these disease are serious, and prevention of hepatitis A and B is achieved through immunization for people who may be at risk. There are also other recognized hepatitis viruses.

Hypoglycaemic – see diabetes

Hypothyroidism A condition that occurs due to a congenital lack of thyroid hormone, which leads to learning disability if left untreated.

Longitudinal study Research that involves the observation or examination of the same group of subjects over time with respect to one or more study variables.

Malaria A parasitic tropical disease, transmitted by mosquito bites, causing fever, shivering, joint pains and vomiting. At least 300 million acute cases of malaria occur worldwide each year, resulting in more than one million deaths annually. Children under 5 years old are most affected and the majority of cases occur in sub-Saharan Africa. Contact with mosquitoes should be avoided by sleeping under chemically treated mosquito nets, and preventive anti-malarial drugs should be taken. Such drugs are important for travellers but are less practical for long-term use by the indigenous population. The aim is to eradicate mosquitoes from malarial areas and scientists are working to develop a vaccine.

Measles A highly infectious viral disease characterized by cold symptoms, a red rash, high temperature. Small red spots with white centres on the inside of the mouth (Koplik's spots) are an early sign. Measles can have severe complications such as pneumonia, middle ear infections and inflammation of the brain (encephalitis). Measles is a common cause of mortality in malnourished children. Prevention is by immunization.

Meningitis The inflammation of the membranes that cover the brain and spinal cord, sometimes accompanied by septicaemia (blood poisoning). There are two main types of meningitis: the milder viral type and the more serious bacterial type, which can be life threatening and requires prompt emergency treatment. Meningitis is very serious so it is important to be able to recognize its signs and symptoms; the Meningitis Research Foundation lists these at http://www.meningitis.org/ (accessed July 2006).

Obesity This occurs when weight gain has increased so much that it is a risk to health. In adults, obesity is defined by assessing a person's body mass index (BMI), which is calculated by dividing their weight in kilograms by the square of their height in metres. In children, obesity is sometimes defined using growth (centile) charts (see above) or by calculating BMI. Childhood obesity has reached epidemic levels in some countries and 22 million children under 5 are estimated to be overweight worldwide.

Phenylketonuria (PKU) An inherited disorder of protein metabolism that causes a rise in the levels of the amino acid phenylalanine in the bloodstream. Untreated this would lead to damage of the central nervous system and intellectual disability. Screening of newborn infants is carried out by testing a spot of blood for phenylalanine (Guthrie test) and enables the condition to be detected before any damage occurs. Treatment is with a phenylalanine-free diet.

Polio (poliomyelitis) A highly infectious disease caused by a virus. It infects the central nervous system and can cause paralysis. The virus enters the body through the nose or mouth and multiplies in the digestive tract. The symptoms are fever, fatigue, headache, vomiting, stiffness in the neck and pain in the limbs. Since the development of a polio vaccine the incidence of the disease has been greatly reduced but there are still countries, particularly in Africa and India, where polio is widespread. Polio particularly affects young children and there is a global eradication programme in place.

Post-traumatic stress disorder (PTSD) An anxiety disorder caused by a serious or frightening event such as abuse or violence. Refugee or asylum-seeking children may suffer PTSD, which may be characterized by a number of symptoms such as recurrent images of the event, nightmares, poor concentration, guilt, anger, or emotional and behavioural problems. Skilled counselling may be required to help the young child come to terms with events.

Pre-term birth Refers to the delivery of a baby before 37 weeks of completed gestation. A full-term pregnancy lasts 40 weeks. Very pre-term infants are born before 32 weeks of gestation; extremely pre-term infants are born before 28 weeks.

Primary health care team (PHCT) This is the health team in the UK which is likely to have the first contact with the patient. The team includes the general practitioner (GP), the midwife, the health visitor, the community nurse and the community psychiatric nurse (CPN). The team is able to refer young children to specialist services such as the dietitian, the speech and language therapist, the paediatrician and to social services.

Puerperal psychosis A rare and severe form of post-natal illness when the mother loses touch with reality and suffers delusions. Puerperal psychosis is an acute, severe mental illness, usually beginning a few days after childbirth. It is a psychiatric emergency, which usually requires hospital care.

Randomized controlled trial (RCT) A research design that involves randomly allocating research subjects into either an experimental group that receives an intervention or to a control group that receives no intervention, and then comparing the two. Medical scientists consider RCTs to offer the most reliable form of scientific evidence because it is the most effective design for eliminating the variety of biases that regularly compromise the validity of medical research. Increasingly, medical scientists are also recognizing the importance of qualitative research, which enables concepts to be developed to aid understanding of the social phenomena that affect health and well-being in natural (rather than experimental) settings, giving due emphasis to the meanings, experiences and views of participants.

Sickle cell disorder A hereditary blood disorder mainly affecting people of African, Indian and Mediterranean descent. In sickle cell disorders there is an abnormality of the haemoglobin in the red blood cells that carry oxygen to the various organs of the body. After the release of oxygen some of the red blood cells assume an abnormal sickle shape, causing the cells to clump together. This may make their passage through smaller blood vessels difficult, leading to pain and inflammatory reactions as the small blood vessels block. Some children are mildly affected but others may experience a more severe range of symptoms that will need ongoing medical treatment and understanding at home and school.

Significant harm The UK Children Act 1989 introduced the concept of significant harm as the threshold that justifies compulsory intervention in family life in the interests of the child. There are no absolute criteria on which to rely when judging what constitutes significant harm. Consideration of the severity of ill-treatment may include the degree and extent of physical harm, the duration and frequency of abuse and neglect, the extent of premeditation, and the degree of threat or coercion. The legal definition of significant harm was amended in the Children Act 2004 to include 'the harm that children see or suffer by seeing or hearing the ill-treatment of another – particularly in the home', thus recognizing domestic violence as being harmful to children.

Social capital Represents the degree of social cohesion in communities. It refers to the processes between people that establish networks, norms and social trust, and facilitate coordination and cooperation for mutual benefit.

Socio-economic status (SES) The National Statistics Office categorizes the population according to occupations. Epidemiologists find these classifications helpful in investigating which disease patterns affect particular groups. The classifications used in the UK are listed below. There is a fine grading of health risks (social gradients) across all the social groups, with children in higher socio-economic groups having less overall risk of ill health than those in poorer socio-economic groups. (There is some evidence of occasional 'reverse social gradients', with children in higher socio-economic groups being more at risk from some allergic conditions, for example.) The list below presents the National Statistics Office's socio-economic classifications.

1.   Higher managerial and professional occupations
   1.1   Large employers and higher managerial occupations
   1.2   Higher professional occupations
2.   Lower managerial and professional occupations
3.   Intermediate occupations
4.   Small employers and own account workers
5.   Lower supervisory and technical occupations
6.   Semi-routine occupations
7.   Routine occupations
8.   Never worked and long-term unemployed

Spina bifida A neural tube (the spine) defect, which is thought to be prevented by taking folic acid in pregnancy. The vertebrae (backbone) usually provide a protective tube of bones with the nerves (spinal cord) running down the middle. In spina bifida, the bones do not close round the spinal cord and the nerves can bulge out on the unborn baby's back and become damaged. This happens very early on in pregnancy, often before the woman even knows she is pregnant. There are three types of spina bifida.

1.   *Spina bifida occulta* (hidden form) where there is a slight defect in the vertebrae, which usually causes no problem. The area is sometimes marked by a tuft of hair or a dimple on the back.
2.   *Spina bifida cystica* where there is a fluid-filled cyst on the back containing meninges (membranes that cover the spine). The spinal cord is not usually damaged so there is little or no disability.
3.   *Myelomeningocele* – this is the most serious form, where the cyst on the back contains spinal cord as well as fluid and meninges. This nerve damage can lead to paralysis below the lesion, and muscular weakness or paralysis of the bowel and bladder. Most children also have hydrocephalus, which is a build-up of spinal fluid in the brain. Treatment is to close the lesion on the back and drain the hydrocephalus.

Systematic review A research process in which all the available evidence about a particular topic is examined. The strength of a systematic review is that the quality of the research is examined and a synthesis made of the relevant studies.

Tetanus A serious and often fatal disease caused by bacteria that live in the soil and in the digestive tract and faeces of many animals, such as dogs, horses, sheep and guinea pigs, and birds such as chickens. Agricultural workers may also harbour the bacteria. Common symptoms are muscle spasms in the jaw (hence the common name lockjaw), difficulty in swallowing, and muscle stiffness and spasm in other parts of the body. Infection can be prevented by immunization.

Theory Presents a systematic way of understanding events or situations. A theory consists of a set of concepts, definitions or propositions that explain or predict.

Tuberculosis (TB) A bacterial infectious disease that commonly affects the respiratory tract but can also affect other organs. Some infected people will show no symptoms but others will develop a chronic cough, spit up blood, and suffer weight loss and night sweats. Treatment is with combinations of antibiotics, and prevention is by immunization with the BCG vaccine. Tuberculosis still presents a major risk, particularly to ethnic groups from areas where the disease is prevalent. The BCG vaccine should be given to high-risk infants and young children.

Vaccine A preparation that contains an antigen consisting of weakened (attenuated) or killed organisms that would otherwise cause a specific disease. A vaccine, under appropriate conditions, will trigger an immune response in the individual, offering them protection without actually having the disease.

Whooping cough (pertussis) A serious bacterial infection that affects the respiratory tract. The disease begins with a cold and a mild cough. The cough develops into frequent spasmodic coughing bouts, which continue until no air is left in the lungs. This is followed by a deep intake of breath that produces a 'whooping' sound as air is gulped into the lungs. The debilitating disease may last for several weeks and is particularly dangerous for babies under the age of 1 year who are unable to 'whoop' air into their lungs. Prevention is by immunization.

References

Abrahams, C. (1994) *The Hidden Victims: Children and Domestic Violence*. London: NCH Action for Children.

Acheson, D. (1998) *Independent Inquiry into Inequalities in Health Report*. London: The Stationery Office.

Ainsworth, M., Blehar, M., Waters, E. and Wall, S. (1978) *Patterns of Attachment*. Hillsdale, NJ: Erlbaum.

Alanen, L. (2001) Exploration in generational analysis, in L. Alanen and B. Mayall (eds) *Conceptualising Child–Adult Relations*. London: Routledge Falmer.

Alderson, P. (1993) *Children's Consent to Surgery*. Buckingham: Open University Press.

Alderson, P. (1995) *Listening to Children. Children, Ethics and Social Research*. London: Barnardo's.

Alderson, P. (2005) Children's rights, in H. Penn (ed.) *Understanding Early Childhood: Issues and Controversies*. Maidenhead: OU Press/Hillsdale, NJ: McGraw-Hill Education Associates.

Alderson, P. and Montgomery, J. (1996) *Health Care Choices. Making Decisions with Children*. London: IPPR.

Alderson, P., Hawthorne, J. and Killen, M. (2005) The participation rights of premature babies, *International Journal of Children's Rights*, 13: 31–50.

Aldridge, J. and Becker, S. (1993) *Children Who Care – Inside the World of Young Carers*. Loughborough: Loughborough University.

Aldridge, J. and Becker, S. (2003) *Children Caring for Parents with Mental Illness: Perspectives of Young Carers*. Loughborough: Loughborough University Young Carers Research Group.

Anders, T., Goodlin-Jones, B. and Sadeh, A. (2000) Sleep disorders, in C.H.J. Zeanah (ed.) *Handbook of Infant Mental Health* (2nd edn). New York: Guilford Press.

Andrew, L. (2004) Beakers for bottles – a health visitor oral health campaign, *Community Practitioner*, 77(1).

Ariès, P. (1962) *Centuries of Childhood*. London: Jonathan Cape.

ASH (Action on Smoking and Health) (2001) *The Impact of Passive Smoking on Children. Passive Smoking – A Summary of the Evidence*. London: ASH.

ASH (Action on Smoking and Health) (2005) Factsheet no. 8, at http://www.ash.org.uk/html/factsheets/html/fact08.html, accessed 2 March 2006.

Attree, P. (2004) Growing up in disadvantage: a systematic review of qualitative evidence, *Child: Care, Health and Development*, 30(6): 679–89.

Audit Commission (1999) *Children in Mind: Child and Adolescent Based Mental Health Services*. London: Audit Commission.

Ballard, C.G., Davis, R., Cullen, P.C. and Mohan, R.N. (1994) Prevalence of post-natal psychiatric morbidity in mothers and fathers, *British Journal of Psychiatry*, 164(6): 782–8.

Barker, D. (1995) Fetal origins of coronary heart disease. *British Medical Journal*, 311: 171–4.

Barker, D.J.P. and Osmond, C. (1987) Infant mortality, childhood nutrition and ischaemic heart disease in England and Wales, *Lancet*, 1: 1077–81.

Barlow, J. and Parsons, J. (2004) Group-based parent-training programmes for improving emotional and behavioural health adjustment in 0–3 year old children (Cochrane Review), *In the Cochrane Library*, 2, Chichester: John Wiley & Sons.

Barlow, J. and Stewart-Brown, S. (2001) Understanding parenting programmes: parents' views, *Primary Health Care Research and Development*, 2: 117–30.

Barlow, J., Coren, E. and Stewart-Brown, S. (2002) Meta-analysis of parenting programmes in improving maternal psychosocial health, *British Journal of General Practice*, 52, 223–33.

Barnes, J. and Lagevardi-Freude, A. (2003) *From Pregnancy to Early Childhood*. London: Mental Health Foundation.

Barrett, H. (2006) *Attachment and the Perils of Parenting*. London: NFPI.

Bartlett, S. (2002) The problem of children's injuries in low-income countries: a review, *Health Policy and Planning*, 17(1): 1–13.

Batchelor, J. and Kerslake, A. (1990) *Failure to Find Failure to Thrive: The Case for Improved Screening, Prevention and Treatment in Primary Care*. London: Whiting & Birch.

Bavolek, S. (1990) Parenting: theory, policy and practice. Research and validation report of the nurturing programmes. Wisconsin, USA: Eau Claire, Family Development Resources, Inc.

Beebe, B. (2000) Constructing mother–infant distress: the microsynchrony of maternal impingement and infant avoidance in the face-to-face encounter, *Psychoanalytic Inquiry*, 20(3): 421–40.

Belsky, J. and Kelly, J. (1994) *The Transition to Parenthood: How a First Child Changes a Marriage*. London: Vermillion.

Belsky, J., Melhuish, T., Barnes, J., Leyland, A. and Romaniuk, H. (2006) Effects of Sure Start local programmes on children and families: early findngs from a quasi-experimental, cross sectional study. *British Medical Journal*, doi:10.1136/bmj.38853.451748.2F (published 16 June 2006).

Benasich, A., Curtis, S. and Tallal, P. (1993) Language, learning and behavioural disturbances in childhood: a longitudinal perspective, *Journal of the American Academy of Child Psychiatry*, 31(3): 585–94.

Benoit, D. (2000) Feeding disorders, failure to thrive and obesity, in C.H.J. Zeanah (ed.) *Handbook of Infant Mental Health* (2nd edn). New York: Guilford Press.

Bibace, R. and Walsh, M. (1980) Development of children's concepts of illness, *Pediatrics*, 66: 912–17.

Bion, W. (1962) *Learning from Experience*. London: Heinemann.

Black, R., Morris, S. and Bryce, J. (2003) Where and why are 10 million children dying every year? *Lancet*, 361: 2226–34.

Blackburn, C., Bonas, S., Spencer, N., Coe, C., Dolan, A. and Moy, R. (2005) Parental smoking and passive smoking in infants: fathers matter too, *Health Education Research*, 20(2): 185–94.

Blair, M., Stewart-Brown, S., Waterston, T. and Crowther, R. (2003) *Child Public Health*. Oxford: Oxford University Press.

Blair, P., Fleming, P., Bensley, D., Smith, I., Bacon, C., Taylor, E., Berry, J., Golding, J. and Tripp, J. (1996) Smoking and the sudden infant death results from 1993–95 case-control study for confidential inquiry into stillbirths and deaths in infancy, *British Medical Journal*, 313: 195–8.

Bluebond-Langner, M. (1978) *The Private Worlds of Dying Children*. New Jersey: Princeton University Press.

BMA (British Medical Association) (1999) *Growing up in Britain: Ensuring a Healthy Future for our Children. A Study of 0–5 Year Olds*. London: BMA.

BMA (British Medical Association) (2001) *Injury Prevention*. London: BMA.

BMA (British Medical Association) (2005) *Preventing Childhood Obesity*. London: BMA.

BMA (British Medical Association) (2006) *Child and Adolescent Mental Health: A Guide for Healthcare Professionals*. London: BMA.

Boddy, J. and Skuse, D. (1994) Annotation: the process of parenting in failure to thrive, *Journal of Psychology and Psychiatry*, 35(3): 401–24.

Bone, M. and Meltzer, H. (1989) The prevalence of disability among children. OPCS surveys of disability in Great Britain, Report 3. London: HMSO.

Bourdieu, P. (1986) The forms of capital, in J.G. Richardson (ed.) *Handbook of Theory and Research for the Sociology of Education*. New York: Greenwood Press.

Bowlby, J. (1969) *Attachment and Loss, Vol. 1: Attachment*. New York: Basic Books.

Bowlby, J. (1973) *Attachment and Loss, Vol. 2: Separation Anger and Anxiety*. New York: Basic Books.

Bowlby, J. (1980) *Attachment and Loss, Vol. 3: Loss, Sadness and Depression*. New York: Basic Books.

Bowlby, J. (1988) *A Secure Base*. London: Routledge.

BPS (British Psychological Society) (1991) *Code of Conduct, Ethical Principles and Guidelines*. Leicester: BPS.

Bradshaw, J. (ed.) (2002) *The Well-being of Children*. London: Save the Children.

Bradshaw, J. (2003) Poor children, *Children and Society*, 17: 162–72.

Brander, N. (2004) My story: bog standards in schools, BBC Action Network, at http://www.bbc.co.uk/dna/actionnetwork/A7812254, accessed 30 December 2005.

Brazelton, T.B. (1995) Neonatal behavioural assessment scale; clinics *in Development Medicine*, 50, London: Blackwell.

Brazelton, T.B. and Cramer, B. (1991) *The Earliest Relationship. Parents, Infants and the Drama of Early Attachment*. London: Karnac.

Brazelton, T.B., Koslowski, B. and Main, M. (1974) The origins of reciprocity. The early mother–infant interaction, in M. Lewis and L. Rosenblum (eds) *The Effects of the Infant on its Caregiver*. New York: John Wiley, pp. 49–76.

Breggin, P. (1998) *Talking Back to Ritalin: What Doctors Aren't Telling You About Stimulants for Children*. Monroe: Common Courage Press.

Breggin, P. and Breggin, G. (1995) The hazards of treating 'attention deficit hyperactivity disorder' with methylphenidate (Ritalin), *Journal of College Student Psychotherapy*, 10(2): 55–72.

Briggs, C. and Cutright, P. (1994) Structural and cultural determinants of child homicide: a cross-national analysis, *Violence and Victims*, 9(1): 3–16.

Bronfenbrenner, U. (1979) *The Ecology of Human Development: Experiments by Nature and Design*. Cambridge, MA: Harvard University Press.

Bronfenbrenner, U. (ed.) (2005) *Making Human Beings Human: Biological Perspectives on Human Development*. London: Sage.

Brown, L. (2003) Mainstream or margin? The current use of family group conferences in child welfare practice in the UK, *Child and Family Social Work*, 8(4): 331–40.

Brunner, E. (1997) Socioeconomic determinants of health: stress and the biology of inequality, *British Medical Journal*, 314: 1472, 17 May.

Bryce, J., Boschi-Pinto, C., Shibuya, K. and Black, R. (2005) WHO estimates the causes of death in children, *Lancet*, 365: 1147–52.

Bull, J., McCormick, G., Swann, C. and Mulvihill, C. (2004) *Ante- and Post-natal Home-visiting Programmes: A Review of Reviews*. London: Health Development Agency.

Bullen, P. and Onyx, J. (1999) Social capital: family support services and neighbourhood and community centres in New South Wales, Concord West, NSW, at www.mapl.com.au/A12.htm, accessed 23 March 2006.

Burridge, R. and Ormandy, D. (eds) (1993) *Unhealthy Housing: Research, Remedies and Reform*. London: E & FN Spon.

Butler, C., van der Linden, M., MacMillan, H.L. and van der Wouden, J.C. (2003) Should children be screened to undergo early treatment for otitis media with effusion? A systematic review of randomized trials, *Child: Care, Health and Development*, 29(6): 425–32.

Butler, D. and Borland, R. (1998) Public education projects in skin cancer prevention: child care, school and college based, *Clinical Dermatology*, 16: 447–59.

Cameron, D. and Jones, I. (1985) An epidemiological and sociological analysis of alcohol, tobacco and other drugs of solace, *Community Medicine*, 7: 18–29.

Campbell, C. (1999) *Social Capital and Health*. London: Health Education Authority.

Campbell, S. (1995) Behaviour problems in pre-school children: a review of recent research, *Journal of Child Psychology and Psychiatry*, 36: 113–49.

Caplan, H., Cogill, S., Alexandra, H., Robson, K., Katz, R. and Kumar, R. (1989) Maternal depression and the emotional development of the child, *British Journal of Psychiatry*, 154: 818–22.

Carlson, C., Cicchietti, D., Barnett, D. and Braunwald, K. (1989) Disorganised/disorientated attachment relationship in maltreated infants, *Child Development*, 25: 525–31.

Carr, S. (2005) Peer educators – contributing to accident prevention, *Community Practitioner*, 78(5), May.

Caspi, A., Moffitt, T., Newman, D. and Silva, P. (1996) Behavioural observations at age 3 years predict adult psychiatric disorders, *Archives of General Psychiatry*, 53: 1033–9.

Cater, S. and Coleman, L. (2006) *Planned Teenage Pregnancy: Views and Experiences of Young People from Poor and Disadvantaged Backgrounds*. Bristol: Policy Press/Joseph Rowntree Foundation.

Central Statistics Office (1995) *Social Trends*. London: HMSO.

Chalmers, B. and Meyer, D. (1994) Preparing women for pregnancy and parenthood: a cross-cultural study, *International Journal of Prenatal and Perinatal Psychology and Medicine*, 6(1): 27–42.

Charlton, T., Abrahams, M. and Jones, K. (1995) Prevalence rates of emotional and behavioural disorder among nursery class children in St Helena, South Atlantic: an epidemiological study, *Journal of Social Behaviour and Personality*, 10: 273–80.

Chieftaz, P., Stavrakakis, G. and Lester, E. (1989) Studies of the affective state in bereaved children, *Canadian Journal of Psychiatry*, 34: 688–92.

Cherlin, A. (1992) *Marriage, Divorce, Remarriage*. Cambridge, MA: Harvard University Press.

Christakis; D., Zimmerman, F., Di Giuseppe, D. and McCarty, C. (2004) Early television exposure and subsequent attentional problems in children, *Child: Care, Health and Development*, 30(5): 559–60.

Christensen, P. and James, A. (2000) *Research with Children: Perspectives and Practices*. London: Falmer.

Chugani, H., Behen, M., Muzik, O., Juhasz, C., Nagy, F. and Chugani, D. (2001) Local brain functional activity following early deprivation: a study of post institutionalised Romanian orphans, *Neuroimage*, 14: 1290–301.

Clark, A. and Moss, P. (2001) *Listening to Young Children. The Mosaic Approach*. London: National Children's Bureau.

Clarke-Stewart, A. (1989) Infant day care: maligned or malignant? *American Psychologist*, 44: 266–73.

Cleaver, H., Unell, I. and Algate, J. (1999) *Children's Needs – Parenting Capacity. The*

Impact of Parental Mental Illness, Problem Alcohol and Drug Use, and Domestic Violence on Children's Development. London: The Stationery Office.

Clulow, C. (1991) Partners becoming parents: a question of difference, *Infant Mental Health Journal*, 12(3): 256–65.

Cohen, N., Menna, R., Vallance, D., Barwick, M., Im, N. and Horodezky, N. (1998) Language, social cognitive processing and behavioural characteristics of psychiatrically disturbed children with previously identified and unsuspected language impairment, *Journal of Child Psychology and Psychiatry*, 39(6): 853–64.

Cohen, N., Muir, E., Parker, C., Brown, M., Lojkasek, M. and Muir, R. (1999) Watch, wait and wonder: testing the effectiveness of a new approach to mother–infant psychotherapy, *Infant Mental Health Journal*, 20(4): 429–51.

Cohen, S., Tyrrell, D. and Smith, A. (1991) Psychological stress and susceptibility to the common cold, *New England Journal of Medicine*, 325(9): 606–12.

Collins, C. and Williams, D. (1999) Segregation and mortality: the deadly effects of racism? *Sociological Forum*, 14: 495–523.

Combes, G. and Schonveld, A. (1992) *Life Will Never be the Same Again*. London: Health Education Authority.

Cooper, P. (2001) The challenges of antenatal prevention of maternal depression, in *Postnatal Depression and Maternal Mental Health: A Public Health Priority*. CPHVA Conference Proceedings 9–12. London: CPHVA.

Coote, A. (2005) But does Sure Start work? *Guardian*, 19 January.

Corsaro, W.A. (2005) *The Sociology of Childhood*. Sage Publications.

Cousins, W. and Wells, K. (2005) 'One more for my baby': foetal alcohol syndrome and its implications for social workers, *Child Care in Practice*, 11(3): 375–83.

Cowan, C. and Cowan, P. (1992) *When Partners Become Parents*. London: Erlbaum.

Cowan, P. and Heatherington, M. (1991) *Family Transitions*. Lawrence Erlbaum.

Cox, J. (1994) Origins and development of the 10-item Edinburgh Post-Natal Depression Scale, in J. Cox and J. Holden (eds) *Perinatal Psychiatry Use and Misuse of the, 10-Item Edinburgh Post-Natal Depression Scale*. London: Gaskell, pp. 115–24.

Crittenden, P. (1988) *Care Index Manual* (3rd Edn). Miami, Fl. Unpublished manuscript available from the author.

Crittenden, P. (1997) *Care-Index Manual*. Miami: Family Relations Institute.

Crittenden, P. (1998) Relationships at risk, in J. Belsky and T. Nezworski (eds) *Clinical Implications of Attachment*. Hillsdale, NJ: Lawrence Erlbaum Associates, pp. 136–76.

Crittenden, P.M. and DiLalla, D.L. (1988). Compulsive compliance: the development of an inhibitory coping strategy in infancy, *Journal of Abnormal Child Psychology*, 16(5), October: 585–99.

Crockenburg, S. and Leerkes, E. (2000) Infant social and emotional development in family context, in C.H. Zeanah Jr (ed.) *Handbook of Infant Mental Health* (2nd edn). New York: Guilford Press.

Croghan, E. (2002) A survey of drinking and toilet facilities in local state schools, *British Journal of Community Nursing*, 7(2).

Currie C., Roberts, C., Morgan, A., Smith, R., Settertobulte, W., Samdal, O. and Barnekow Rasmussen, V. (eds) (2004) *Young People's Health in Context: International Report from the HBSC 2001/02 Survey*. WHO Policy Series: *Health Policy for Children and Adolescents*, Issue 4. Copenhagen: WHO Regional Office for Europe.

Davis, J. and Watson, N. (2000) Disabled children's rights in everyday life: problematising notions of competency and promoting self-empowerment, *International Journal of Children's Rights*, 8(3): 211–28.

Day, A. (2001) The challenges of detecting and managing PND in a multicultural society, in *Postnatal Depression and Maternal Mental Health: A Public Health Priority*. CPHVA Conference Proceedings 24–28. London: CPHVA.

Dearden, C. and Becker, S. (2004) *Young Carers in the UK: The 2004 Report*. London: The Children's Society.

Deleuze, G. and Guattari, F. (1987) *A Thousand Plateaus: Capitalism and Schizophrenia*. London: Athlone Press.

DfES (Department for Education and Skills) (2000) *Summary of the Education Regulations (Nutritional Standards for School Lunches)*. Nottinghamshire: DfES.

DfES (Department for Education and Skills) (2003). *Every Child Matters*. London: The Stationery Office.

DfES (Department for Education and Skills) (2004) *Every Child Matters: Change for Children*. London: The Stationery Office.

Doak, C., Adair, L., Bentley, M., Monteiro, C. and Popkin, B. (2005) The dual burden household and the nutrition transition paradox, *International Journal of Obesity*, 29: 129–36.

Dobash, R.E. and Dobash, R.P. (1980) *Women, Violence and Social Change*. London: Routledge.

DoH (Department of Health) (1997) *Local Authority Circular LAC(97) 15 Family Law Act 1996 Part IV. Family Homes and Domestic Violence*. London: Department of Health.

DoH (Department of Health) (1998) *The Health of Young People 1995–97*. London: The Stationery Office.

DoH (Department of Health) (2000) *Protecting Children, Supporting Parents: A Consultation Document on the Physical Punishment of Children*. London: Department of Health.

DoH (Department of Health) (2002) *National School Fruit Scheme. Information for Schools*. London: DoH.

DoH (Department of Health) (2004a) *Choosing Health, Making Healthier Choices Easier*. London: The Stationery Office.

DoH (Department of Health) (2004b) *National Service Framework for Children, Young People and Maternity Services*. London: DoH.

DoH/DfES (Department of Health/Department for Education and Skills) (2004)

National Service Framework for Children, Young People and Maternity Services. London: The Stationery Office.

DoH/DfES/HO (Department of Health, Department for Education and Employment, and Home Office) (2000) *Framework for the Assessment of Children in Need and their Families.* London: The Stationery Office.

Doherty, W. and Whitehead, D. (1986) The social dynamics of cigarette smoking: a family systems perspective, *Family Process*, 25: 453–9.

Dominey, N. and Radford, L. (1996) *Domestic Violence in Surrey: Towards an Effective Inter-agency Response.* London: Roehampton Institute/Surrey Social Services.

Dorling, D. (1995) *A New Social Atlas of Britain.* Chichester: Wiley.

Douglas, H. and Ginty, M. (2001) The Solihull Approach: evaluation of changes in the practice of health visitors, *Community Practitioner*, 74: 222–4.

Dowdney, L. (2000) Annotation: childhood bereavement following parental death, *Journal of Child Psychology and Psychiatry*, 41(7): 819–30.

Doyle, W. (1994) Nutritional status of school children in an inner city area, *Archives of Disease in Childhood*, 70(5): 376–81.

DSS (Department of Social Security) (1999a) *Households Below Average Income: A Statistical Analysis 1979–1995/96.* London: HMSO.

DSS (Department of Social Security) (1999b) *Opportunity For All: Tackling Poverty and Social Exclusion, The First Annual Report.* London: HMSO.

Duncan, G., Brooks-Gunn, J. and Klebanov, P. (1994) Economic deprivation and early childhood development, *Child Development*, 65(2): 296–318.

Dunn, J. (1983) Sibling relationships in early childhood, *Child Development*, 54: 787–811.

Dunn, J. (1988) *The Beginnings of Social Understanding.* Oxford: Blackwell.

Dunn, J. (2005) Naturalistic observations of children and their families, in S. Greene and D. Hogan *Researching Children's Experience.* London: Sage.

Dunn, J. and Deater-Deckard, K. (2001) *Children's Views on their Changing Families.* York: Joseph Rowntree Foundation.

Dwivedi, K.N. and Harper, P.B. (2004) *Promoting the Emotional Well-being of Children and Adolescents and Preventing their Ill Health.* London: Jessica Kingsley.

Dwyer, T. and Ponsonby, A. (1996) The decline of SIDS: a success story for epidemiology, *Epidemiology*, 7: 323–5.

Eammons, K. (2001) A randomised control trial to reduce passive smoke exposure in low-income households with young children, *Pediatrics*, 108(1): 18–24.

Edwards, J., Franklin, S., Hirsch, E., Price, F. and Strathern, M. (1993) *Technologies of Procreation.* London: Routledge.

Efron, D. (2005) ADHD: the need for system change (editorial comment), *Journal of Paediatric Child Health*, 41: 621–2.

Eiser, C. (1989) Children's concepts of illness: towards an alternative to the stage approach, *Psychology and Health*, 3: 93–101.

Eiser, C. (1993) *Growing Up with a Chronic Disease.* London: Jessica Kingsley Publications.

Elfer, P. (2005) Observation matters, in L. Abbott and A. Langston (eds) *Birth to Three Matters: Supporting the Framework for Effective Practice*. Maidenhead: OUP/ McGraw-Hill.

Elfer, P., Goldschmied, E. and Selleck, D. (2003) *Key Persons in the Nursery: Building Relationships for Quality Provision*. London: Fulton.

Elliot, M. (1988) *Keeping Safe*. Sevenoaks: Hodder & Stoughton.

Ennew, J. (1986) *The Sexual Exploitation of Children*. Cambridge: Polity Press.

Evangelou, M. and Sylva, K. (2002) *The Effects of PEEP on Children's Development: Progress Towards Effective Early Childhood Interventions*. London: DfES.

Every Child Matlers (2005) Factsheet Common Assessment Framework Dfes: London www.everychildmatters.gov.uk/_files/3576A50122D70628E7C53972 803022BE. doc, accessed June 2006.

Expert Maternity Group (1993) *Changing Childbirth (Parts 1 and 2)*. London: HMSO.

Falicov, C. (1995) Training to think culturally: a multidimensional comparative framework, *Family Process*, 134(4): 373–88.

Fantuzzo, R., Boruch, A., Beriama, A. and Atkins, M. (1997) Domestic violence and children: prevalence and risk in five major US cities, *Journal of the American Academy of Child and Adolescent Psychiatry*, 36: 116–22.

Fazel, M. and Stein, A. (2003) Mental health of refugee children: comparative study, *British Medical Journal*, 327, 19 July.

Fitzpatrick, M. (2005) Why can't the *Daily Mail* eat humble pie over MMR? *British Medical Journal*, 33, November: 1148.

Fogelman, K. and Manor, O. (1988) Smoking in pregnancy and development into early adulthood, *British Medical Journal*, 297: 1233–6.

Foley, P., Roche, J. and Tucker, S. (eds) (2001) *Children in Society. Contemporary Theory Policy and Practice*. Hampshire: Palgrave.

Fonagy, P., Redfe, S. and Charman, T. (1997) The relationship between belief desire reasoning and a projective measure of attachment security (SAT), *British Journal of Developmental Psychology*, 15: 51–61.

Fonagy, P., Steele, M., Steele, H., Higgitt, A. and Target, M. (1994) Theory and practice of resilience, *Journal of Child Psychology and Psychiatry and Allied Disciplines*, 35: 231–57.

Fonagy, P., Gergely G., Jurist, E. and Target, M. (2004) *Affect Regulation, Mentalization and the Development of the Self*. London: Karnac.

Foster, K., Lader, D. and Cheesborough, S. (1997) *Infant Feeding*. London: HMSO.

Foster, G., Makufa, C., Drew, R. and Kralovec, E. (1997) Factors leading to the establishment of child headed households: the case of Zimbabwe, *Health Transition Review*, 7, supp. 2: 152–66.

Frank, J., Tatum, C. and Tucker, S. (1999) *On Small Shoulders: Learning from the Experiences of Former Young Carers*. London: The Children's Society.

Franklin, B. (ed.) (2002) *The New Handbook of Children's Rights*. London: Routledge.

Gallup Organization (1995) *Disciplining Children in America: A Gallup Poll Report.* Princeton, NJ: Gallup.

Gardner, D. (1956) *The Education of Young Children.* London: Methuen.

Gaskin, I. (1987) *Babies, Breastfeeding and Bonding.* South Hadley, MA: Bergin & Garvey.

Gatrad, A.R., Brown, E., Notta, H. and Sheikh, A. (2003) Palliative care needs of minorities, *British Medical Journal*, 327: 176–7.

Gershoff, E. (1997) *The Short- and Long-term Effects of Corporal Punishment on Children: A Meta-analytical Review.* Austin, TX: University of Texas.

Gibbons, J., Gallagher, B., Bell, C. and Gordon, D. (1995) *Development After Physical Abuse in Early Childhood.* London: HMSO.

Gill, T. (1992) *Parenting under Pressure.* Cardiff: Barnardo's.

Gittens, D. (1998) *The Child in Question.* London: Macmillan.

Glanz, K., Rimer, B.K. and Lewis, F.M. (2002). *Health Behavior and Health Education. Theory, Research and Practice.* San Francisco: Wiley & Sons.

Glass, N. (1999) Sure Start: the development of an early intervention programme for young children in the United Kingdom, *Children and Society*, 13: 257–64.

Glass, N. (2005) Surely some mistake? *Guardian*, 5 January.

Glew, G. (2005) Bullying, psychosocial adjustment and academic performance in elementary school, *Archives of Pediatric and Adolescent Medicine*, 159: 1026–31.

Glover, V. (2001) Ante-natal and post-natal mood: the effects on the fetus and child, *Post-natal Depression and Maternal Mental Health: A Public Health Priority.* London: CPHVA Conference Proceedings.

Glover, V. and O'Connor, T. (2002) Effects of antenatal stress and anxiety implications for development and psychiatry, *British Journal of Psychiatry*, 180(5): 389–95.

Golombok, S. (2000) *Parenting. What Really Counts.* London: Routledge.

Golombok, S. and Tasker, F. (1994) Children in lesbian and gay families: theories and evidence, *Annual Review of Sex Research*, 5: 73–100.

Golombok, S., Spencer, A. and Rutter, M. (1983) Children in lesbian and single-parent households: psychosexual and psychiatric appraisal, *Journal of Child Psychology and Psychiatry*, 24: 551–72.

Gopfert, M., Harrison, P. and Mahoney, C. (1999) *Keeping the Family in Mind: Participative Research into Mental Ill-health and How it Affects the Whole Family.* North Mersey Community Health Trust: Barnardo's/Save the Children.

Gorin, S. (2004) *Understanding what Children Say: Children's Experiences of Domestic Violence, Parental Substance Misuse and Parental Health Problems.* London: JRF/NCB.

Graham, H. and Power, C. (2004) Childhood disadvantage and health inequalities: a framework for policy based on lifecourse research, *Child Care, Health and Development*, 30(6): 671–8.

Green, R., Mandel, J., Hotvedt, M., Gray, J. and Smith, L. (1986) Lesbian mothers and their children. *Archives of Sexual Behaviour*, 15: 167–84.

Gregory, J. and Lowe, S. (2000) *National Diet and Nutrition Survey: Young Children Aged 4–18 years. Vol. 1: Report of the Diet and Nutrition Survey.* London: The Stationery Office.

Griffiths, L., Tate, R. and Dezateux, C. (2005) The contribution of parental and community ethnicity to breastfeeding practices: evidence from the Millennium Cohort Study, *International Journal of Epidemiology*, 34(6): 1378–86(9).

Gritz, E., Tripp, M., James, A., Carvajah, M., Harrist, R., Mueller, N., Chamberlain, R. and Parcel, G. (2005) An intervention to promote preschool children's sun protection: effects of Sun Protection is Fun! *Preventive Medicine*, 41: 357–66.

Gross, D., Fogg, L. and Tucker, S. (1995) The efficacy of parent training for promoting positive parent–toddler relationships, *Research in Nursing and Health*, 18: 489–99.

Gunnar, M. (1998) Quality of early care and buffering of neuroendocrine stress reactions. Potential effects on the developing human brain, *Preventive Medicine*, 27: 208–11.

Gussy, M., Waters, E., Walsh, O. and Kilpatrick, N. (2006) Early childhood caries: current evidence for aetiology and prevention, *Journal of Paediatrics and Child Health*, 42(1–2): 37–43.

Haines, A. and Smith, R. (1997) Working together to reduce poverty's damage, *British Medical Journal*, 314: 529.

Hall, D. and Elliman, D. (2003) *Health for all Children.* Oxford: Oxford University Press.

Hall, H., McDavid, K., Jorgensen, C. and Kraft, J. (2001) Factors associated with sunburn in white children aged 6 months to 11 years, *American Journal of Preventive Medicine*, 20(1): 9–14.

Hallett, C. and Prout, A. (eds) (2003) *Hearing the Voices of Children.* London: Routledge.

Hapgood, R., Kendrick, D. and Marsh, P. (2000) How well do socio-demographic characteristics explain variation in childhood safety practices? *Journal of Public Health Medicine*, 22(3): 307–11.

Harbourview Injury and Prevention Research Center (2001) *Cochrane Collaboration Systematic Review Database.* Seattle, WA: HIPRC.

Hawthorne, J., Jessop, J., Pryor, J. and Richards, M. (2003) *Supporting Children through Family Change: A Review of Interventions and Services for Children of Divorced and Separating Parents.* York: Joseph Rowntree Foundation.

Hedin, L.W., Grimstad, H., Moller, A., Schei, B. and Janson, P.O. (1999) Prevalence of physical and sexual abuse before and during pregnancy among Swedish couples, *Acta Obstricia et Gynecologica Scandinavica*, 78(4): 310–15.

Heinecke, M.H. and Guthrie, D.G. (1992) Stability and change in husband–wife adaptation, and the development of the positive parent–child relationship, *Infant Behavior and Development*, 15: 109–27.

Helman, C. (2000) *Culture, Health and Illness* (4th edn). London: Arnold.

Henderson, L., Kitzinger, J. and Green, J. (2000) Representing infant feeding:

content analysis of British media portrayals of bottle feeding and breast feeding, *British Medical Journal*, 321: 1196–8.

Hester, M., Pearson, C. and Harwin, N. (2000) *Making an Impact: Children and Domestic Violence. A Reader.* London: Jessica Kingsley.

Hiley, C. and Morley, C. (1994) Evaluation of government's campaign to reduce risk of cot death, *British Medical Journal*, 309: 703–4.

Hill, A. and Waterston, C. (2002) Fat teasing in pre-adolescent children: the bullied and the bullies, *International Journal of Obesity*, 26: S20.

HM Government (2006) Working together to safeguard children: a guide to interagency working to safeguard and promote the welfare of children, at http://www.everychildmatters.gov.uk/_files/CCE39E361D6AD840F7EAC9DA 47A3D2C8.pdf, accessed July 2006.

HMSO (2001) *ONS Annual Reference Volume DH3 Series. Mortality Statistics: Childhood, Infant and Perinatal.* (Generic) Report ref ID: 6747.

Hoddinott, P. and Pill, R. (1999) Qualitative study of decisions about infant feeding among women in the east end of London, *British Medical Journal*, 318: 30–4.

Holaday, B., La Monagne, L. and Marciel, J. (1994) *Issues in Comprehensive Paediatric Nursing*, 17: 15–27.

Holden, G., Geffner, R. and Jouriles, E. (1998) *Children Exposed to Marital Violence: Theory Research and Applied Issues.* Washington, DC: American Psychological Association.

Holzheimer, L., Mohay, H. and Masters, I. (1998) Educating young children about asthma: comparing the effectiveness of a developmentally appropriate asthma education video tape and picture book, *Child: Care, Health and Development*, 24(1): 85–99.

Hopkins, J. (1996) The dangers and deprivations of too-good mothering, *Journal of Child Psychotherapy*, 22(3).

Horgan, G. (2001) *A Sense of Purpose: The Views and Experiences of Young Mothers in Northern Ireland about Growing Up.* Belfast: Save the Children.

Horton, E. (ed.) (2005) *Working with Children 2006–07. Facts Figures and Information.* London: NCH.

Horwath, J. (ed.) (2001) *The Child's World.* London: Jessica Kingsley.

Hossain, Z., Field, T., Gonzalez, J. and Malphurs, J. (1994) Infants of 'depressed' mothers interact better with their non-depressed fathers, *Infant Mental Health Journal*, 15(4): 348–57.

House, J. and Williams, D. (2000) Understanding and reducing socio-economic and racial/ethnic disparities in health, in B. Smedley and S. Syme (eds) *Promoting Health Intervention Strategies from Social and Behavioral Research.* Washington, DC: National Academy Press, pp. 57–86.

Howarth, C., Kenway, P., Palmer, R. and Miorellie, R. (1999) *Monitoring Poverty and Social Exclusion.* York: Joseph Rowntree Foundation/London: New Policy Institute.

Howe, D. (2005) *Child Abuse and Neglect Attachment, Development and Intervention.* New York: Palgrave Macmillan.

HPA (Health Promotion Agency) (2001) *Eating for Health? A Survey of Eating Habits among Children and Young People in Northern Ireland.* Belfast: The Health Promotion Agency for Northern Ireland.

Hughes, H. (1988) Psychological and behavioral correlates of family violence in child witnesses and victims, *American Journal of Orthopsychiatry*, 58: 77–90.

Hughes, H., Parkinson, D. and Vargo, M. (1989) Witnessing spouse abuse and experiencing physical abuse: a double whammy? *Journal of Family Violence*, 4: 197–209.

Hughes, P. (2003) Curriculum contexts: parents and communities, in G. MacNaughton (ed.) *Shaping Early Childhood: Learners, Curriculum and Contexts.* Berkshire: Open University Press.

Isabella, R. and Belsky, J. (1995) Marital change during the transition to parenthood and security of infant–parent attachment, *Journal of Family Issues*, 6: 505–22.

Jack, G. and Jordan, B. (1999) Social capital and child welfare, *Children and Society*, 13: 242–56.

Jackson, T. (2002) Both sides now, *British Medical Journal*, 325: 603, 14 September.

Jaffe, P., Hurley, D. and Wolfe, D. (1990) Children's observations of violence: 1. Critical issues in child development and intervention planning. *Canadian Journal of Psychiatry*, 35(6): 466–9.

James, A. and Prout, A. (1997) *Constructing and Reconstructing Childhood.* London: Routledge Falmer.

James, A., Jenks, C. and Prout, A. (1998) *Theorizing Childhood.* Oxford: Polity.

James, W., Nelson, M. and Ralph, A. (1997) Socio-economic determinants of health. The contribution of nutrition to inequalities in health, *British Medical Journal*, 314: 1545–9.

Jarvis, M. and Wardle, J. (1999) Social patterning of individual health behaviours: the case of cigarette smoking, in M. Marmot and R.G. Wilkinson (eds) *Social Determinants of Health.* OUP.

Jenner, S. (1988) The influence of additional information, advice and support on the success of breast feeding in working class primiparas, *Child: Care, Health and Development*, 14: 319–28.

Johnson, Z. and Molloy, B. (1995) The Community Mothers Programme – empowerment of parents by parents, *Children and Society*, 9(2): 73–83.

Johnson, Z., Howell, F. and Molloy, B. (1993). Community Mothers Programme: randomised controlled trial of non-professional intervention in parenting. *British Medical Journal*, 306: 1449–52.

Johnson, Z., Molloy, B., Scallan, E., Fitzpatrick, P., Rooney, B., Keegan, T. and Byrne, P. (2000) Community Mothers Programme – seven year follow-up of a randomised controlled trial of non-professional intervention in parenting, *Journal of Public Health Medicine*, 22(3): 337–42.

Jones, R. and Belsey, E. (1977) Breast feeding in an inner London borough: a study of cultural practices, *Social Science Medicine*, 11: 175–9.

Joseph Rowntree Foundation (2006) What will it take to end child poverty in the UK?, at http://www.jrf.org.uk/child-poverty/, accessed 20 July 2006.

Keller, H., Scholmerich, A. and Eibl-Eibelsfeldt, I. (1988) Communication patterns in adult–infant interaction in western and non-western cultures, *Journal of Cross Cultural Psychiatry*, 19: 427–45.

Kelly, J. (1967) The influence of native customs in obstetrics in Nigeria, *Obstetrics and Gynaecology*, 30: 608–12.

Killian, B. (n.d.) A structured group therapy programme for children affected by HIV/AIDS, poverty and violence, at http://www.psychology.unp.ac.za/Documents/bjk_Group%20Therapy%20Colour.pdf, accessed June 2006.

Kim, T.I., Shin, Y.H. and White-Traut, R.C. (2003) Multisensory intervention improves physical growth and illness rates in Korean orphaned newborn infants, *Research in Nursing and Health*, 26(6): 424–33.

Kirkpatrick, M., Smith, C. and Roy, R. (1981) Lesbian mothers and their children: a comparative survey, *American Journal of Orthopsychiatry*, 51: 545–51.

Kitzinger, S. (1982) The social context of birth: some comparisons between childbirth in Jamaica and Britain, in C. MacCormack (ed.) *Ethnography of Fertility and Birth*. London: Academic Press, pp. 181–203.

Klaus, M. and Kennel, J. (1982) *Parent–Infant Bonding*. St Louis: Mosby.

Klinnert, M., Campos, J., Sorce, J., Emde, R. and Svedja, M. (1983) Emotions as behaviour regulators: social referencing in infancy, in R. Plutchik and H. Kellerman (eds) *Emotion: Theory Research and Experience* 2. New York: Academic Press, pp. 57–86.

Kmietowicz, Z. (2000) More services needed for bereaved children, *British Medical Journal*, 320: 893.

Konofal, E., Lecendreux, M., Arnulf, I. and Mouren, M. (2004) Iron deficiency in children with attention deficit disorder, *Archives of Pediatric Adolescent Medicine*, 158: 1113–15.

Korbin, J. (1989) Fatal maltreatment by mothers: a proposed framework, *Child Abuse and Neglect*, 13: 481–9.

Kreppner, J.O., Connor, T. and Rutter, M. (2001) Can inattention/overactivity be an institutional deprivation syndrome? *Journal of Abnormal Child Psychology*, 29: 513–28.

Kurdek, L. and Siesky, A. (1980) Children's perceptions of their parents' divorce, *Journal of Divorce*, 3: 339–78.

Laevers, F. (1997) *A Process-oriented Child Monitoring System for Young Children*. Leuven: Centre for Experiential Education.

Lamborn, S., Mounts, N. and Steinberg, L. (1991) Patterns of competence and adjustment among adolescents from authoritative, authoritarian, indulgent and neglectful families, *Child Development*, 62: 1049–65.

Laming, H. (2003) *The Victoria Climbie Inquiry. Report of an Inquiry by Lord Laming*. London: The Stationery Office.

Lansdown, G. and Lancaster, P. (2001) Promoting children's welfare by respecting their rights, cited in G. Pugh (ed.) *Contemporary Issues in the Early Years* (3rd edn). London: Paul Chapman.

Lawrence, P. and Wiffen, J. (2002) *Family Group Conferences: Principles and Practice Guidance*. Essex: Barnardo's/Family Rights Group/NCH.

Leather, S. (1996) *The Making of Modern Malnutrition: An Overview of Food Poverty in the UK*. London: The Caroline Walker Trust.

LeVine, R., Dixon, S., LeVine S., Richman, A., Leiderman, P., Keefer, C. and Brazelton, T.B. (1994) *Child Care and Culture: Lessons from Africa*. Cambridge: Cambridge University Press.

Lewis, M., Feiring, C., McGuffoy, C. and Jaskir, J. (1984) Predicting psychopathology in six year olds from early social relations, *Child Development*, 55: 123–36.

Liabo, K., Gibbs, J. and Underdown, A. (2004) *Group-based Parenting Programmes and Reducing Children's Behaviour Problems. Highlight no. 211*. London: NCB.

Linnet, K., Dalsgaard, S. and Obel, C. (2003) Maternal lifestyle factors in pregnancy, risk of attention deficit disorder and associated behaviours: review of the current evidence, *American Journal of Psychiatry*, 160: 1028–40.

Llewellyn, N. (1993) The use of PCA for paediatric post-operative pain management, *Paediatric Nursing*, 5.

Loh, C. and Vostanis, P. (2004) Perceived mother–infant relationship difficulties in postnatal depression, *Infant and Child Development*, 13(2): 159–71.

Lowes, L., Gregory, J. and Lyne. P. (2004) Newly diagnosed childhood diabetes: a psychosocial transition for parents? *Journal of Advanced Nursing*, 50(3): 253–61.

Lucas, P. and Liabo, K. (2004) *Breakfast Clubs and School Fruit Schemes. Highlight no. 206*. London: NCB.

Lyons, C. (2000) *Loving Smack or Lawful Assault? A Contradiction in Human Rights Law*. London: IPPR.

Maattanen, K. (2001) *Dialogical Baby Dance – A Parent's Guide*. South Eastern Health Centre at Herttoneime.

Maccoby, E. and Martin, J. (1983) Socialization in the context of the family. Parent–child interaction, in P. Mussen (ed.) *Handbook of Child Psychology*. New York: John Wiley.

MacNaughton, G. (2005) *Doing Foucault in Early Childhood Studies: Applying Post-structural Ideas*. Oxford: Routledge.

Main, M. and Hesse, E. (1990) Parents' unresolved traumatic experiences are related to infant disorganised attachment status: is frightening and/or frightening behaviour the linking mechanism? in M.T. Greenberg and D. Cicchetti (eds) *Attachment in the Pre-school Years*. Chicago: University of Chicago Press.

Manby, M. (2005) Evaluation of the impact of the Webster–Stratton parent–child videotape series of participants in a Midlands town in 2001–2002, *Children and Society*, 19: 316–28.

Marsh, A. and McKay, S. (1994) *Poor Smokers*. London: Policy Studies Institute.

Martini, M. and Kirkpatrick, J. (1981) Early interactions in the Marquesas Islands, in T. Field, A. Sostek, P. Vietze, and P. Leiderman (eds) *Culture and Early Interactions*. Hillsdale, NJ: Lawrence Erlbaum.

Marx, J. (1997) Iron deficiency in developed countries: prevalence, influence of lifestyle factors and hazards of prevention, *European Journal of Clinical Nutrition*, 51: 491–4.

Maslow, A. (1970) *Motivation and Personality* (2nd edn). New York: Harper Row.

Mason, M. (1992) The integration alliance: background and manifesto, in T. Booth, W. Swann, M. Masterton and P. Potts (eds) *Learning For All 2: Policies for Diversity in Education*. London: Routledge/OU.

Mayall, B. (1994) *Negotiating Health. Primary School Children at Home and School*. London: Cassell.

Mayall, B. (2002) *Towards a Sociology for Childhood*. London: Routledge Falmer.

McClean, M. (2004) *Together and Apart: Children and Parents Experiencing Separation and Divorce*, Foundations Ref 314. York: Joseph Rowntree Foundation.

McCormick, M., Shapiro, S. and Starfield, B. (1981) Injury and its correlates among 1-year-old children, *American Journal of Diseases of Children*, 135: 159–63.

McGhan, S., Reutter, L., Hessel, P., Melvin, D. and Wilson, D. (2002) Developing a school asthma policy, *Public Health Nursing*, 19(2): 112–23.

McLanahan, S. and Sandefur, G. (1994) Growing up with a single parent: what helps, what hurts? Cambridge, MA: Harvard University Press.

McLaughlin, C. (ed.) (2004) *Research on Divorce Separation and Family Change: Messages for Practitioners*. York: Joseph Rowntree Foundation.

McLean, D. and Gallagher, R. (1998) Sunscreens: use and misuse, *Dermatologic Clinics*, 16: 219–24.

McLeroy, K., Bibeau, D., Steckler, A. and Glanz, K. (1988) An ecological perspective on health promotion, *Health Education Quarterly*, 15: 351–77.

McNeish, D. and Roberts, H. (1995) *Playing it Safe*. Barkingside: Barnardo's.

Meins, E. (1997) *Security of Attachment and the Social Development of Cognition*. Hove: Psychology Press.

Meins, E. (2006) *Developmental Outcomes of Joint Attention and Maternal Mind-mindedness*. University of Durham: Department of Psychology. http://www.esrc.ac.uk/ESRCInfoCentre/Plain_English_Summaries/LLH/health_wellbeing/index376.aspx?ComponentId=9957&SourcePageId=11769 (date accessed July 2006)

Meins, E., Fernyhough, C., Fradley, E. and Tuckey, M. (2001) Rethinking maternal sensitivity: mothers' comments on infants' mental processes predict security of attachment at 12 months, *Journal of Child Psychology and Psychiatry*, 42(5): 637–48.

Meltzer, H., Gatward, R., Goodman, R. and Ford, T. (2000) *The Mental Health of Children & Adolescents in Great Britain*. London: The Stationary Office.

Merriam-Webster (2006) at http://en.wikipedia.org/wiki/Mental_state, accessed 14 May 2006.

MHF (Mental Health Foundation) (1999) *Bright Futures. Promoting Children and Young People's Mental Health*. London: The Mental Health Foundation.

Middleton, L. (1999) *Disabled Children: Challenging Social Exclusion*. Oxford: Blackwell Science.

Miller, L. (2002) *Observation Observed. An Outline of the Nature and Practice of Infant Observation* (video and booklet). London: The Tavistock Clinic.

Miller, L., Rustin, M., Rustin, M. and Shuttleworth, J. (1989) *Closely Observed Infants*. London: Duckworth.

Miller, T. (2000) Losing the plot: narrative construction and longitudinal childbirth research, *Qualitative Health Research*, 10(3): 309–23.

Minde, K. and Minde, R. (1977) Behavioral screening of pre-school children: a new approach to mental health, in P. Graham (ed.) *Epidemiological Approaches in Child Psychiatry*. London: Academic Press, pp. 139–64.

Moffitt, T. (1993) Adolescence limited and life course persistent antisocial behavior: a developmental taxonomy, *Psychological Review*, 100: 674–701.

Molbak, K., Gottschau, A., Aaby, P., Hojlyng, N., Ingholt, L. and Da Silva, J. (1994) Prolonged breast feeding, diarrhoeal disease, and the survival of children in Guinea-Bissau, *British Medical Journal*, 308: 1403–6.

Molyneux, E., Riordan, F., Andrew, I. and Walsh, A. (2006) Acute bacterial meningitis in children presenting to the Royal Liverpool Children's Hospital, Liverpool, UK and Queen Elizabeth Central Hospital in Blatyre, Malawi: a world of difference, *Annals of Tropical Paediatrics: International Child Health*, 26(1): 29–37(9), March.

Mooney, J. (1994) *The Hidden Figure: Domestic Violence in North London*. London: Islington Council.

Morrow, V. (1998) *Understanding Families. Children's Perspectives*. London: NCB.

Morrow, V. (1999) Conceptualising social capital in relation to the well-being of children and young people: a critical review, *Sociological Review*, 47(4): 744–65.

Muir, E. (1999) *Watch, Wait, and Wonder: A Manual Describing a Dyadic Infant-led Approach to Problems in Infancy and Early Childhood*. Canada: Hincks-Dellcrest Institute.

Mullen, C. and Smithson, R. (2000) *Community Child Accident Prevention Project. Using Home Visits to Promote Child Safety in Deprived Areas*. Belfast: Co-operation and Working Together (CWT).

Mullender, A. and Morley, R. (1994) *Children Living with Domestic Violence: Putting Men's Abuse of Women on the Child Care Agenda*. London: Whiting & Birch.

Munro, E. (2002) *Effective Child Protection*. London: Sage.

Munro, S.A., van Niekerk, A. and Seedat, M. (2006) Childhood unintentional injuries: the perceived impact of the environment, lack of supervision and child characteristics, *Child: Care, Health and Development*, 32(3): 269–79(11), May.

Murdoch, G. (1949) *Social Structure*. New York: Macmillan.

Murray, C. and Lopez, A. (1996) *Global Burden of Disease: A Comprehensive Assessment of Mortality and Disability from Diseases, Injuries and Risk Factors in 1990 and Projected to 2020*. Boston: Harvard School of Public Health/WHO, World Bank.

Murray, L. (1992) The impact of postnatal depression on infant development, *Journal of Child Psychology and Psychiatry*, 33: 543–61.

Murray, L. (2001) *How Postnatal Depression can Affect Children and Families. Postnatal Depression and Maternal Mental Health: A Public Health Priority*. London: CPHVA Conference Proceedings.

Murray, L. and Andrews, L. (2000) *The Social Baby*. London: The Children's Project.

Murray, L. and Cooper, P. (1997) Effects of postnatal depression on infant development, *Archives of Disease in Childhood*, 77: 99–101.

Murray, L., Fiori-Cowley, A. and Hooper, R. (1996) The impact of post-natal depression and associated adversity on early mother–infant interactions and later infant outcomes, *Child Development*, 67: 2512–26.

Must, A. and Strauss, R. (1999) Risks and consequences of childhood and adolescent obesity, *International Journal of Obesity*, 23: S2–S11.

Nelson, C. and Bosquet, M. (2000) Neurobiology of fetal and infant development: implications for infant mental health, in C.H. Zeanah Jr (ed.) *Handbook of Infant Mental Health* (2nd edn). New York: Guilford Press.

NESS (National Evaluation of Sure Start) (2005) *Early Impacts of Sure Start Local Programmes on Children and Families*. Research Report NESS/2005/FR/013, at http://www.surestart.gov.uk/_doc/P0001867.pdf, accessed 12 January 2006.

Neugebauer, R. (1989) Divorce, custody and visitation; the child's point of view, *Journal of Divorce*, 12: 153–68.

Newman, T. (2004) *What Works in Building Resilience?* Barkingside: Barnardo's.

Nobes, G. and Smith, M. (1997) Physical punishment of children in two-parent families, *Clinical Child Psychology and Psychiatry*, 2: 271–81.

Nolan, M.L. (1997) Antenatal education – where next? *Journal of Advanced Nursing*, 25: 1198–204.

NSO (National Statistics Online) (2006) Lone parents in employment, at http://www.statistics.gov.uk/cci/nugget.asp?id=409, accessed 2 April 2006.

Nutbeam, D. (1998) *Health Promotion Glossary*. Geneva: WHO.

O'Riordan, D., Geller, A., Brooks, D., Zhang, Z. and Miller, D. (2003) Sunburn reduction through parental role modelling and sunscreen vigilance, *Journal of Pediatrics*, 142(1): 67–72.

Oakley, A. (1980) *Women Confined: Towards a Sociology of Childbirth*. Oxford: Martin Robertson.

Ofsted (2004) *Childminding: Guidance to National Standards. Revisions to Certain Criteria.* Version 2. London: Ofsted Publications Centre.

Olfson, M., Marcus, S., Weissman, M. and Jensen, P. (2002) National trends in the use of psychotropic medications by children, *Journal of the American Academy of Child and Adolescent Psychiatry*, 41: 514–21.

Onozawa, K., Glover, V., Adams, D., Modi, N. and Kumar, C. (2001) Infant massage improves mother–infant interaction for mothers with post natal depression, *Journal of Affective Disorders*, 63: 201–7.

ONS (Office for National Statistics) (2005) http://www.statistics.gov.uk/StatBase/Source.asp?vlnk=101&Pos=2&ColRank=1&Rank=272, accessed December 2005.

OPCS (Office of Population Censuses and Surveys) (1994) *Child Accident Statistics 1993.* London: HMSO.

Parr, M. (1998) A new approach to parent education, *British Journal of Midwifery*, 6(3): 160–5.

Patterson, G. (1986) The contribution of siblings to training for fighting: a microsocial analysis, in D. Olweus, J. Block and M. Radke-Yarrow (eds) *Development of Anti-social and Pro-social Behaviour.* New York: Academic Press, pp. 235–61.

Patterson, G., Reid, J. and Dishion, T. (1992) *A Social Learning Approach 4. Antisocial Boys.* Ontario: Castalia Publishing Company.

Pavis, S., Masters, H. and Burley, S. (1996) *Lay Concepts of Positive Mental Health and How it Can be Maintained.* Edinburgh: University of Edinburgh.

Payne, L. (2003) So how are we doing? A review of the concluding observations of the UN committee on the rights of the child: United Kingdom, *Children & Society*, 17(1): 71–4.

Peltola, H., Patja, A., Leinikki, P., Valle, M., Davidkin, I. and Paunio, M. (1998) No evidence for measles, mumps and rubella vaccine associated inflammatory bowel disease or autism in a 14 year prospective study (research letters), *Lancet*, 351: 1327–8.

Percival, J. (2002) Protecting children from passive smoking, *Community Practitioner*, 75(5): 165–6.

Percy, P. and Barker, W. (1986) The child development programme, *Midwife, Health Visitor and Community Nurse*, 22: 235–40.

Petterson, S. and Burke Albers, A. (2001) Effects of poverty and maternal depression on early child development, *Child Development*, 72(6): 1794–1813.

Petticrew, M. and Roberts, H. (2004) Child public health and social welfare: lessons from the evidence, *Child: Care, Health and Development*, 30(6): 667–9.

Piaget, J. and Inhelder, B. (1969) *The Psychology of the Child.* London: Routledge & Kegan Paul.

PIPPIN (2000) *Your Baby as a Person* (training notes). London: PIPPIN.

Pollitt, E. and Matthews, R. (1998) Breakfast and cognition: an integrative summary, *American Journal of Clinical Nutrition*, 67(4): 804S–13S.

Popkin, B. (2001) The nutrition transition and obesity in the developing world, *Journal of Nutrition*, 131: 871S–873S.

Prentice, A. (2005) The emerging epidemic of obesity in developing countries, *International Journal of Epidemiology* (advance access, published 2 December 2005), at http://ije.oxfordjournals.org/cgi/content/abstract/dyi272v1, (accessed 1 January 2006).

Priestly, M. (ed.) (2001) *Disability and the Life Course*. Cambridge: Cambridge University Press.

Prochaska, J. and DiClements, C. (1983) Stages and processes of self-change of smoking: toward an integrative model of change, *Journal of Consulting and Clinical Psychology*, 51(3): 390–5.

Prout, A. (2005) *The Future of Childhood*. Oxford: Routledge.

Pryor, J. and Rodgers, B (2001) *Children in Changing Families*. Oxford: Blackwell.

Putnam, R. (2000) *Bowling Alone – The Collapse and Revival of American Community*. New York: Simon & Schuster.

Puura, K., Davis, H., Papadopoulou, K., Tsiantis, J., Ispanovic-Radojkovic, V., Rudic, N., Tamminer, T., Turunen, M., Dragonas, T., Paradisiotou, A., Vizakou, S., Roberts, R., Cox, A. and Day, C. (2002) The European Early Promotion Project: a new primary health care service to promote children's mental health, *Infant Mental Health Journal*, 23(6): 606–24.

Rauh, V., Achenbach, T., Nurcombe, B., Howell, C. and Teti, D. (1988) Minimizing adverse effects of low birthweight: four-year results of an early intervention program, *Child Development*, 59: 544–53.

Raynor, P. and Rudolf, M. (2000) *Clues from Children's Mealtimes. Insights into Managing Infant and Toddler Eating Behaviour* (training video for health professionals). University of Leeds: Media Services.

Redshaw, M., Rivers, R. and Rosenblatt, D. (1985) *Born too Early*. Oxford: Oxford University Press.

Reilly, J.J., Dorosty, A.R. and Emmett, P.M. (1999) Prevalence of overweight and obesity in British children: cohort study, *British Medical Journal*, 319: 1039.

Renfrew, M., Dyson, L., Wallace, L., D'Souza, L., McCormack, F. and Spiby, H. (2005) *Breast Feeding for Longer – What Works? Systematic Review Summary*. London: National Institute for Health and Clinical Excellence.

Reyes, L. and Manalich, R. (2005) Long-term consequences of low birth weight, *Kidney International*, 68, Supp. 97: S107–S111.

Richman, N. (1974) The effects of housing on pre-school children and their mothers, *Developmental Medicine and Child Neurology*, 16: 53–8.

Roberts, H. (2000) *What Works in Reducing Inequalities in Child Health?* London: Barnardo's.

Roberts, H., Smith, S.J. and Bryce, C. (1993) Prevention is better …, *Sociology of Health and Illness*, 15: 447–63.

Roberts, I. and Pless, B. (1995) For debate: social policy as a cause of childhood accidents: the children of lone mothers, *British Medical Journal*, 311: 925–8.

Robertson, J. and Robertson, J. (1989) *Separation and the Very Young.* London: Free Association Books.

Robins, L. (1991) Conduct disorder, *Journal of Child Psychology and Psychiatry*, 32: 193–212.

Robinson, L., McIntyre, L. and Officer, S. (2005) Welfare babies: poor children's experiences informing healthy peer relationships in Canada, *Health Promotion International*, 20(4).

Rodriguez, C. (2003) Parental discipline and abuse: potential effects on child depression, anxiety, and attributions, *Journal of Marriage and Family*, 65(4): 809–17.

Royal College of Paediatrics and Child Health (2002) *Helpful Parenting.* London: Royal College of Paediatrics and Child Health.

Royal College of Physicians (2003) *Tobacco Smoke Pollution: The Hard Facts.* London: RCP.

Runyan, D., Hunter, W., Socolar, R., Amaya-Jackson, L., English, D., Landsverk, J., Dubowitz, H., Browne, D., Bangdiwala, S. and Mathew, R. (1998) Children who prosper in unfavourable environments: the relationships to social capital, *Pediatrics*, 101 (I pt 1): 12–18.

Rustin, M. (1989) Observing infants: reflections on methods, in L. Miller, M. Rustin, M. Rustin and J. Shuttleworth (eds) *Closely Observed Infants.* London: Duckworth.

Rutter, M. and Smith, D. (1995) *Psychosocial Disorders in Young People. Time Trends and their Causes.* John Wiley & Sons Ltd.

Ruxin, J., Paluzzi, J., Wilson, P., Tozan, Y., Kruk, M. and Teklehaimanot, A. (2005) Emerging consensus in HIV/AIDS, malaria, tuberculosis and access to essential medicines, *Lancet*, 365: 618–21.

Schaffer, H. and Emerson, P. (1964) The development of social attachments in infancy, *Monographs of the Society for Research in Child Development*, 29(93), whole no. 94.

Scheper-Hughes, N. (1993) *Death without Weeping: Violence of Everyday Life in Brazil.* California: University of California Press.

Schore, A. (1994) *After Regulation and the Origin of the Self: The Neurobiology of Emotional Development.* New Jersey: Erlbaum.

Schore, A. (2001) The effects of secure attachment relationship on the right brain development, affect regulation and infant mental health, *Infant Mental Health Journal*, 22: 7–66.

Scott, S., O'Connor, T. and Futh, A. (2006) *What Makes Parenting Programmes Work in Disadvantaged Areas?* York: Joseph Rowntree Foundation.

Scottish Office (1999) *Towards a Healthier Scotland.* London: The Stationery Office.

Seedhouse, D. (1986) *Health: The Foundations for Achievement.* Chichester: John Wiley & Sons.

Seeley, S. (2001) Strengths and limitations of the Edinburgh Post-natal Depression Scale, in *Postnatal Depression and Maternal Mental Health: A Public Health Priority.* CPHVA Conference Proceedings 9–12. London: CPHVA.

Seipp, C. (2002) Asthma attack: when 'zero tolerance' collides with children's health, at http://www.reason.com/0204/fe.cs.asthma.shtml, (accessed 14 June 2006.)

SEU (Social Exclusion Unit) (1999) *Teenage Pregnancy: A Report by the Social Exclusion Unit*. London: TSO.

Shah, R. and Hatton, C. (1999) *Caring Alone. Young Carers in South Asian Communities*. London: Barnardo's.

Sharpe, D., Hay, D., Pawlby, S. and Schumucher, G. (1995) The impact of post natal depression on boys' intellectual development. *Journal of Child Psychology and Psychiatry*, 36: 1315–37.

Shemilt, I., O'Brien, M., Thoburn, J., Harvey, I., Belderson, P., Robinson, J., Camina, M. and School Breakfast Clubs Evaluation Group (2002) School breakfast clubs, children and family support, *Children and Society*, 17(2): 100–12.

Shohaimi, S., Welch, A., Bingham, S., Luben, R., Day, N., Wareham, N. and Tee Khaw, K. (2004) Residential area deprivation predicts fruit and vegetable consumption independently of individual educational level and occupational social class: a cross sectional population study in the Norfolk cohort of the European Prospective Investigation into Cancer, *Journal of Epidemiology and Community Health*, 58: 686–91.

Slade, A. and Cohen, L. (1996) The process of parenting and the remembrance of things past, *Infant Mental Health Journal*, 17: 183–97.

Sloper, P. (1996) Needs and responses of parents following the diagnosis of childhood cancer, *Child: Care, Health and Development*, 22(3): 187–202.

Smart, C. and Neale, B. (1999) *Family Fragments?* Cambridge: Polity Press.

Smart, C., Neale, B. and Wade, A. (2001) *The Changing Experience of Childhood: Families and Divorce*. Cambridge: Policy Press.

Smith, A., Taylor, N., Gollop, M., Gaffney, M., Gold, M. and Heneghan, M. (1997) *Access and other Post-separation Issues*. Dunedin, NZ: Children's Issues Centre.

Smith, J., Brooks-Gunn, J. and Klebanov, P. (1997) The consequences of living in poverty for young children's cognitive and verbal ability and early school achievement, in G. Duncan and J. Brooks-Gunn (eds) *Consequences of Growing Up Poor*. New York: Sage, pp. 132–89.

Smith, M., Bee, P. and Nobes, G. (1995) Parental control within the family: the nature and extent of parental violence to children, in Department of Health, *Messages from Research*. London: HMSO.

Sonuga-Barke, E., Daley, D., Thompson, M., Laver-Bradbury, C. and Weeks, A. (2000) Parent-based therapies for pre-school attention deficit/hyperactivity disorder: a randomised, controlled with a community sample, *Journal of the American Academy of Child and Adolescent Psychiatry*, 40(4): 402–8.

Spencer, N. (2000) *Poverty and Child Health* (2nd edn). Oxfordshire: Radcliffe Medical Press.

Spohr, H.-L. and Steinhausen, H.C. (eds) (1996) *Alcohol, Pregnancy and the Developing Child*. Cambridge, MA: Cambridge University Press.

Sroufe, A. (1995) *Emotional Development: The Organisation of Emotional Life in the Early Years*. Cambridge: Cambridge University Press.

Staab, D., Diepgen, T., Fartasch, M.. Kupfer, J., Lob-Corzilius, T., Ring, J., Scheewe, S., Scheidt, R., Schmid-Ott, G., Schnopp, C., Szczepanski, R., Werfel, T., Wittenmeier, M., Wahn, U. and Gieler, U. (2006) Age-related educational programmes for children with atopic eczema. *British Medical Journal*, 332: 933–8.

Stagg, G.D., Wills, G. and Howell, M. (1989) Psychopathology in early child witnesses of family violence, *Topics in Early Childhood Special Education*, 9: 73–87.

Stallard, P. (1993) The behaviour of 3 year old children: prevalence and parental perception of problem behaviour: a research note, *Journal of Child Psychology and Psychiatry and Allied Disciplines*, 34: 413–21.

Stanton, W., Janda, M., Baade, P. and Anderson, P. (2004) Primary prevention of skin cancer: a review of sun protection in Australia and internationally, *Health Promotion International*, 19(3): 369–78.

Statistics Canada (1993) *The Violence Against Women Survey*. Canada: Centre for Justice Statistics.

Steele, H., Steele, M. and Fonagy, P. (1996) Associations among attachment classifications of mothers, fathers and their infants, *Child Development*, 67: 541–55.

Stein, A., Gath, D., Bucher, J., Bond, A., Day, A. and Cooper, P. (1991) The relationship between post natal depression and mother–child interaction, *British Journal of Psychiatry*, 158: 46–52.

Stern, D. (1986) *The Motherhood Constellation*. London: Karnac/United Nations Children's Fund.

Stern, D. (1998a) *The Interpersonal World of the Infant*. London: Karnac.

Stern, D. (1998b) *The Motherhood Constellation*. London: Karnac.

Stewart-Brown, S. (1998) Editorial: Emotional wellbeing and its relation to health: physical disease may well result from emotional distress, *British Medical Journal*, 317: 1608–9.

Stinco, G., Favot, F., Quinkenstein, E., Zanchi, M., Valent, F. and Patrone, P. (2005) Children and sun exposure in the northeast of Italy, *Pediatric Dermatology*, 22(6): 520–4.

Strassberg, Z., Dodge, K., Pettit, C. and Bates, J. (1994) Spanking in the home and children's subsequent aggression toward kindergarten peers, *Development and Psychopathology*, 6: 445–62.

Strathern, M. (1992) *After Nature: English Kinship in the Late Twentieth Century* (Lewis Henry Morgan Lectures). Cambridge: Cambridge University Press.

Sure Start (n.d.) http://www.surestart.gov.uk/aboutsurestart/, accessed 20 March 2006.

Sure Start (2001) *A Guide for Fourth Wave Programmes*. Nottingham: DfEE Publications.

Sure Start Plus evaluation (2005) *Supporting Teenagers who are Pregnant or Parents.* Sure Start Plus National Evaluation. London: SSRU Institute of Education.

Sustain (2005) The Children's Food Bill. *Why We Need a New Law, Not More Voluntary Approaches.* London: Sustain.

Svanberg, P.O. (1998) Attachment, resilience and prevention, *Journal of Mental Health*, 7(6): 543–78.

Svanberg, P.O. (2005) Promoting attachment security in primary intervention using video feedback: the Sunderland Infant Programme. Draft paper.

Tanaka, S. (2005) Parental leave and child health across OECD countries, *Economic Journal*, 115: F7–F28.

Taylor, A. (1985) Antenatal classes and the consumer mothers' and fathers' views, *Health Education Journal*, 44(2): 79–82.

Templeton, S.K. (2005) Expert tells doctors: let the youngest premature babies die, *The Times*, 5 June: 4.

Thurlbeck, S. (2000) Growing up in Britain (review), *British Medical Journal*, 320: 809.

Timimi, S. (2005) *Naughty Boys: Anti-social Behaviour, ADHD and the Role of Culture.* Hampshire: Palgrave Macmillan.

Towner, E., Dowsell, T., Mackereth, C. and Jarvis, S. (2001) *What Works in Preventing Unintentional Injuries in Children and Young Adolescents. An Updated Systematic Review.* London: Health Development Agency.

Toynbee, P. (2004) Inequality is fattening, *Guardian*, 28 May.

TPU (Teenage Pregnancy Unit) (2006) Teenage pregnancy targets and indicators, at http://www.dfes.gov.uk/teenagepregnancy/dsp_content.cfm?pageId=96, accessed 20 July 2006.

Trevarthan, C. and Aitkin, J. (2001) Infant intersubjectivity: research, theory and clinical applications, *Journal of Child Psychology and Psychiatry*, 42(1): 3–48.

Trickett, P. and Putnam, F. (1998) Developmental consequences of child sexual abuse, in P. Trickett and C. Schellenbach (eds) *Violence Against Children in the Family and the Community*. Washington, DC: American Psychological Association, pp. 39–56.

Underdown, A. (1998) Investigating techniques used in parenting classes, *Health Visitor*, 71(2): 65–8.

Underdown, A. (2000) *When Feeding Fails.* London: The Children's Society.

Underdown, A. (2002) 'I'm growing up too fast': messages from young carers, *Children and Society*, 16: 1–4, January.

UNICEF (2001a) *A League Table of Child Deaths by Injury in Rich Nations.* Innocenti Research Centre. Florence: UNICEF.

UNICEF (2001b) *A League Table of Teenage Births in Rich Nations.* Innocenti Research Centre. Report Card no. 3. Florence: Innocenti Research Centre.

UNICEF (2001c) *The State of the World's Children.* Oxford: Oxford University Press.

UNICEF UK (2004) *Children's Rights and Responsibilities* (leaflet), at http://www.unicef.org.uk/tz/resources/resource_item.asp?id=32, accessed 11 July 2006.

UNICEF (2005) *Child Poverty in Rich Countries*. Innocenti Research Centre. Report Card no. 6. Florence: Innocenti Research Centre.

UNICEF UK Baby Friendly Initiative (n.d.) http://www.babyfriendly.org.uk/ukstats.asp prevalence, accessed 10 May 2005.

United Nations (n.d.) http://www.un.org/rights/dpi1765e.htm, accessed 10 May 2005.

United Nations (1989) *The United Nations Convention on the Rights of the Child*. New York: United Nations.

United Nations (1995) *Children's Rights. Background Note*. Published by the United Nations Department of Public Information, *DPI/1765/HR–December 1995, http://www.un.org/rights/dpi1765e.htm, accessed 20 June 2006.

Upton, M., Watt, G., Smith, G., McConnachie, A. and Hart, C. (1998) Permanent effects of maternal smoking on offsprings' lung function, *Lancet*, 352: 453.

US Census Bureau (2006) http://www.infoplease.com/ipa/.html, Infoplease © 2000–2006 Pearson Education, publishing as Infoplease. 28Mar.2006<http://www.infoplease.com/ipa/A0004393.html>.http://infoplease.com/ipaA0004393.html, accessed 29 April 2006.

Van den Boom, D. (1995) Do first year intervention effects endure? Follow-up during toddlerhood of a sample of Dutch irritable infants, *Child Development*, 66: 1798–1816.

Van Eederwegh, M., Bieri, M., Parrilla, R. and Clayton, P. (1982) The bereaved child, *British Journal of Psychiatry*, 140: 23–9.

Van Eederwegh, M., Clayton, P. and Van Eederwegh, P. (1985) The bereaved child: variables influencing early psychopathology, *British Journal of Psychiatry*, 147: 188–94.

Van-Ijzendoorn, M.H. (1997) Attachment, emergent morality and aggression: toward a socioemotional model of antisocial behaviour, *International Journal of Behavioral Development*, 21(4): 703–27.

Vincenten, J. and Michalsen, A. (2002) Priorities for child safety in the European Union: agenda for action, *Injury Control and Safety Promotion*, 9(1): 1–8.

Vostanis, P., Grattan, E. and Cumella, S. (1998) Mental health problems of homeless children and families: longitudinal study, *British Medical Journal*, 316: 899–902.

Vygotsky, L. (1978) *Mind in Society: The Development of Higher Mental Processes*. Cambridge, MA: Harvard University Press.

Vylder, S. De (2000) The big picture, *Children's Rights Information Network Newsletter*, 13: 11–13.

Wainright, P. (2002) Dietary essential fatty acids and brain function: a developmental perspective on mechanisms, *Proceedings of the Nutrition Society*, 61(1): 61–9.

Wakefield, A.J., Murch, S., Anthony, A., Linnell, J., Casson, D., Malik, M., Berelowitz, M., Dhillon, A., Thomson, M., Harvey, P., Valentine, A., Davies, S. and

Walker-Smith, J. (1998) Ileal-lymphoid-nodular hyperplasia, non-specific colitis, and pervasive developmental disorder in children, *Lancet*, 351: 637–41.

Wallerstein, J. and Kelly, J. (1980) *Surviving the Breakup: How Children and Parents Cope with Divorce*. New York: Basic Books.

Wallerstein, N. (2002) Empowerment to reduce health disparities, *Scandinavian Journal of Public Health*, 30 (supp. 59): 72–7.

Wang, X., Wang, Y. and Kang, C. (2005) Feeding practices in 105 counties of rural China, *Child: Care, Health and Development*, 31(4): 417–23.

Wanless, D. (2002) *Securing our Future: Taking a Long Term View*. London: HM Treasury.

Waterston, E., Evans, D. and Murray-Lyons, L. (1990) Is pregnancy a time of changing drinking and smoking patterns for fathers as well as mothers? An initial investigation, *British Journal of Addiction*, 85: 389–96.

Webster-Stratton, C. (1999) Researching the impact of parent training programmes on child conduct problems, in E. Lloyd (ed.) *Parenting Matters: What Works in Parenting Education?* Barkingside: Barnardo's.

Weinstein, J., Yarnold, P. and Hornung, R. (2001) Parental knowledge and practice of primary skin cancer prevention: gaps and solutions, *Pediatric Dermatology*, 18(6): 473–7.

Werner, E. (1996) Vulnerable but invincible: high risk children from birth to adulthood, *European Child and Adolescent Psychiatry*, 5 (supp. 1): 47–51.

Whitehead, R. and Douglas, H. (2005) Health visitors' experiences of using the Solihull Approach, *Community Practitioner*, 78(1): 20–3.

WHO (World Health Organization) (1948) *The Constitution of the World Health Organization*. WHO, Chronicle 1.

WHO (World Health Organization) (1986) *Ottawa Charter for Health Promotion*. Geneva: WHO.

WHO (World Health Organization) (1997) *Atlas of Mortality in Europe*. Geneva: WHO.

WHO (World Health Organization) (2006) http://www.who.int/en/, accessed 11 March 2006.

Wickberg, B. and Hwang, C. (1997) Screening for postnatal depression in a population based Swedish sample, *Acta-Psychiatrica-Scandinavica*, 95(1): 62–6.

Wilkinson, R. (1996) *Unhealthy Societies: The Afflictions of Inequality*. London: Routledge.

Wilkinson, R. (1999) Health, hierarchy and social anxiety, in N. Adler, M. Marmaot, B. McEwan and J. Stewart (eds) *Annals of the New York Academy of Sciences*; 896. *Socioeconomic Status and Health in Industrial Nations: Social, Psychological and biological pathways*. New York: New York Academy of Sciences pp. 71–102.

Williams, J., Wake, M. and Hesketh, K. (2005) Health related quality of life of overweight and obese children, *Journal of American Medicine*, 293(1): 70–6.

Willow, C. and Dugdale, L. (1998) *It Hurts You Inside*. London: NCB.

Wilson, A. and Edwards, J. (2003) *Schools and Family Change: Schools Based Support for Children Whose Parents Have Separated.* York: Joseph Rowntree Foundation.

Winnicott, D. (1960) The theory of parent–infant relationships, *International Journal of Psychoanalysis,* 41: 585–95.

Winnicott, D. (1966) *The Family and Individual Development.* New York: Basic Books.

Wocadlo, C. and Rieger, I. (2006) Social skills and nonverbal decoding of emotions in very preterm infants at school age, *European Journal of Developmental Psychology,* 3(1): 48–70.

Women's Aid (1995) *Domestic Violence, the Social Context.* Dublin: Women's Aid.

Woodhead, M. and Faulkner, D. (2000) Subjects, objects or participants? Dilemmas of psychological research with children, in P. Christensen and A. James (eds) *Research with Children: Perspectives and Practices.* London: Falmer.

Woods, S., Springett, J., Porcellato, L. and Dughill, L. (2005) 'Stop it, it's bad for you and me': experiences of and views on passive smoking among primary school children in Liverpool, *Health Education Research Theory and Practice,* 20(6): 645–55.

Woolfson, L. (2004) Family well-being and disabled children: a psychosocial model of disability-related child behaviour problems, *British Journal of Health Psychology,* 9(1): 1–13.

Woolfson, L. and Grant, E. (2006) Authoritative parenting and parental stress in parents of pre-school and older children with developmental disabilities, *Child: Care, Health and Development,* 32(2): 177–84.

Worden, J. (1996) *Children and Grief: When a Child Dies.* New York: Guilford Press.

Wright, C. (2005) Growth charts for babies, *British Medical Journal,* 330: 1399–1400, 18 June.

Wright, C. and Talbot, E. (1996) Screening for failure to thrive – what are we looking for? *Child: Care Health and Development,* 22(4): 223–34.

Wright, C., Callum, J., Birks, E. and Jarvis, S, (1998) Effects of community based management in failure to thrive: a randomised control trial, *British Medical Journal,* 317: 571–4.

Zeanah, C. and Benoit, D. (1995) Clinical applications of a parent perception interview in infant mental health, *Infant Psychiatry,* 4(3): 539–54.

Zeanah, C.H. Jr (ed.) (2000) *Handbook of Infant Mental Health* (2nd edn). New York: Guilford Press.

Zielhuis, G., Rach, G. and van den Broek, P. (1990) The natural course of otitis media with effusion in preschool children, *European Archives of Oto- rhino-lanyngology,* 247(4): 215–21.

Index

PARENTS MATTER

SUPPORTING THE BIRTH TO THREE MATTERS FRAMEWORK

Edited by Lesley Abbot and Ann Langston

This book explores the important role of parents and the extended family in the lives of babies and young children. It complements and extends the DfES Birth to Three Matters framework, which supports practitioners in working with children aged birth to three, and builds on the information provided in the companion book *Birth to Three Matters: Supporting the Framework of Effective Practice* (Open University Press, 2004).

Written by academics, practitioners and policy makers interested or involved in the development of the Birth to Three Matters framework, this book argues that parent engagement is essential for developing partnerships within communities in order to give children the best start in life, and shows how this can be achieved. The book:

- Discusses ways in which services may be developed to involve parents more fully in the care and education of babies and young children

- Looks at the powerful role of parents and grandparents in the lives of children

- Considers how skilled practitioners can manage relationships to provide support for both parents and children at difficult times

- Explores the ways in which parents can be helped to fulfil their own needs at the same time as meeting their children's needs

- Includes discussion of families whose children have special needs or disabilities

Parents Matter is essential reading for early years professionals and students on courses in Early Education, as well as policy makers, professional development trainers, local authority trainers, social workers and health visitors who work with very young children.

Contents: *List of contributors – Preface – Acknowledgements – Why parents matter – Becoming a family – Grandparents matter – Everyday activities at home: Meeting our developmental needs with our young children – 'Don't you tell me what to do' – Parents and child protection matter – Evaluating 'better beginnings' – Health matters to families – 'Arty farty nonsense?' Working with parents in the art gallery – Special lives: Working with parents of children with special educational needs and disabilities – 'Observe more... do less": The approaches of Magda Gerber to parent education – Young parents matter – Children and parents matter: Research insights from integrated child and family services in Australia – Future matters – Index.*

200pp   0 335 21980 2 Paperback   0 335 21981 0 Hardback

EARLY CHILDHOOD STUDIES
A MULTIPROFESSIONAL PERSPECTIVE

Edited by Liz Jones, Rachel Holmes and John Powell
"A celebration of the tremendous strides made towards the achievement of a multiprofessional early years workforce, and a challenge to those responsible for training the next generation of professionals... Students and trainers, policy makers and practitioners have a duty to be knowledgeable, to be able to reflect on their beliefs and practice and to articulate concerns, share their views, convey their enthusiasm and act as advocates for young children. This book will help them do just that."
Lesley Abbott OBE, Manchester Metropolitan University

Early Childhood Studies critically engages the reader in issues that relate to young children and their lives from a multiprofessional perspective. Whilst offering a theoretically rigorous treatment of issues relating to early childhood studies, the book also provides practical discussion of strategies that could inform multiprofessional practice. It draws upon case studies to help the reader make practical sense of theoretical ideas and develop a critical and reflective attitude. Hard and pressing questions are asked so that beliefs, ideas, views and assumptions about notions of the child and childhood are constantly critiqued and reframed for the post-modern world.

The first part of the book explores the early years, power and politics by looking at child rights, the politics of play, families, and working with parents and carers. The second part explores facts and fantasies about childhood experiences, such as anti-discriminatory practice, the law, child protection, and health issues. The final section encourages the reader to explore what childhood means from historical, ideological and cultural perspectives, and looks at how popular assumptions arise.

This is a key critical text for early childhood students, academics and researchers, as well as practitioners who want to develop their reflective practice.

216pp   0 335 21485 1 Paperback   0 335 21486 X Hardback

LEARNING FROM SURE START
WORKING WITH YOUNG CHILDREN AND THEIR FAMILIES

Edited by Jo Weinberger, Caroline Pickstone and Peter Hannon

" ... an easy-to-read evaluation of a trailblazer local programme ... packed with helpful information such as pointers for the future, pie charts and parents' stories (not translated into dry 'research' speak) ... It renewed my passion and reminded me why I got involved in Sure Start in the first place"
Nursery World

"This book demonstrates the key strength of Sure Start, its breadth of vision ... It shows how with the right effort, statutory and voluntary organisations can work side by side. It also shows how important it is to engage local people in finding solutions, blending professional and community support to strengthen both ... Learning from Sure Start is a significant contribution to the evidence base on what works for young children and families."
Naomi Eisenstadt, Director, Sure Start Unit

Sure Start, an exciting initiative in early childhood care and education with families in the UK, has been developing new forms of community-focused early interventions, with the aim of having all children 'ready to flourish' when they start school.

This book, the first of its kind, is the result of a close collaboration between one local programme and a university over a five year period. The contributors all have first hand experience as practitioners or researchers in the Sure Start programme at Foxhill & Parson Cross in Sheffield, which has provided a wide range of new services. Contributors:

- Describe various services within health, education and social welfare

- Examine implications of the development of inter-agency theory and practice for planning and delivery of services for children

- Evaluate methods that were employed

- Identify what worked and what didn't

- Indicate lessons that can be drawn from experience

This is indispensable reading for students of early childhood and early years practitioners, policy makers, and researchers.

Contents: *Foreword – Contributors – List of abbreviations – Part One: Introduction – Why we should learn from Sure Start – Listening to families: a survey of parents' views – Part Two: Improving and emotional development – Family support – 'Connecting with our kids' parenting programme – Meeting the needs of teenage parents – Part Three: Improving health – Low birth – Supporting breast feeding mothers – The impact of Sure Start on health visiting – Child safety scheme – Part Four: Improving children's ability to learn – Quality of play and learning opportunities – Community teaching in a Sure Start context – Screening and language development – Media, popular culture and young children – A dialogic reading intervention programme for parents and preschoolers – Part Five: Strengthening families and communities – Community involvement – The Young Families' Advice Service – Community research – Part Six: What have we learned? What do we need to know? – Bringing it together: the role of the programme manager – Looking to the future – Appendices – Index.*

304pp   0 335 21638 2 Paperback   0 335 21639 0 Hardback